ME, I'M AFRAID OF VIRGINIA WOOLF

Alan Bennett first appeared on the stage in 1960 as one of the authors and performers of the revue *Beyond the Fringe*. His stage plays include *Forty Years On, Getting On, Habeas Corpus, The Old Country* and *Enjoy*, and he has written many television plays, notably *A Day Out, Sunset Across the Bay, A Woman of No Importance* and the series of monologues, *Talking Heads*. An adaptation of his television play *An Englishman Abroad* was paired with *A Question of Attribution* in the double bill *Single Spies*, first produced at the National Theatre in 1988. This was followed in 1990 by his adaptation of *The Wind in the Willowsr* and in 1991 by *The Madness of King George III*, both produced at the National Theatre. His stage version of *The Lady in the Van* was first seen in the West End in 1999.

ALAN BENNETT

Me, I'm Afraid
of Virginia Woolf

ff

faber and faber

First published in this collection 2003
by Faber and Faber Limited, 3 Queen Square London WC1N 3AU

Typeset by Country Setting, Kingsdown, Kent CT14 8ES
Printed in England by Mackays of Chatham plc, Chatham, Kent

A CIP record for this book is available from the British Library

ISBN 0–571–22042–8

2 4 6 8 10 9 7 5 3 1

CONTENTS

Introduction by Alan Bennett
vii

A Day Out
I

Sunset Across the Bay
29

A Visit from Miss Prothero
67

Me, I'm Afraid of Virginia Woolf
89

Green Forms
127

The Old Crowd
159
Introduction by Lindsay Anderson 161

Afternoon Off
211

INTRODUCTION

Revisiting these plays twenty to thirty years after they were written ought, I would have thought, to provide insights into the time when I was putting them together and into the person I was at that time.

I'm not sure that they do. To younger readers they may seem old-fashioned and even antique, but they always were even at the time of writing. Writing and recollection are inextricable and I never felt that I was chronicling my own times, simply because so much of the dialogue came out of my remembrance of childhood.

The places were from childhood, too – Leeds and its back streets, where I was brought up, Morecambe where we used to go on holiday, locations that were even then disappearing as we filmed. In Leeds particularly was this the case, on two occasions demolition crews working in the next street to where we were shooting. This at least was contemporary, the wrecking of England's provincial cities and the break-up of their social structure the background to many of these plays.

In 1971 I had written two plays, *Forty Years On* and *Getting On*, but had no notion of how to write a TV play, still less a TV film, the actual word 'film' still trailing enough glamour to make me feel slightly intimidated. I began to jot down scraps of northern dialogue with no notion of the characters into whose mouths they might go and with no notion of a plot, either, though I knew I wanted it to have a pre-First World War setting.

These jottings eventually turned into *A Day Out* (1971), a road movie of sorts, only the road was a succession of back lanes and even cart tracks that takes an Edwardian cycling club from Halifax to Fountains Abbey. Pathetically literal-minded, I remember worrying that this was a little far for a group to cycle on the machines of the time and whether the BBC Script Department would on that score alone find it implausible. They did find it implausible, though not because the cyclists had too far to go but because, in the script editor's view, the play didn't go far enough; didn't go anywhere, in fact. It was at this point a rather military-looking producer at White City got hold of it, and dismissed these objections by saying, 'Well, it goes to Fountains Abbey and back which is quite far enough for me,' and briskly put it into production.

This was Innes Lloyd, whom I've written about elsewhere (*Writing Home*, 1994, pp. 000–000), and who produced everything I wrote for the BBC over the next twenty years. Without him many of my plays would not have got to the screen and our collaboration, always happy and fruitful, was the best and the longest working relationship I've had in my life. My other collaborator, who directed all the plays in this volume apart from *The Old Crowd*, was Stephen Frears. To both of them I owe an immeasurable amount.

BBC Television in the early seventies was only distantly related to what it has since become, with the atmosphere then discernibly derived from what had prevailed on BBC Radio. From its inception radio had proved a haven for the odd and the eccentric, a ramshackle set-up that found room for the flotsam of the literary world, stalled writers, indolent poets, the seemingly unemployable and the downright drunk. To such as these the BBC was above all a patron, easy-going, generous and not too demanding. But that the forties and fifties should also have been the golden age of radio says something about the nature of patronage, with waste (or at any rate slack) an essential component.

Some of this easy-going but richly productive atmosphere carried over into television in its early days, with certain programmes outstanding in nurturing talent: *Tonight*, the early-evening magazine programme, and *Monitor*, the arts programme, were both umbrellas under which many young film-makers learned their trade. The atmosphere was notably relaxed and for me as for many of my contemporaries television began as a kind of playground or a school where you learned as you went along, making your mistakes on the blackboard with the nation the class. I served an apprenticeship in two of Ned Sherrin's late-night shows, *Not So Much a Programme* and *The Late Show*, successors to *That Was the Week That Was*, writing and performing in sketches live every Saturday night.

In terms of quality of output, which was often outstanding, this unfrenzied approach was not a wasteful way of working. But it was unpredictable, and not easy to control or to quantify, so when in the seventies the BBC began getting in management consultants and embarked on a series of reorganisations, what had always been the traditional BBC approach both in radio and TV was an early casualty. If I regret the supposedly streamlined organisation that eventually emerged, this is not just nostalgia, but an almost ecological regret for the loss of a habitat – the wetlands of the mind, perhaps, the draining of a friendly fen which had long sheltered several struggling or endangered species.

One such was a type of tough, often gruff middle-aged woman, single very often, though not always, who was the prop and stay of whatever department she was assigned to. She would know the BBC inside out and be versed in all its administrative short cuts. Unabashed by money, rank or celebrity, such women ruled the roost in their departments much as senior civil servants did in Whitehall. It's a well-known story, but it was one such who was manning the desk at TV Centre when the King of Norway arrived to visit the Director of Programmes. She called the office in question, then turned back to the distinguished visitor. 'I'm sorry. Did you say the King of Norway or the King of Sweden?'

Happily, such women (and they were always women) made the jump from radio to television, and were quick to master 'crossing the line' and the mysteries of continuity – knowing how many bites had been taken out of a sandwich at the cut, how far down the cigarette had been smoked and all the petty but essential expertise of film-making. Tireless, loyal and unsung, with names like Kay, Thelma and Joan, they lived for the Corporation and, versed in its logic and lore, took many a now famous director through his first shooting script and pointed them towards Hollywood.

Smokers all, and fond of a snifter in the BBC Club, there aren't many of them left, their few successors catching their deaths in draughty doorways at the back of the building, still pulling on a guilty fag. Once, though, they were the backbone of the BBC, and I am happy to have seen them in their pride.

Another difference between productions then and now was that there was never a long-drawn-out process haggling about money, such as generally has to be gone through today. It's true that, being a model producer, Innes Lloyd shielded me from any such concerns, and it was also true that being a much-trusted figure in the BBC his approval carried weight and was often recommendation enough. At this time in the early seventies single plays were accepted as part of the BBC's remit; they were seldom commercial nor, in the days before co-productions with transatlantic companies, could they be expected to make their money back. But even the most modest plays were part of a tradition of BBC drama, inherited from the radio, which with two or three plays a week had built up a regular and informed audience. The play was still the thing.

That is, of course, no longer the case today. Single plays are made into events; there's no sense of them being part of a repertory or of any tradition at all. An audience that was sophisticated and educated to the drama has been prodigally abandoned. I just count myself lucky that in 1971 I managed to catch the wave.

Back then I used to attend all the rehearsals of my plays and go on location with the films. I am more gregarious than I like to think, and I found filming an enjoyable process. It got one out of the house and away from the typewriter. To be filming in a strange place with a group of congenial people seemed to me then the best sort of holiday. Inevitably, though, the more I did the more an element of the chore came into it. But so it is with most things. Sooner or later in life everything turns into work, including work.

I learned lessons, some of them quite basic. If I had a function it was as unofficial dialogue coach, particularly on the northern pieces. I learned the hard way that though it's possible to give an actor the pronunciation of a word, it's unwise to tamper with its emphasis. In *A Day Out*, Baldring (played by Paul Shane) gets off his bike after a long ride and remarks: 'My bum's numb,' the emphasis rightly falling on 'numb'. Paul, however, put it on 'bum', with the implication that while his bum might be numb, the rest of him remained vibrantly alive. I queried this emphasis and he made valiant but unsuccessful attempts to correct it. Subsequent experience has shown me that the more a phrase is repeated, the less meaning it has, and the harder it is to get right. At such times the writer's function is not all that different from that of, say, the props man or the make-up girl, who dash onto the set just before a take to tweak a doyley into position or powder a nose. And it was at moments like this, getting an actor to repeat 'My bum's numb' for the seventeenth time, that I began to wonder if this was a proper profession for an adult person.

A propos dialogue, I notice that in *A Day Out*, which was my first attempt to write in a northern idiom, I also tried to transcribe how it should be spoken. This sometimes makes the speaker seem gormless, and the more of this kind of dialogue I wrote the less I concerned myself about pronunciation and left it to the actor. Later I was happy to find my instinct confirmed by Thomas Hardy:

> An author may be said fairly to convey the spirit of intelligent peasant talk if he retains the idiom, compass and characteristic expressions, although he may not encumber the page with obsolete pronunciations of the purely English words and with mispronunciations of those derived from Latin and Greek. In the printing of standard speech hardly any phonetic principle at all is observed; and if a writer attempts to exhibit on paper the precise accents of a rustic speaker he disturbs the proper balance of a true representation by unduly insisting upon the grotesque element; thus directing attention to a point of inferior interest; and diverting it from the speaker's meaning, which is by far the chief concern where the aim is to depict the men and their natures rather than their dialect form.
>
> Thomas Hardy
> quoted in Robert Gittins, *The Older Hardy*, p. 16

Sunset Across the Bay (1974) was my second television play and is here printed for the first time. It's about a couple living in Leeds whose dream has always been to retire to Morecambe. When they do, they find they are lonely and unhappy, and the husband ends up having a fatal heart attack, leaving his wife to face the future alone in this place of their dreams. In some ways the couple are not unlike my parents, except the wife is more querulous than my mother and the husband less gentle than my father. But much of their language is the same and their attitudes: Mr Palmer gets up at six o'clock and paces the promenade, just as my father did when we were on holiday in Morecambe, and Mrs Palmer is every bit as cautious in company as my mother.

I had to consider these similarities when I was writing it because my parents had not long retired, not actually to Morecambe but to a village in Craven which was not all that far away, and they were often there. Unlike the couple, though, their retirement was very happy, if marred by illness, and in 1974, when I had written the play but it had not yet been filmed, my father had a heart attack and died, leaving my mother in much the same position as the widow in the film. Anyone who writes will be familiar with the feeling of involuntary prediction it sometimes involves, so having written my father's death I felt I had helped to occasion it. My mother never felt this or saw either of them in the characters I had created. 'They're from Leeds,' she said, 'and we're from Leeds, but that's as far as it went. Mind you, it was grand seeing Morecambe.'

A Visit from Miss Prothero and *Green Forms* were both shot in the studio and were the first plays in which I worked with Patricia Routledge and Prunella Scales, whose voices I cannot help but hear when I read the text.

The same applies to *Me, I'm Afraid of Virginia Woolf*, which marks the beginning of another long association, this time with Thora Hird. I wasn't a prolific enough writer for the actors I worked with to form any sort of repertory but, as any playwright or director would confirm, to work with an actor whom you know and trust halves the labour and makes it a joy.

Things could always go wrong, though, and I can never watch a tape of *Me, I'm Afraid of Virginia Woolf* without cringing at its final minute. It's not at all plain where the action is going (and wasn't plain to me when I was writing it) but five minutes from the end (when Hopkins gets it together with his student, Skinner) it turns into a love story. As they both grin cheekily there is a wonderful swelling (on the sound track, at least) and in comes *South Pacific* and 'I'm as corny as Kansas in August,' climaxing with 'I have found me a wonderful guy.' Back in 1978 this was rather bold, except that in transmission the sound was (as I've always thought deliberately) faded down at this point for one of those needless announcements (since discontinued) saying, 'Hugh Lloyd is currently appearing in *Run for Your Life* at the Vaudeville Theatre.' So no danger there, and the nation's moral sensibilities remained unassaulted.

It wouldn't happen now, of course, and maybe in its small way the play and others like it (though more explicit) are part of the reason why.

Another sexual cop-out occurred more inadvertently at the end of *Afternoon Off*. The play tells the story of Lee, a Chinese waiter who spends his afternoon off looking for Iris, a girl whom he has been told fancies him. He eventually finds her, but she is in bed with the waiter who's given him the information in the first place, so at the end of the play he lies on his bed in his underpants, feeling not a little sorry for himself. In such circumstances a wank would be excusable and indeed in the final shot his hand begins to stray across his belly towards his thigh. Which is fine, except that the cut comes too soon for the purpose of the movement to be established – an omission which in these more explicit days would be inexcusable. But it was the last shot of the film, we were behind schedule and into overtime already, so it's hardly surprising that the moment was snatched. That one can muff such a moment is, I suppose, one of the differences between film-making in England and film-making in Hollywood.

About *The Old Crowd* I'll let Lindsay Anderson speak for himself (see page 161). It caused more of a rumpus than all the other plays put together and indeed anything else I've ever written. This was partly due to Lindsay's flair for publicity and his ability to get people's backs up: the actual piece still seems to me quite mild. But to be abused and the play vilified was for me a novel experience which I was surprised to find wasn't entirely disagreeable. If I haven't written anything like it since it's not because I learned my lesson, just that nothing similar has occurred.

A Day Out

CAST AND CREDITS

First shown in black and white on BBC2 on 24 December 1972

ACKROYD	John Normington
SHORTER	James Cossins
WILKINS	Philip Locke
SHUTTLEWORTH	David Waller
MR TETLEY	Don McKillop
ERNEST TETLEY	Bernard Wrigley
GIBSON	David Hill
EDGAR APPLETON	Paul Greenwood
BALDRING	Paul Shane
BOOTHROYD	Brian Glover
CROSS	Paul Rosebury
MRS ACKROYD	Helen Fraser
MRS SHORTER	Maggie Jones
PLAIN GIRL	Rosalind Elliott
PRETTY GIRL	Sharon Campbell
FIRST BROTHER	George Fenton
SECOND BROTHER	Anthony Andrews
MOTHER	Dorothy Reynolds
FLORENCE	Virginia Bell
Directed by	Stephen Frears
Designed by	Jeremy Bear
Music by	David Fanshawe

TITLE SEQUENCE.
A northern mill town on a Sunday morning in Summer 1911. Deserted mills, the double gates of the mills closed. Silent machinery through grimy mill windows.
'Sunday May 17' superimposed.

[17 May 1911 wasn't a Sunday. I had several letters to this effect.]

A stream tumbling into the mill dam. Dingy streets. The sound of the five-minute bell of a church. A clock showing 7.55.

INT. ACKROYD'S. DAY.
Close shot of mustard being spread thick on sandwiches. A sleepy, plump young woman in nightgown, her hair down, is cutting the sandwiches and wrapping them in paper. She pops a bit in her mouth. Behind her, two young children are asleep in bed in a corner. The house is untidy, full of objects, stuffed birds, pictures, books, butterflies. An upright piano.

EXT. ACKROYD'S. DAY.
Ackroyd is outside feeding his rabbits and doing up buttons at the same time. His bike is in the yard by the rabbit hutches. He comes in.

INT. ACKROYD'S. DAY.
MRS ACKROYD (*whispering*) Is two enough? And there's a bit of spice cake.
   Ackroyd, a sandy-haired, distracted, young-old man, has a little cap on and knickerbockers: his cycling gear. He kisses her.
ACKROYD Pipe.
   He rummages round, and eventually she finds it down the side of the armchair.

EXT. ACKROYD'S. DAY.
He sets off, butterfly net and panniers on his bike. She stands at the door watching him go, then goes out into the little garden and closes the gate after him, as eight o'clock strikes behind her . . .

5

INT. SHORTER'S HOUSE.
... and strikes also over next shot: but it is a different clock. A cardboard box, open. Tissue paper being folded back to reveal a new knickerbocker suit and cap. The cap is taken out and tried on reverently in front of the mirror by Shorter, a middle-aged man in underwear. He fingers the badge on the cap. The Shorters' house is very spick and span. It gleams. While Shorter is admiring himself in the wardrobe mirror, his wife turns down his stocking-tops, prinking and patting him.
MRS SHORTER Grown men, gadding off on bikes. And on a
    Sunday.
    Shorter makes to go out.
    Where are you going?
SHORTER I'm only going down t'yard.
MRS SHORTER You're not going down t'yard in that. Take it off
    this minute. (*She makes him take off the cap and jacket.*) And be
    sharp.

EXT. SHORTER'S HOUSE.
We see him setting off on his bicycle, very upright, very neat, and the further away he gets from his wife, the more self-assured and self-satisfied he becomes.

INT. WILKINS'S HOUSE.
Wilkins, an old-fashioned young man, tiptoes through the hall of his mother's house in his stockinged feet, carrying his boots. He tiptoes past the hall table on which there is a hymn book, a Bible and a neat pair of white gloves. His bike is standing in the vestibule. He puts his boots down, opens the door very quietly, and wheels his bike out. The wheel catches the door and he freezes. Then he comes back in for his boots. As he does so a woman's voice shouts from upstairs.
VOICE (*of Wilkins's mother*) Gregory!
    Wilkins freezes again, his boots in his hand, his hand on the door-knob. Silence from upstairs. Agonised look at hymn book etc. He goes out very carefully and quietly, closing the door behind him.

EXT. SHUTTLEWORTH'S.
Mr Shuttleworth is just edging his bike out of the passage by his shop, a Men's Outfitters. An old youth brings out a chair to help him mount. Mr Shuttleworth is in late middle age, a figure of substance and some

dignity. He is the chairman of the Cycling Club, to whom everyone defers; in fact he is a man of straw. He is mounting his bicycle rather unsteadily when Ackroyd wheels into view, so they ride off together.

ACKROYD Morning, Mr Shuttleworth.

MR SHUTTLEWORTH Good morning, Arthur.

ACKROYD It's a grand day for it.

MR SHUTTLEWORTH It is. It is that.

EXT. BOOTHROYD'S HOUSE.

Boothroyd is pumping up his tyres. Baldring bikes by very slowly.

BALDRING Well, I put th'alarum on.

BOOTHROYD Th'alarum! Keep going.

He mounts his bike and they ride off together.

EXT. WAR MEMORIAL.

The meeting place is at the War Memorial set up for the dead of the Boer War. Gibson is riding round and round in the road, watched by a small boy in a chatterbox cap, whom he occasionally pretends to run down. He pinches the boy's cap and rides off with it.

GIBSON Here, got yer hat. Come on. Get yer hat.

Mr Shuttleworth is sat on the seat with Shorter, looking at a map.

MR SHUTTLEWORTH It's a fair ride, Mr Shorter.

SHORTER Easy stages, Mr Shuttleworth. Easy stages.

MR SHUTTLEWORTH No, we won't overdo it.

SHORTER And we've got all day.

BOOTHROYD That is if we can get started. Saddle up, Mr Shorter.

There should be some friction between Shorter and Boothroyd, who is a Socialist.

MR SHUTTLEWORTH Do you want to see the map, Percy?

Percy is Mr Baldring, who is fat and lazy.

BALDRING No. No. I'll take it on trust.

SHORTER Come on then, Percy, be sharp.

BALDRING All in good time. All in good time.

MR SHUTTLEWORTH Take it steady, lads. Shall you bring up the rear, Percy?

BALDRING I expect so, Mr Shuttleworth. I generally do.

The two other members of the party are Mr Tetley and his son, Ernest. Ernest is simple. He doesn't talk in any distinguishable way, but roars incomprehensibly. On his account Mr Tetley tends to sit apart from the rest. He is an oldish man. He and Ernest ride a tandem.

MR TETLEY Hold on a second. The lad's lace is undone.
He gets off the tandem to fasten it, and Ernest lets go of the bike.
Hold the bike, Ernest.
Ackroyd tries to hold it.
No. Leave him, Cyril, he can do it.

ACKROYD Please yourself.
Ernest roars.
That'll do Ernest. Come on.

WILKINS Wish we could get off. It's me mam.

ACKROYD Don't worry, Gregory. We'll protect you.

GIBSON Fancy being afraid of your mam at your age.

SHORTER We're just lacking one of the full complement, Mr Shuttleworth. Mr Appleton.

GIBSON (*calling out from his bike*) Who're we waiting on?

ACKROYD Edgar.

WILKINS He's happen not coming.

ACKROYD Nay, he told me he wor coming.

SHORTER We mun be off, I reckon. What do you say, Mr Shuttleworth?
Mr Shuttleworth is consulting his watch.

MR SHUTTLEWORTH Ay. He'll happen catch us up.

SHORTER Punctuality is the politeness of kings, that's what I say.
Shot of the setting off.

INT. EDGAR'S ROOM.
Edgar Appleton's digs. Untidy, clothes strewn about. He is fast asleep. Young, handsome, a bit of a card. His landlady knocking softly at the door, not particularly anxious to wake him. She is blousy, and rather sweet on him, and will linger slightly in the hope of seeing him dress. There is a cup of cold tea by the bed.

LANDLADY You haven't drunk your tea, Mr Appleton. It's after eight. I've been shouting. You'll have to get your skates on.
Edgar shoots out of bed and dresses very quickly.

EXT. EDGAR APPLETON.
Cut to Edgar pedalling off, down back lanes, carrying his bike down some steps and over a field by a recreation ground. Cut to:

8

EXT. MAIN PARTY.
Main party pedalling through the town.
MR TETLEY Don't be turning round, Ernest. You'll have us over.
  *Mr Shuttleworth leading, flanked by Mr Shorter, touching hats to
  the few passers-by. Shorter waving children out of the way. Wilkins
  looks unhappily at the caretaker unlocking the chapel, who watches
  as they pass.*
ACKROYD Look out, Gregory. You've been spotted.
  *They all laugh. Slow faces watching them as they go. No hurry.
  No rush. No obvious interest. Heavy faces in close-up. Women in
  shawls, a child in clogs. A milkman riding on the back of his cart.
  They are at the foot of the hill leading out of the town and they
  dismount and begin to climb. Cut in shot of Edgar still trying to
  catch up.*

INT. CROSS'S HOUSE.
*Cut to a middle-class interior, a doctor's house, seen in a mirror behind
the face of a thin, pale young man in front of a cheval glass, dressed
and ready. He is a handsome, delicate-looking youth. His name is
Cross. He walks to the door and we see that he limps. He has a surgical
boot on.*

INT. CROSS'S SECOND BEDROOM.
*Cut to interior of another bedroom. His mother's face, lying sideways on
the pillow, eyes open. Listening to the uneven sound of his footsteps
going down the stairs. Her husband asleep beside her.*

INT. CROSS'S HALL.
*A maid in the hall. Cut to Cross against the glass doors of the hall. The
house is set above the town, with a drive, and steps up to the door.*

EXT. CROSS'S HOUSE. DRIVE AND ROAD.
*He limps to his bike, but once on it he is freed from his deformity,
cycling round and round the drive. His mother is watching him from
the window as he rides out to the gate.*
*The road outside Cross's house is the road up which the cycling club is
toiling. He waits for them.*
*Mr Shuttleworth would plainly like to take this excuse for a rest, but
they go on.*

SHORTER Fall in behind, Mr Cross.

CROSS Mr Shorter. Good morning, Mr Shuttleworth.

ACKROYD Now then, Gerald.

CROSS Arthur. Hurry yourself up, Edgar!

Edgar is coming up behind. The others are pushing their bikes, but Edgar rides his, standing up on the pedals in order to overtake them. Cross falls in behind, alongside Edgar.

EXT. TOP OF HILL.

The numbers are now complete, and as they reach the summit of the hill, still pushing their bikes, the sun comes out. They are on the edge of the moors, and the town (Halifax or Hebden Bridge) is below them. The older ones sit down to have a bit of a rest. Gibson, Edgar and Cross stay on their bikes.

ACKROYD Here we are. The heights of Babylon.

SHORTER Worst bit over.

BALDRING Ay. I think I'll just have five minutes.

SHORTER You're not jiggered already, Mr Shuttleworth?

MR SHUTTLEWORTH Just taking in the view, Mr Shorter. Just taking in the view.

ACKROYD There's your dark Satanic mills, Gerald.

WILKINS Where's t'chapel. I can't see t'chapel.

GIBSON It's down there, look. Can't you see your mam waving her fist at thee?

WILKINS Shut up.

ACKROYD See, do you see Mason's? Down there. Do you see?

BOOTHROYD Them's them new houses, Mr Shuttleworth. They've getten built up right to West Vale.

MR SHUTTLEWORTH I can remember when all that were fields. It's where my grandma lived.

ACKROYD There's going to be nought left o't'country if they're not careful. When I were little you could stand on t'steps o't'Corn Exchange and see t'moors. Nowadays there's nought but soot and smoke and streets and streets.

BOOTHROYD Ay, but there's all this. It'll be a long time before they build up England.

EXT. DIFFERENT PART.

Shots of them cycling along. They are coming flying down a hill.

ACKROYD Hey up, lightning.

BOOTHROYD Last one at t'bottom's a cissy, Mr Shorter.

Suddenly the tandem comes through the middle of the group.

MR TETLEY (*shouting*) Can't stop . . . can't stop . . . no brakes.

*The tandem crashes. The others look back at the scene of the crash.
No damage has been done. Ernest mumbles a lot, while Mr Tetley
fixes the handlebars of the bike.*

[This crash wasn't in the script, but occurred while we were
shooting. Fortunately the actors remained in character and the
camera kept turning.]

EXT. DIFFERENT PART.

*Shots of them cycling along easily now, down hills, through moors and
fields, in their characteristic ways: Edgar with no hands, Shuttleworth
and Shorter leading the way, but passed and re-passed by the more
adventurous ones. Close shots of the actual mechanical workings of the
bikes – pedals, etc., and a close shot of the strap arrangement that
enables Cross to keep his boot in the pedal.*

EXT. PUB.

The party arrives outside a pub.

MR SHUTTLEWORTH Here we are, lads.

They get off their bikes and leave them in the hedge.

I hope you'll allow me to do the honours. It's my birthday this
year.

SHORTER Mr Shuttleworth, you have a wry tongue. A wry
tongue, Mr Shuttleworth. A right wry tongue.

MR SHUTTLEWORTH Good morning. Give them all their
pleasure, landlord, and let me know the damage.

[A speech improvised by the actor David Waller, at this time
working with the Royal Shakespeare Company.]

They sit drinking their beer at tables in the pub garden.

BALDRING This'll lay the dust a bit.

EDGAR Ay, this is right beer, this is. Make your hair curl. This'll
put lead in your pencil, Gerald.

SHORTER There's some folks have too much lead in their pencil,
I reckon.

EDGAR Who're you taking that for?

Cross is carrying out a bottle of lemonade.

GIBSON It's Arthur. He's temperance.

BOOTHROYD No, I like a drink, but I don't go mad with it.

ACKROYD I've seen that many families ruined with it.

GIBSON By, that looks strong stuff, Arthur. Here, let's have a sup.
He snatches the glass.

ACKROYD Nay, give us it here. Sithee . . . damn you, you've spilt it.
You lout.

GIBSON Shurrup, you great lass.

BOOTHROYD It's not the drink does harm. It's the social
consequences, that I'm reckoning on. Drink retards progress.
Did you ever think why we haven't had a revolution in this
country? There's two reasons. One is drink, and the other
paradoxically is Methodism . . .
*The camera has meanwhile drifted away from Boothroyd, though
his voice continues over the next sequence, showing:*

EXT. THE ORCHARD AND KITCHEN GARDEN BEHIND PUB.

BOOTHROYD (*voice over*) . . . both of them in their different ways,
distracting the mind of man from his immediate social
conditions. Putting him into a false Nirvana. Intoxicated with
beer, intoxicated with heaven. It's the same thing. Nirvana.
*Baldring is sat happily on the earth closet in the garden with the
door open, listening drowsily to the birds. He also (in 1911) has a
wristwatch on.*

EXT. DIFFERENT PART.
*Cycling along again. They halt at a gate while Mr Shuttleworth
consults the map.*

MR SHUTTLEWORTH I think we can take advantage of a short cut
here, Mr Shorter. Hey, lads. Short cut here.
Mr Shuttleworth goes through first, Shorter holding the gate.

SHORTER Thank you, Mr Shuttleworth.
*They come up against a gate. Along it is strung a line of dead rooks
and moles.*

ACKROYD Poor little buggers.
Gibson touches one of the moles gingerly.
Why do they have to hang 'em up?

GIBSON It's like a warning to the others.

ACKROYD How do you mean . . . a warning? What're they

warning 'em about? They're born moles, aren't they? They can't do ought about it. Barmpots.

They cycle on. Close up of Shuttleworth's back tyre which is gradually deflating. Mr Shuttleworth tries to glance round at it as he rides, wobbling, almost coming off and stopping.

MR SHUTTLEWORTH Hold it, lads. Quite flat, I'm afraid.

Shorter and Ackroyd dismount and look at the tyre, and gradually the ones ahead stop and ride back. Shorter takes charge, first of all upending the bike.

MR SHUTTLEWORTH Mind my paintwork, Mr Shorter.

SHORTER I'm doing my best, Mr Shuttleworth.

BOOTHROYD Take it steady, take it steady. Don't fullock it.

Baldring is already sat down and half asleep.

BALDRING Ay, take it steady.

BOOTHROYD A bowl of water's the first requirement. All hands to the pumps. You make a better door than a window, lad.

Ackroyd goes and knocks at a cottage and comes back with a bowl of water.

MR SHUTTLEWORTH I've never been mechanically minded, for all I ride a bicycle.

SHORTER No.

MR SHUTTLEWORTH I wouldn't know where to start.

BOOTHROYD You're an artist, Mr Shuttleworth.

MR SHUTTLEWORTH Well, that way on, any road.

SHORTER There's an art in *this*, like there is in all these things. Now, everybody. Don't wander off. This halt isn't on the agenda, you know.

BALDRING (*asleep*) I'll keep in the vicinity, Mr Shorter.

BOOTHROYD What're you reading then, Gerald?

Cross shows him.

Allus got your nose in a book. Is it a tale? Oh ay, H. G. Wells. Is it a good one?

CROSS Yes. Yes it is.

BOOTHROYD *He's* a socialist, too. Does it come through?

CROSS A bit, I suppose. Yes, a bit.

BOOTHROYD That's good.

The tyre bubbles air in the bowl of water.

MR TETLEY There she blows.

MR SHUTTLEWORTH It is aggravating.

MR TETLEY Gumption, that's what's required.

SHORTER A puncture of this size is a serious business. It can jeopardise the whole wall of the tyre. Is that tacky yet, Mr Ackroyd?

Meanwhile Gibson is taunting Ernest with a lemonade bottle, pretending to give him a drink, then taking the bottle away.

MR TETLEY Ernest! Come over here, Ernest!

The puncture is almost mended. In close up we see a small box from the puncture outfit opened and powder rubbed onto the newly applied patch, as in voice over Shorter says:

SHORTER Apply it to the affected part and dust with the powder provided.

MR SHUTTLEWORTH Champion, champion.

While the puncture is being mended, Edgar gives the glad eye to a woman watching the proceedings from her cottage doorway. He pops his bike against the hedge, and is about to go in when her husband, who has been bending down behind the hedge, straightens up and confronts Edgar.

EDGAR Oh heck!

MAN Morning.

EDGAR How do you do.

When someone throws the water away after the puncture is mended, it goes quite close to Shorter.

SHORTER Mind out. This suit's new on.

BALDRING By, I'm hot. I wish I'd never put a vest on. (*He peels an apple, very carefully and fastidiously.*)

GIBSON What you do that for? T'skin's the best part.

BALDRING For them as likes it. For them as likes it.

Gibson takes the skin, and waits for the core. Baldring looks at Gibson, then throws it away.

GIBSON (*going after it*) Soft bugger.

BALDRING I think I'll just have five minutes.

CROSS It doesn't seem like Sunday, somehow.

BOOTHROYD It would if you were in t'mill all week like most folks.

WILKINS They'll miss me, you know. It's my morning for taking t'plate round.

EXT. ANOTHER PART.

The puncture mended, they are cycling along again, Boothroyd singing 'Did you not hear my lady, / Go down the garden singing'.

[These shots, redolent of high Edwardian summers, had to be abandoned because of the bitter weather, the chestnut trees scarcely in leaf, let alone in flower.]

They cycle past a line of village boys, all in their Sunday best, walking along a white and dusty road in Indian file. The front one looks round. They ride along in clouds of white dust, in bright sunshine, then under chestnut trees. They ride through puddles. A watersplash. Some going over the bridge, and others the adventurous way through the stream. One man riding a carthorse. A farm cart, with the mother and father up front and the daughter facing over the back of the cart.

Edgar rides for a while with his hand on the back of the cart while she giggles, until her mother looks round, the father whips up the horse and Edgar nearly goes flying.

Riding very slowly along, Mr Shuttleworth farts. Edgar giggles and Ackroyd winks. A dog runs after Mr Shuttleworth, barking and snapping at his ankles.

SHORTER Take no notice, Mr Shuttleworth. He's more frightened of you than you are of him.

WILKINS Be careful. We don't want hydrophobia.

GIBSON Gerron, you little bugger.

SHORTER Don't race it, don't race it. You make it worse. And watch your language.

EXT. DIFFERENT ROAD SECTION.

They are cycling along.

ACKROYD Breathe in, breathe this air.

They pass a manure heap and are thrown into confusion.

EDGAR By heck! Smell that!

ACKROYD Breathe in! It's a grand country smell, is that. It fair does you good.

CROSS (*imitating him*) Make your hair curl will that, Edgar. (*And winks.*)

They lift their bikes over a stile.

SHORTER Mind your oily great bike on my socks, Edgar. You've no thought. They've no thought, Mr Shuttleworth. Allow me.

He helps Mr Shuttleworth with his bike.

EXT. FIELD.

The party wheel their bikes across a field.

SHORTER Mind where you're putting your feet. This field's in a
disgusting state.

WILKINS That's one good thing about Halifax . . . no cows.

EDGAR Oh I don't know. I've come across one or two cows in
Halifax.

SHORTER Damnation.

ACKROYD Never mind. It's good clean muck.

SHORTER My missus doesn't distinguish between sorts of muck,
Mr Ackroyd. Muck is muck to her. And it's anathema.

Baldring and Boothroyd cycling along a road. Boothroyd is singing.

BOOTHROYD

'O, saw you not my lady, out in the garden there;
Shaming the rose and lily, for she is twice as fair.'

[Everything conspired against making this a lyrical film. In the
text I had given this and another song ('O maiden, my maiden')
to Boothroyd, intending them to mark moments of sadness
and warmth. Boothroyd was played by Brian Glover. No
slouch at acting, Brian does not sing in tune. The moment still
has a limited pathos: it's a man who can't sing, trying to.]

*Various shots of individual members of the group cycling along. They
cross a final field and come to a halt overlooking some monastic ruins.*

ACKROYD Here we are. Journey's end.

MR SHUTTLEWORTH Well, isn't that a picture?

BALDRING I know one thing. My bum's numb.

They go down to the ruins, and the afternoon is spent there.

EXT. THE RUINS.

*The party is sitting by the stream in the abbey ruins eating their
sandwiches. Some have lunch in handkerchiefs, others in odd bits of
newspaper which they read. Mr Shuttleworth takes no part in the
conversation but has the largest and most elaborate lunch of all, which
he eats with deliberation and contentment, oblivious of the envious eyes
cast on it.*

GIBSON I reckon we ought to share.

SHORTER Share! But you've only got two scrutty little
sandwiches. I've got some spice cake.

ACKROYD Did you know sandwich isn't an original word? In
olden days they didn't have sandwiches. They were brought
in by the Earl of Sandwich (*mouth full*), hence the name.
Gibson tries to pinch some of Wilkins's lunch.

WILKINS Take your hands off. You can have a bit of my cake, but
I'm hanged if I'm sharing.

BOOTHROYD In my day that was known as paternalism.

SHORTER Well in my day it was known as generosity.

GIBSON (*eating*) It's as hard as the devil.

WILKINS They'll just be coming out now. They'll think I'm poorly.
I never miss. Happen they'll go round home and find out.

EDGAR Nay, that's not what you've got to worry about, Gregory.
It's him up there writing it all down. 'Sunday May 17, 1911.
Skipped chapel. T'singing from Mount Zion sounds a bit thin
today, Peter. Have we got somebody off?'

CROSS 'It's Wilkins, O Lord. He's . . . he's gone cycling.'

EDGAR 'Wilkins? Gone cycling! Cycling? And him a Deacon.
Write it down, lad, write it down.'
*Mr Shuttleworth wanders round the abbey, earnestly examining the
ruins. At one point during his wanderings he comes upon Gibson,
who is carving his initials on a pillar.*

MR SHUTTLEWORTH That's not going to get us any further, is it,
Eric?

GIBSON Sorry, Mr Shuttleworth.
Who has already passed on. Gibson looks after him.

MR SHUTTLEWORTH If we all went round carving our names,
there'd soon be no ruins left. Desist, lad, desist.
Ackroyd and Boothroyd are also doing a tour.

ACKROYD They were Cistercian monks here. From Cîteaux in
France. (*He has a guide book.*)

GIBSON What made 'em want to come here for, soft things?

BOOTHROYD It's an unnatural life, separating yourself off like
that.

ACKROYD 'They always selected sites of great remoteness, away
from the temptations of civilisation.'
Gibson laughs coarsely.

BOOTHROYD You don't always want to be with men. You don't
always want to be with your own sort. You want variety, a
mixture.

ACKROYD Ay, but there would be all sorts, carpenters, builders, gardeners . . . it wouldn't be as if they were all parsons.

BOOTHROYD There wouldn't be any kids, would there? And allus getting down on their knees. It's no sort of life . . . You want to get out and get something done, not be stuck here waiting for it to happen, waiting for God to put things right.

ACKROYD No. No . . .

Conversation fading.

. . . it would be a little community.

In some of these conversations we do not see the talkers, but simply a meadow, covered in long grass. Occasionally someone sits up above the level of the grass or a hand comes up to swat a fly with a cap.

[A remnant of the original script and its presumption of high, cloudless days. In retrospect I think this sequence was no great loss: there is a limit to the interest of grass as a shot.]

Baldring, as usual, has found himself a comfortable spot.

BALDRING I think I'll just have five minutes.

EXT. STEPPING STONE. STREAM.
Mr Shuttleworth, Edgar, Shorter and one or two others are sat by the stepping stones. Edgar is skimming stones across the river.

CROSS That's a good one.

Two girls start to come across the stepping stones. One pretty, one plain. Edgar aims a stone which splashes them, upsets the balance of the pretty one who teeters on the edge of a stone, hitching up her skirts and shouting with delight. This is watched in strained silence by the men on the bank.

MR SHUTTLEWORTH She's a well-set-up lass is that.

SHORTER I think you've caught the mood of the company, Mr Shuttleworth.

The girls reach the shore.

PLAIN GIRL Grown men. You ought to be ashamed of yourselves.

Edgar tosses another stone, which sends the pretty girl into more laughter and brings shouts of protest from the others.

SHORTER Nay, Edgar, mind out. That's gone on Mr Shuttleworth's trousers.

ACKROYD It's grand to get away from folks. Just fancy being fastened in.

BOOTHROYD You see, I see Man going on from strength to
strength. And it's a pretty straight road now, I reckon. We're
finished with wars now. Folks won't stand for it. It's not us that
makes wars. Worker's not going to take up arms against
worker.

ACKROYD You'll not alter folks, Henry, I don't care what you say.

BOOTHROYD This'll seem like a dark age one day. A dark age.

EDGAR If it's that easy, why hasn't it happened before?

*Two youths in white shirts and riding breeches skirt the edge of the
trees on large horses, looking incuriously at the trippers as they water
the horses in the stream. Ackroyd catching butterflies with a net.*

[Cut, alas. The butterflies were in charge of a butterfly handler
(*sic*). The scene was set up and on a shout of 'Action' the
butterfly handler loosed his troop of Thespian cabbage whites.
Whereupon the poor creatures took one look at the bitter
weather and promptly fell dead of hypothermia.]

*These scenes should overlap in time, so that when one scene is being
played another is going on in the background.*

SHORTER They've no nobility about them, women. It's all
mundane. One day to the next. No large view. No theory. All
practice.

*Nobody is listening to him. Ackroyd is feeding a squirrel, enticing it
nearer and nearer with food. Gibson creeps up behind him and
throws a coat over it.*

[The butterfly handler doubled as a squirrel handler. The
squirrel, though hardier than its butterfly colleagues, was in its
way equally intractable. Animal handlers invariably claim an
exact knowledge of the habits and intentions of their charges.
This is seldom the case.]

GIBSON That's copped him.

ACKROYD Damn you. (*He tries to kick Gibson.*)

BOOTHROYD Nay, fair does, Arthur. They're nobbut rats.

GIBSON Soft bugger.

At the ruins Ernest sits with his feet in the water, roaring.

BOOTHROYD Are you singing, then, Ernest?

Ernest roars.

MR TETLEY That's right.

They smile.
The next speech should be dreamlike, casting a spell which will be
broken by the gunshots. As Boothroyd speaks in voice over we see
close-ups of Boothroyd, Cross, Shuttleworth, Shorter, Wilkins,
Ackroyd, Edgar and Ernest.

[Another sequence which, due to the weather, had to be shot
in close-up on the actors rather than in wide shot on the actors
in a summer landscape.]

BOOTHROYD This century, it's like letting the kids out into the
fields. We're encamped on the edge of the twentieth century.
Like an army after toiling upwards through slavery, wars,
oppression, century after century. And now we're over the hill,
into a great green place. You come up over the top of the hill
and see it stretched out before you, the twentieth century.
The calm is suddenly broken by the sound of reverberating shots.

INT. NAVE OF ABBEY.
The gaunt, ruined walls. More shots. A gamekeeper is shooting rooks,
watched by Gibson. He shoots more, and they fall to the ground.
Gibson makes to fetch the birds.
GAMEKEEPER Let the dog do it, man. That's what it's for.
Ackroyd and Wilkins come running in. And stop sheepishly when
they see what's happening. The shots should be sudden, mysterious.
No alarm. But puzzlement and mystery.
As the shots sound, Cross is wandering through woods and under-
growth, having awkwardly crossed the stepping stones, once slipping
with his bad leg into the water. He wanders through the woods and
on the far side comes out onto a lawn in front of a country house.

EXT. LAWN. COUNTRY HOUSE.
Two ladies are sat under a tree and their husbands play croquet. As
Cross watches, a procession of butler and two maids comes out very
formally with tea.
MOTHER (*calling*) Florence! Flo–o–rence! Te–a–a!
She stands up and looks towards the edge of the wood where Cross is
standing. He steps back and turns away as the two young men on
horseback appear. They wave to the croquet party. Cross goes back
through the wood.

EXT. STREAM. WOODLAND EDGE.
A girl is coming through the trees. She is about fifteen. She stings
herself on a nettle.
FLORENCE Damn. (*seeing him*) I stung my hand.
CROSS Get a dock leaf.
  He picks a dock leaf and puts it on her wrist. Distant calls of
  'Florence.' 'Tea. Tea.' 'Florence.'
FLORENCE Thank you. You'll catch it if they find you here, you
  know.
  The gamekeeper who has been shooting in the ruins comes through
  the undergrowth.
GAMEKEEPER Now then, young fellow me lad. You've no
  business here.
  Girl still dusting down her frock.
FLORENCE It's all right, Gateacre.
GAMEKEEPER (*still suspicious*) Her Ladyship's calling, miss.
FLORENCE I don't know why you have to shoot on a Sunday,
  Gateacre.
GAMEKEEPER Pests, miss. Pests. (*turning away and going off*
  disgruntled) They don't know it's Sunday. (*turning and almost*
  shouting it back at her) Vermin ain't no Sundays.
  The girl is going back through the wood with Cross. She sees
  he limps.
FLORENCE Have you hurt yourself?
CROSS No. (*Lifts his boot.*)
FLORENCE Oh, sorry. Sorry. *I* stutter.
  He shrugs and they both smile.
  Come for tea.
  He hesitates and she pulls his coat.
  Come on.
  They come out into the sunlight on the edge of the lawn.

EXT. LAWN.
MOTHER There she is. Oh. (*And looks askance at Cross.*)
  Harrison, you'd better bring another cup.
  The maid runs off across the lawn. Cross and the girl walk away
  to the other side of the lawn, as the two gentlemen playing croquet
  raise their hats, and go to the tea table. Faint conversation drifts
  after them.

I don't know. I don't say anything. Nothing surprises me any more.

Intermingled with Cross talking to the girl.

AUNT Sad face. Sad face.

MOTHER That boot won't help the grass one bit.

GIRL Have you come far?

CROSS Halifax.

FLORENCE Forsyth. Could we have some cake. Do you mind having a bad leg? Or is that rude? People don't mention it. I am pert.

CROSS I do mind. It isn't rude. People don't mention it. You are pert.

They laugh.

It's all right on a bike. Then you're like everybody else.

FLORENCE Or a horse. I know someone who rides beautifully and she's a terrible . . . cripple.

Cross looks over at the tea party.

My mother and my aunt. And these are my brothers.

The two young men run onto the lawn. They wave and stand talking at the tea table or sprawl on the grass. Snatches of conversation drift over.

MOTHER Someone Florence found in the undergrowth. Isn't it exciting?

Though it is quite plain that exciting is not what it is at all.

FIRST BROTHER Give you a game.

SECOND BROTHER Florence, give you a game. We'll take you on.

FLORENCE Do you play croquet? Come on. It's terribly easy. We can be partners. Be a sport.

Cross shakes his head.

CROSS I couldn't. No, I couldn't, honestly.

FIRST BROTHER We're really none of us much good.

CROSS No. Thank you. No.

They play and he watches.

FLORENCE I'm having the good mallet.

SECOND BROTHER Right. Then it's me to start.

He hits ball through the hoop first time. Florence messes up her shot.

FLORENCE Oh useless.

Boy turns back to croquet her ball.

No, Arthur, please. It's not fair.

22

FIRST BROTHER Sorry, Florence.

FLORENCE I've hardly started.

Her brother fetches it a great whack and sends it shooting across the lawn.

Damn.

She runs after it. It has ended up quite near where Cross's abandoned tea cup stands on the edge of the lawn.

Look you should have . . .

But Cross has disappeared. Forsyth comes over to take the tea cup away, as Florence stares at the rustling trees.

FIRST BROTHER You are a frightful tart, Florence.

EXT. ANOTHER PART OF THE WOOD.

By the bank of the stream, Edgar and the pretty girl lie in the grass. He has his hand inside her blouse. She watches him unsmiling and seemingly unresponsive. He tries to get his hand up her leg. It is all quite awkward, with the noise of clothes unbuttoning and the rustle of her dress very much in the foreground. The plain girl is sulking on the far bank of the stream.

PLAIN GIRL Come on, Connie . . . Your ma won't half play pop with you, Connie Sinker.

FLIRT She won't know. (*Pause.*) Louisa . . . Louisa.

PLAIN GIRL What?

FLIRT She won't know.

PLAIN GIRL I shall tell her.

EDGAR She won't.

PLAIN GIRL I shall.

EDGAR Take no notice.

PLAIN GIRL Connie.

Connie is too busy with Edgar.

Connie. Connie.

EXT. ABBEY RUINS.

Baldring sits silent among the ruins. Cross watches. Ackroyd is catching butterflies. He puts them in a killing bottle.

[Cut. See above. No bottle was necessary: the air was killer enough.]

ACKROYD It's a kind of gas, you see. They don't feel anything. It just puts them to sleep.

A shot of them moving about in sunken parts of the ruins, the old drains and passages. So that their heads and shoulders are above ground, the rest hidden, as if they were in trenches. And above this the rumble of thunder. It ought to be another moment like the guns first sounding, a sudden pause and a slight alarm.

[Cut, again because of the weather. This scene makes the same point as is made by the (altered) ending of the film at the War Memorial, but it makes it better because less explicitly.]

BOOTHROYD Are we going to have a game, then?

GIBSON Aye, come on.

CROSS Bags foggy. Foggy innings. Come on, be sharp.

SHORTER This is consecrated ground, you know.

ACKROYD It never is. It's where they had their dinners. (*to Baldring*) Come on, Percy.

BALDRING I'd rather just spectate.

ACKROYD Nay, come on.

BALDRING I'll just field for a bit, then.

TETLEY Can Ernest play?

BOOTHROYD Can he play?

TETLEY Ay, I think he's all right. Do you want to play cricket, Ernest?

Ernest roars.

BOOTHROYD Aye, all right.

TETLEY 'Appen just let him field, he'll be all right.

BOOTHROYD Come on then.

They play and Mr Shorter takes first go.

Look out, let Wilfred Rhodes have a go.

WILKINS We'll get into trouble, playing in here.

Shorter whacks the ball into the water.

In t'river's out.

SHORTER It never is.

Baldring goes to retrieve the ball from the water and in doing so glances up at the archway over the stream.

BALDRING That's interesting. Do you see what they've done there? Them arches, they've buttressed it. We'd never do that now. We'd brace it. You don't buttress now. Mind you, they're grand buttresses, are them. T'feller as laid them stones knew what he was doing.

WILKINS He'd be a monk.

BALDRING I don't care if he were Charley Peace. He could lay
right bricks.

Mr Shuttleworth calls out.

MR SHUTTLEWORTH It says there's an echo. Hoo-ooh!

*He positions himself, consulting the guide book, and calls out again,
but not a bit self-consciously. Boothroyd looks up from the game and
winks at one of the others. Mr Shuttleworth calls out again. This
time there is an echo and he nods, satisfied, and comes on past where
Boothroyd and co. are playing cricket.*

BOOTHROYD Everything all right, Mr Shuttleworth?

MR SHUTTLEWORTH Yes. Oh yes, yes.

Shorter looks and Wilkins throws the ball.

GIBSON Owzat!

WILKINS Out, you're out, Mr Shorter.

SHORTER I never were.

WILKINS You were.

SHORTER Which is t'wicket?

WILKINS That's t'wicket.

Points to a bit of the wall.

SHORTER I were thinking that were t'wicket.

Points to another bit.

BOOTHROYD Well then. You're out then.

SHORTER No, I'm not.

GIBSON You are.

SHORTER Well I'm not playing then.

ACKROYD Nay, come on. Disputed decision, here, Mr
Shuttleworth. Would you care to arbitrate?

Gibson bowls and hits Shorter.

GIBSON You're out now anyway. BBW.

SHORTER What's that.

GIBSON Bum before wicket.

SHORTER I'm not having that sort of language.

He throws down the bat.

GIBSON I don't know. It's nobbut a game. Are we playing or
aren't we? Here, catch, Ernest.

He hurls the ball at Ernest, who roars.

MR TETLEY Nay, give over.

The game breaks up and the players drift away.

EXT. ABBEY GATES.
They are ready to set off back. Wilkins picks flowers.
SHORTER Late setting off, late going back. I don't know. Where is he?
CROSS Edgar!
BALDRING Edgar! Come on, sithee. We're late.
Gibson comes round a corner on his bike to find Mr Shuttleworth having a pee behind a buttress.
GIBSON Sorry, Mr Shuttleworth.
MR SHUTTLEWORTH Just obeying a call of nature.
CROSS Edgar!
BOOTHROYD Come on then, lads. Saddle up. Back to the rhubarb fields.
SHORTER Aye, time we were off.

EXT. ANOTHER PART OF THE WOOD.
VOICES OFF Edgar! Edgar!
Edgar pushes the girl away and gets up.
EDGAR I mun go. (*He runs off into the trees, stopping to call back to the girl.*) I can't stop. We're a club.
GIRL (*disgustedly*) Club!

EXT. A ROAD.
The others have set off. A shot of them silhouetted against the sky, climbing a hill. Edgar catches up with them.
EDGAR Lads.
BOOTHROYD Been lakin' cricket. You missed a right good game, Edgar.
He winks at Shorter.
GIBSON He's been lakin' a better game nor that, haven't you, Edgar?

EXT. ABBEY RUINS.
The girl rides through the empty ruins, then through the wood towards the road taken by the cyclists.

EXT. ROAD AND HILL.
SHORTER I shall sleep tonight. All this country air.
Mr Shuttleworth nods. He looks worried.

EXT. ROAD BY THE WOODS.
Florence waits by the road, hoping to see Cross.

EXT. A HILL.
They are still coming up the hill, but not within sight of where Florence
is waiting, when Mr Shuttleworth suddenly steers into Shorter.
SHORTER Nay, look out, you'll have me over.
MR SHUTTLEWORTH I think I'm going to have to sit down.
SHORTER Nay, come on, Mr Shuttleworth. We've only just set off.
    Mr Shuttleworth has passed out. They lay him down by the side
    of the road and loosen his collar.
    Are you all right?
ACKROYD He looks bad.
    He calls to the others who are still going up the hill.
    Nay, hold on.
SHORTER You've had a funny turn.
MR SHUTTLEWORTH Ay, I have. I have that.
ACKROYD You've done too much. Are you all right?
MR SHUTTLEWORTH I'm all right now. I've happen done too
    much.
SHORTER You're not so young as you were.
BOOTHROYD It were perhaps summat you had. Pork's a funny
    thing, I always think. And you were having pork.
MR SHUTTLEWORTH Aye. I was. Happen so.
BOOTHROYD I always steer clear of pork.
    Edgar and Gibson are standing apart.
EDGAR He's too old to be bikin' about.
GIBSON That's put a right damper on things, that has.
ACKROYD How do you feel now?
MR SHUTTLEWORTH I'm right enough. I don't feel ought clever,
    but I'm right enough.

EXT. COUNTRY HOUSE AND LAWN.
The lawn empty. Croquet mallets left. Lights going on. Maid collecting
croquet sticks. Mother calling 'Flo–rence'.

EXT. ROAD NEAR WOODS.
Florence, still waiting. She hears her mother calling and slowly turns
back into the wood.

27

EXT. HILL.

They begin climbing the hill again, slowly.

SHORTER And take it easy, Mr Shuttleworth. We don't want to
lose our founder-member.

*They come up to the crest of the hill, where Florence had been
waiting, but by now she has gone. It is getting dark. They ride along,
slowly silhouetted against the sky. Boothroyd sings 'O Maiden,
My Maiden'. The last shot is of them going over the edge of the
hill back into the abyss again.*

[The original script ended here, on a sequence of shots of the
cyclists wending their way home against the evening sun –
country roads, long shadows, lovely light – a perfect end to
an almost perfect day, with the abyss not so much Halifax
as the war to come. The weather put paid to such a sequence;
the end we filmed (in the rain) is a poor substitute:]

EXT. WAR MEMORIAL.

*The War Memorial from which the expedition set off at the start of the
film. It is now some years later. The Great War is over and the names of
new dead have been inscribed on the column. Those gathered round the
Memorial sing the hymn 'O Valiant Hearts . . .' Among them we see
Mr Shuttleworth, Wilkins, Shorter and Cross. As the hymn ends they
look at the wreaths at the foot of the monument. Shorter points with
his umbrella at one particular wreath. It is from the cycling club and
carries its emblem. They turn away and we hold on the Memorial for
the closing credits.*

Sunset Across the Bay

CAST AND CREDITS

MAM	Gabrielle Day
DAD	Harry Markham
BERTRAM	Bob Peck
WOMAN IN FLATS	Christine Buckley
WOMAN S HUSBAND	Bill Pilkington
CANTEEN LADY	Elizabeth Dawn
GATEKEEPER	Peter Wallis
REMOVAL MAN	Paul Shane
WORKMAN	Joe Beloher
ARTHUR	Albert Modley
MRS.LONGSTAFF	Betty Alberge
NEWSAGENT	Marjorie Sudall
1ST MAN IN TEA BAR	Clifford Kershaw
2ND MAN IN TEA BAR	Joe Kenyon
MILKMAN	Bernard Wrigley
BORING WOMAN	Jill Summers
BRICKLAYER	Bert Palmer
MAN IN GARDEN	Allan Bowlas
MISS PASSMORE	Madge Hindle
PIANIST	Neil Anderton
MISS VENABLES	Patricia Mason
MRS LIVERSIDGE	Nora Pollitt
CONDUCTOR	Harold Graham
HOTEL WAITER	John Gee
PASSER-BY	Sam Shed
DOCTOR	William Hoyland
NURSE	Julia Lang
WOMAN IN POST OFFICE	Gwen Harris

Directed by	Stephen Frears
Designed by	Moira Tait
Music	William Davies

INT. MAM AND DAD'S HOME. BEDROOM. NIGHT.
The bedroom of a Victorian terrace house at night.
Dialogue under credits.
MAM What're you thinking?
DAD There'll be that cellar to clear out.
MAM It'll all get done.
DAD It needs sorting through.
MAM Funny not going upstairs to bed. Take a bit of getting used
    to. When Bertram was little, in the war, the sands were all
    mined, do you remember? Barbed wire and girders to stop the
    parachutists. And Heysham, that was all mined too. We never
    had a proper holiday then, did we?
DAD I was working.
MAM These days it's all holidays.
DAD Get to sleep. I've got to be up at six, you know. I'm not
    retired yet.

INT./EXT. FLATS. LEEDS. DAY.
A half-demolished, half-developed slum area in Leeds. Wortley, say,
or Beeston, seen through one of the windows of a high rise block.
Sound of railways. Shuntings. Diesel klaxons.
Shot first through window from outside. Two women, looking out. They
are talking but we don't hear them. Both sixtyish. One in her hat and
coat, the other doing housework.
The whole of this scene wants to be slow and disconnected. They aren't
really talking to one another, or listening much.
Mam, the one in her hat and coat.
MAM How do you clean the outside?
    Woman opens window, which swivels round.
    Sudden noise from streets and railway, shut off again as she closes
    the window.
    I've always wondered what was on the other side of that wall.
WOMAN It's easy to follow. I've done in no time. When is it he
    finishes?

MAM Today.

WOMAN Today?

MAM The Edinburghs are all down. And the Hancocks. It's wicked is that. They were grand houses. By, I'm smothered in here.

WOMAN I've got used to it. And when're you off?

MAM Not for a bit yet. A week or two. You know. There's all sorts to see to. Fancy, you can see the cemetery.

WOMAN What?

MAM I shall be glad when we get off. It's like going on your holidays. All the preparations and you get stalled before you start.

WOMAN It'll be all holiday now.

EXT. LIFT IN FLATS. DAY.
They are outside the flat, the woman pressing the lift button several times, and again when it doesn't come.
She is taking some washing downstairs.

MAM Them folks next door have gone. They've cut the gas off. There's only us left out of everybody we knew in our street. I go along to the end now and I never see one person to speak to.
Woman gets her washing awkwardly into the lift, as Mam watches.
The lift door tries to close too soon.

WOMAN If I had the architect that designed this place I'd pause his backside. Press G.

INT. WORKS CANTEEN. DAY.
The canteen is almost empty, a few men just finishing off their tea and going.
The canteen women clearing up, talking distantly, wiping tables, collecting salts and peppers, putting sauce bottles on a tray.
Dad sitting alone at a table, his face reflected in an electric toaster, with an inscription on the shiny, stainless-steel side.

CANTEEN LADY Is that what they've given you?

DAD Ay, it is.

CANTEEN LADY Thirty-five years.

DAD Ay.

CANTEEN LADY Do you like toast?

INT. WORKS. LOCKER ROOM. DAY.
Some lads are having a sly smoke in a corner.
They look a bit cocky as Dad comes in, but he doesn't take much notice
of them.
Goes to his locker, takes what's left of his things and leaves the door
open.

EXT. WORKS GATE. DAY.
Large time-clock.
DAD Sam.
    He hands in his keys to the gateman, who has a game leg.
SAM Are you off, then?
DAD Yes. Ay.
SAM It's the first time you've ever beaten the clock.
DAD It is. It is that.
SAM See you look after yourself.
DAD And you too.
SAM You're off to the seaside, then?
DAD Ay. It's been, like, her ambition. Now the lad's in Australia
    there's nobody to keep us here. I've got some cousins up at
    Pudsey but I don't see them one year's end to the next.
SAM We always go the other side. Scarborough.
DAD Except I think it feels to do you more good, the west coast.
    My missus thinks so.
SAM And they decide, don't they? Look out, they're here.
    A bell goes in the works.
    Have you got somewhere to live?
DAD Oh ay. We've got a flat.
SAM Off you go, then. Send us a postcard.
DAD Ta ra.
    The first workmen begin to run out of the works, run past him as he
    goes through the gates.

EXT. LEEDS. DAY.
Montage of journey home.
Shots of him on his way home.
Crossing railway sidings with his tea-can. A bridge. A recreation
ground. An underpass under a new road. A half-derelict street on the
edge of demolition area.

INT. MAM AND DAD'S TERRACE HOUSE. DAY.
Dad sat at the table, still with his cap and coat on.
The toaster is on the table.

MAM They pee in that lift, you know. I didn't like to say so. You
 can smell it. They must know.

DAD Are you not going to read it?

MAM I am. I'm just looking for my reading glasses. Oh yes. That
 is nice. It is, isn't it? You'd have thought young Braithwaite
 would have been there, when you've been with them that long.

DAD Old Mr Braithwaite would have been there. This chap
 didn't even know my name. He had to look at his bit of paper.

MAM It's with them being taken over. They don't know anybody.

DAD There were two women under-clippers getting a presentation
 and they only came six years since.

MAM Save the bit of paper. I'll send it our Bertram.

DAD They won't want it.

MAM They would. They'll want to see it, I know.
 Dad puts the toaster on the sideboard.
 We don't want it on the sideboard.

DAD Well, where do you want it?

MAM Well, Dad, we don't. It's not like an ornament. What do
 you fancy for your tea?

DAD What is there?

MAM There's that brisket to finish off.

DAD That'll do.
 They are having their tea. He is making toast with the toaster.

MAM I expect it'll be all toast for a bit, now.

EXT. BUSY SHOPPING STREET IN THE CENTRE. LEEDS. DAY.
Voices over.

MAM I used to right like a trip into town. Every Thursday I used
 to come. They were such grand shops. Nowadays there's no
 pleasure in it. These days, they've all gone mad.

DAD 'Leeds: Motorway City of the Seventies.' Wall of Death
 more like.

MAM I don't wonder folk shop in Harrogate. We're here on
 sufferance, pedestrians. It all has to be cars nowadays. If they
 could translate folks into cars they would. Mind you, prices are
 wicked. I don't know how folks manage now.

EXT. LEEDS CITY MARKET BUILDING. DAY.
Voices over.

MAM Everything has to be washed now. Potatoes. Carrots. And
they don't keep the same once they've been washed. And it all
has to be in bags. And that's all to pay for. Do you wonder stuff
costs more? It'll be a new experience for me, buying
vegetables. Dad's always kept us well supplied.

DAD Stuff always comes on at a rush somehow. One minute it's
all carrots, and the next you're eating cabbage every day. I've
never gauged it out right, somehow. Still, we've had some
grand rhubarb. A real purifier is rhubarb, cleans the
bloodstream.

EXT. ALLOTMENTS. DAY.
Some neat and well kept up, others derelict. A railway in the distance.

DAD If there's owt you want, Arthur, you'd better take it. They'll
only thieve it.

ARTHUR Have you not got a garden there, then?

DAD It's a flat. Downstairs has the garden.
*There are some lads playing on the edge of the allotments. They come
by, maybe on bikes. One of them has a plant pot balanced on a
stick.*
The two old men watch them silently.

EXT. ALLOTMENTS. LATER. DAY.
Dad is clearing out some pots, where there is a toad.

DAD Here. See. Now then – are you coming to the seaside?

ARTHUR They live to a great age, do toads.

DAD Ay. Well, they never move, do they? He never moves from
one week's end to the next, do you then? (*He surveys the
allotments.*) I've seen rabbits here. And a fox once. Right in the
middle of Leeds.
*They lock up their sheds and set off home, both with laden carrier
bags, passing the lads on the way.*
We wanted a bungalow, but they're ridiculous.

ARTHUR Ay, well. The seaside, they will be.

DAD We only got this because of our Bertram. Property's
ridiculous now. Course they'd have re-housed us up New
Wortley if we'd wanted.

ARTHUR Oh ay?

DAD But we didn't fancy. She wanted a change.

ARTHUR How is the lad?

DAD It's their winter now, you know. I say winter, it's never right
cold.

ARTHUR I wouldn't like it.

DAD You're as bad as my missus.

ARTHUR It's a long way off.

DAD She feels it. But I tell her. Australia, it's not the other end of
the world. Not nowadays.

INT. FLAT. LEEDS.

*High flats as before except that the woman's husband is sat watching
television.*

WOMAN We haven't got room. Not for a piano. Where would it go?

MAM I don't like to sell it. It belonged to my grandma.

HUSBAND You could put it in the *Evening Post*.

MAM It came from Sheffield. I'd like it to be somebody we know.
It's got a lovely tone. She was a beautiful player.

HUSBAND There's pianos in every night.

MAM She used to play all sorts, just rattle it off, at sight.

WOMAN I remember.

MAM I've been sorting out one or two bits of things. There's
them pillow-cases. And that's a tray cloth. It came from Hong
Kong.

WOMAN Don't you want it?

MAM We've got too much stuff. Half of it we never use. You don't
realise until you start sorting it out. That's a little tray cloth
that came from our Nora's. That's all hand-done. Bertram
brought it home from Malaya.

WOMAN Are they all right?

MAM (*with snaps*) I've got a letter in my bag. Lynne's going to be
bonny.

WOMAN Aren't they brown? He looks right American now, does
Bertram.

MAM Where? I don't think so.

WOMAN I do.

MAM That's Jennifer. We've never seen her. She'll be three.
Sydney's the seaside.

WOMAN Yes. There's the bridge there.

WOMAN Weren't you in Sydney, Frank?

HUSBAND San Francisco.

WOMAN Oh yes. There's a bridge there too, isn't there? You get mixed up. Frank's been all over.

MAM Isn't that a bonny frock? They often go to the beach when he's finished work.

WOMAN You'll all be at the seaside now, one way or another.

MAM I shan't miss Leeds.

WOMAN What's left of it.

INT. FLAT. LEEDS. LATER.
Woman returning when Mam has gone, husband still watching TV.

WOMAN Trying to palm us off with their piano. What do we want with a piano?
She opens the tray cloth and holds it up, looking at it.

INT. HOME. DOWNSTAIRS. NIGHT.
The night before moving.
Carpets rolled. Furniture ready for going.

INT. HOME. BEDROOM. NIGHT.

MAM My mother was a great worker for the Conservatives. That was with having a shop. She was in the Primrose League. That seems to have gone out now. All that. Empire Day. Do you remember?
She sings to the tune of 'John Brown's Body'.
Empire Day is the 24th of May,
Empire Day is the 24th of May,
Empire Day is the 24th of May,
Ta-tee-ta-tee-ta-ta.

DAD Wisht. Singing. It's three o'clock in the morning.

MAM The kids all used to get dressed up and parade about. Things used to come round then, regular, year in year out. One minute they'd all be laking marbles, next minute it'd be whip and top. Skipping. Chalking patterns on their tops. You never see it now.

DAD You never see them with their trousers' bottoms hanging out either. Or no socks.

MAM Well, we were happy.

DAD I'm not saying we weren't happy.

MAM We've lived round here all our lives. Courting in the
   cemetery.

DAD Only that once.

MAM It was my teeth you fell for.

DAD What? Oh ay.

MAM I had lovely teeth. Fancy . . .

DAD What?

MAM I've slept in this bedroom twenty-seven years and I've
   never seen that before.

DAD What?

MAM That crack in the ceiling.

DAD Where?

MAM There.

DAD I have.

MAM Well, I haven't. It's like a man smoking a pipe.

INT. HOME. DOWNSTAIRS. MORNING.
Removing.
The men are just carrying out the piano.

REMOVER This isn't to go, is that right?

OTHER REMOVER They're putting it in a sale.

REMOVER You won't get much for this, you know. Pianos.
   They're giving them away.

MAM I've not seen 'em. And wipe your feet.

REMOVER It's not the show house, missus. They're pulling it
   down. Slums.
   There is a banging upstairs.

MAM Slums? They never are. What's he doing?

INT. HOME. BEDROOM. DAY.
*Dad is dismantling the double bed, banging at the corner of the iron
frame with a hammer and a block of wood.*

MAM You've no need to be doing that. Tufnell's do all that. They
   said leave it as it is.

DAD You bang that while I hold it level.

MAM All this performance.

DAD I've always done this bed. I know how it . . . bang it, Mam,
go on. Frame. Mind your fingers.
Bed dismantled.
MAM I still think I ought to have scrubbed down.

INT. HOME. DOWNSTAIRS. DAY.
WORKMAN I've come to cut the gas off.
DAD They can't wait, can they?
WORKMAN Do you mind if we start putting the boards up?
DAD What boards?
WORKMAN On the windows. For the vandals.
MAM Vandals. What do you think they are? What's all this . . .
(*waving at the derelict street*) That's vandals. Vandals that live out
at Adel and Lawnswood. Vandals with big cars. Vandals that get
on the council and haven't the sense they were born with.
They're the vandals.
DAD Nay, lass.

INT./EXT. HOME. DOWNSTAIRS. DAY.
*They are in their best clothes and ready for going, with two or three
cases. They are waiting for a taxi.*
MAM We can't even make a cup of tea.
*She wanders about the house, while Dad stands at the door waiting
for the taxi.*
(*of the tiled fireplace*) We only had that put in in 1956. That was
a waste of money. Slums. They never are.
DAD It's here.
*They get into the taxi. Groups of workmen watching, demolishing
other houses. A big fire burning. They are waved off by one old
woman from a dirty house.*
(*through the window*) It's like leaving a bloody battlefield.

EXT. JOURNEY TO BUS STATION.
*Taxi drives through Tong Road, Wellington Road area, towards the bus
station.*
Same with Mam asking him how much he tips the taxi driver.

EXT. LEEDS BUS STATION.
Mam and Dad waiting for the bus.

41

MAM What's 13.36?

DAD Twenty-five to.

MAM It all has to be different. I don't know. Hey.

The dog is smelling their cases.

DAD Get out, you nasty narrow, lamppost-smelling article.

He catches the owner's eye, but is unabashed.

BUS SEEN FROM OUTSIDE. DAY.

Mam silently pointing things out through the window.

INT. BUS. DAY.

MAM That's where I first went out to work.

DAD There's St Matthew's.

MAM That's all new. This'll be the new by-pass.

EXT. OUTSKIRTS OF LEEDS. DAY.

They pass a sign saying 'Leeds Thanks Careful Drivers'.

MAM Leeds thanks careful drivers. Drivers again. What about everybody else? It's all drivers.

DAD Anyway, we're off.

MAM Ay. Bye-bye, mucky Leeds.

INT. THE BUS. DAY.

MAM (*undertone*) It's one of them buses with a lavatory. Are you going to go?

DAD I don't want to go.

MAM I do.

DAD Well, go then.

MAM I don't like folks to know I'm going.

DAD She's been twice already. (*of another passenger*) She were in there before we got to Stanningley. Anyway, what's it matter what folks think? We're retired now.

MAM All right. Hold my bag.

She goes. The bus is by now on a motorway.

Mam returns and doesn't say anything for a bit.

I went.

DAD Yes.

MAM It's very ingenious. They've got it in where they generally put the luggage under the stairs. Where the conductor usually is. You want to go.

DAD I don't.

MAM That's your trouble. No spirit of adventure.

Pause.

I wonder where it goes.

DAD What?

MAM You know –

Pause.

I expect it's scattered on the central reservation.

They both crack with laughing, and we see their laughing faces through the bus window – maybe passing a motorway signpost saying 'Morecambe and Carnforth'.

EXT. FLAT (SEMI-DETACHED HOUSE). MORECAMBE. DAY.

Taxi arrives outside the semi-detached house, the upper floor of which is their flat.

Tufnell's van is outside, the furniture still being carried in.

The house is at the back edge of Morecambe, well distant from the sea, by the railway.

They go up to the door, which is open. A rather prissy fiftyish woman is putting newspapers down, the steps already being amply covered with them.

WOMAN You've got here safely, then?

MAM Yes.

WOMAN I'm Mrs Longstaff.

MAM How do you do?

MRS LONGSTAFF They've been trailing in and out all afternoon. Still, it's not every day, is it?

Mam and Dad go upstairs to their front door, which is at the top of the stairs.

INT. MORECAMBE FLAT. DAY.

Mam and Dad walk round the flat, the furniture all over the place. They look out of the windows.

MAM I wish we had our own entrance.

A little knock on the door.

MRS LONGSTAFF I thought you might like a cup of tea.

DAD Thank you very much.

MRS LONGSTAFF And a cake or two. I made them myself.

DAD Thank you. See, Mam.

43

MAM Thank you, yes.

MRS LONGSTAFF You come from Leeds?

DAD Yes.

MRS LONGSTAFF Lots of people here from Leeds. Home from home. Retired people. You're retired, I suppose.

MAM Yes.

MRS LONGSTAFF What sort of thing?

MAM Metal casings.

DAD (*overlapping*) Engineering.

MRS LONGSTAFF My nephew is in engineering. On the management side, of course. Nothing like that here, of course. No industry at all. That's a great boon. Have you got everything now?

DAD Ay, yes. We haven't a lot of stuff.

MRS LONGSTAFF No, well, you don't want it when you're getting on, do you?

DAD No

MRS LONGSTAFF Anyway, I'll leave you. Anything you want, just knock on my door. (*Mrs Longstaff exits.*)

DAD That was nice of her.

MAM How old do you reckon she was?

DAD Fifty-odd.

MAM Talking about getting on. I can't bide everybody wanting to know your business. This is poor tea. It's like medicine.

DAD We've no need to whisper.

MAM She might hear.

DAD She can't.

MAM I don't want her telling t'tale.

DAD We can't always be whispering. Come on.

MAM That's the trouble with flats. You never know who's listening.

DAD Nay, come on, Mam, we've only just got here. I don't know about tea, but these cakes are as hard as wuz.

MAM Well, we can't put them in the dustbin. She'll see.

DAD Save 'em. I'll give 'em to the seagulls.

They take off their coats and start putting the place straight. Maybe putting the bed up.

INT. BEDROOM. NIGHT.

The first night.

MAM Dad.

DAD What?

MAM Listen.

DAD What?

MAM Is that the sea?

DAD Traffic.

A dog is barking intermittently.

I hope that's not a feature. It's been yap-yap-yap all flaming night.

MAM It doesn't feel like our bed, somehow, this. There used to be a right dip there.

DAD It's flitting. It gets shaken about.

MAM Could you drink some tea?

DAD It's two o'clock in the morning.

MAM Well, we're retired now.

INT. BEDROOM. NIGHT. LATER.

MAM Shh. (*She tastes it and looks at it under the light.*) Tea has a right funny taste here.

DAD It's the water, so you'd better get used to it.

MAM How much did you give them removal men?

DAD Fifty p.

MAM That's a lot. Have we done right, do you think? It's like being able to have a choice makes it so difficult. We've never had a proper choice before. Its always been Leeds. There wasn't anywhere else we could have gone though, was there?

DAD Australia.

MAM What would we do in Australia? It's all for young 'uns. And we wouldn't have stopped here.

DAD Where?

MAM Leeds. Well we couldn't, could we?

DAD No.

MAM I wouldn't go in one of them tall blocks. Moortown, Seacroft. I don't want to be dumped on the outskirts. New estates, they're all hooligans. They find all sorts in them lifts. If we'd had a lass it would have been different. Lasses, they're always popping in.

45

DAD It's too late to start now.
   They laugh.
MAM Sssh. She'll wonder what's going on.

INT. BEDROOM. NEXT MORNING.
Dad looks at clock. Six o'clock.
Mam is fast asleep. He gets up quietly, and gets dressed.
MAM What's up?
DAD I'm just going out, a bit of a walk.
MAM Why, what time is it?
DAD Six o'clock. Go back to sleep.
   He shuts the door quietly, tiptoes down the stairs and out into the
   suburban avenue.

EXT. MORECAMBE. EARLY MORNING.
Shot of Dad walking along in the early morning sunshine past the
silent houses.
Then walking up the long road to the front.
Shot of him walking along the front, breathing in and obviously
enjoying himself.
He spots a tea bar open on the front and crosses the road, but goes into
a newsagents first.

INT. NEWSAGENTS. DAY.
DAD Have you got a Leeds paper?
NEWSAGENT We've got a *Bradford Argus.*
DAD That's not a Leeds paper.
NEWSAGENT Well, it's thereabouts.

INT. TEA BAR. DAY.
Dad is very cheery and talkative. Another man having a cup of tea
next to him.
DAD Nay, that's never tea.
MAN You get rheumatism from strong tea.
DAD First I ever heard of it.
MAN You do. Our lass was riddled with rheumatism and the first
   thing the doctor did was to take her off strong tea.
DAD And did it do any good?
MAN Well, I couldn't sup that anyroads.

The man is a holidaymaker in white open shirt and dark suit,
probably like Dad unable to lie abed although he's on his holidays.
I can't lie in, even on my holidays.

DAD I'm the same.

MAN Visitor?

DAD No. I live here. Retired.

MAN God, they're stopping them soon these days, aren't they?

DAD I'm sixty-five..

MAN Don't look it. Whereabouts?

DAD Leeds.

MAN Leeds.

ANOTHER MAN (*getting up*) Well, some of us have got jobs to go to.

DAD Sort of time do you call this? In Leeds we'd have been hard
at it by this.

EXT. MORECAMBE. LEADING TO FLAT. DAY.
Dad walking back through suburban streets. Mam is already up, and
waves to him from the window.

INT. FLAT. DAY.
Mam and Dad are cleaning up the flat. Dad is painting.

DAD The fellow that invented emulsion paint deserves a medal.

MAM There's a woman been sat in that window all morning.

DAD Five minutes and it's dry.

MAM You'd think she'd have something better to do.

DAD I don't think it needs another coat. What do you think?

MAM She could make a start scouring that step. It's disgusting.
What?

DAD Will that do?

MAM It's champion. It's a classy colour, is that. There's no muck
is there, see. Leeds, you could be scrubbing all day and it'd still
be black.

EXT. FLAT. DAY.
Doorstep of the house.

MAM Just a pint.

MILKMAN Any extras? Cream, eggs, yogurt?

MAM Yogurt? No. You have to be brought up to stuff like yogurt.

MILKMAN Put new life into you.

MAM It's funny stuff, I always think. Anyway, you can't be branching out into yogurt at our age.

MILKMAN Go on, live a bit.

MAM Maybe we'll have a little thing of double cream on Sundays.

MILKMAN Sorry, don't deliver Sundays.

MAM They did in Leeds.

FLAT, FROM HOUSE OPPOSITE.
Point of view of woman opposite:
A. Mam and Dad arranging furniture.
B. Re-arranging furniture, until the room is more or less shipshape.
C. Mam hanging curtains, which shut out the view, and end the scene.

EXT. BUS STOP. DAY.
Mam and Dad are waiting for the bus to take them up the long road to the sea front.

EXT. SEAFRONT. DAY.
Getting off the bus on the seafront.
Walking arm in arm among the crowds along the front.

MAM They were from Leeds.

DAD Yes?

MAM He used to be an inspector on the buses.

DAD I'll say one thing. It's not crowded.

MAM No. It's nice.

DAD In summer you'd have to fight your way along here.

EXT. SEAFRONT. DAY. LATER.
Shelter facing sea, on promenade.
Mam is writing postcards, and watching people go by.

MAM It's no wonder the mills are closing. Skirts are that short. Look at her. There's no material there.

DAD It beats Wellington Road does this.

BORING WOMAN Grand morning.

DAD Ay.

BORING WOMAN Fair feels to do you good.

DAD Ay.

BORING WOMAN Would you like a toffee?

MAM No thank you, we shall be having our dinner soon.

BORING WOMAN I don't have dinner. I have my main meal at night.

MAM Oh yes.

BORING WOMAN Ever since I lost my husband.

MAM That's right.

BORING WOMAN I don't feel to want as much, somehow. I think you don't.

MAM No.

EXT. SEAFRONT. DAY.

DAD Yon's a boring woman. Talk, talk, talk, and when it's all done she's said nowt.

MAM It's happen because her husband died.

DAD I bet he were after a bit of peace and quiet.

MAM Look at this feller's trousers.

EXT. BOARDING HOUSES. DAY.

Mam and Dad walking past boarding houses.
Holidaymakers sat outside waiting for their lunch.
Boarding-house front windows, with cruets and 'Vacancies' signs.

MAM (*voice over*) We've stayed at some shocking places. Shocking. Of course it's different now, with these package holidays. They have to provide a bit more. In the old days landladies could do what they want. Right dictators. And you're not your own master. Ten o'clock and they like you out, and it doesn't matter if it's raining, there's no stopping in. Course they all call themselves private hotels now, you see. Central heating, television. And television, you have to have the programmes they want, you're not free. No . . .

INT. FLAT. EVENING.

The flat. Mam and Dad are sitting at home.

MAM I'm glad we've got our own place. I wouldn't fancy poling back to digs every day. Do you remember that place we stayed, that woman with the bald husband?

DAD That was at Cleveleys.

MAM She hit our Bertram, did that woman. 'No sand in the bedroom.'

DAD He used to have to do everything, that feller. Washed up,
  laid the tables . . . she never did a hand's turn.
MAM You were that hungry you used to put sauce on bread.
  Then she tippled to that and took the sauce away.
DAD And it was a seven-mile walk to the lavatory.
MAM These days folks wouldn't stand for it.
DAD What's the time?
MAM Five past five. Why?
DAD Nowt. They do seem long days.

EXT. MONTAGE. DAY.
A. The promenade. Mam and Dad sat on a seat, watching passers-by.
B. The pier. Mam and Dad sat on a seat watching a man fishing.
C. The sands. Dad asleep against the promenade wall, Mam paddling.
D. Floral Hall. Mam and Dad listening to the orchestra. Dad asleep.

EXT. OUTSIDE CAFÉ. DAY.
MAM Shall we have our dinner out? I mean, just for a change?
DAD We can if you want.
MAM It'd save us going back.
  They look at menu outside café.
  Seventy-five p. for plaice and chips and tartare sauce. They
  don't know what to charge. And that doesn't include tea and
  bread and butter.
DAD You'd have to fill up on tartare sauce. Come on.

INT. ITALIAN RESTAURANT (EMPTY). DAY.
MAM They've altered this place. It used to be a right grand old-
  fashioned place.
DAD It'll do. I'm fed up of trailing round.
MAM It's all continental. I've been coming here for years. Waiters
  now. It used to be waitresses.
  A waiter brings menus.
  See. Where are my reading glasses? What do you think, Dad?
DAD I don't know. What do you think?
MAM We were wanting something like . . . well, is there anything
  like Welsh Rarebit?
  The waiter smiles, uncomprehending.

WAITER Yes?

MAM Welsh Rarebit.

DAD Cheese on toast.

WAITER Is toasted cheese, here?

He points out a dish on the menu.

MAM Is it? It doesn't look like toasted cheese to me. Are you sure?

WAITER So. Si.

DAD Well, we'd better have that.

MAM Can we have some tea and bread and butter, to go with it?

WAITER Is roll and butter.

MAM Oh. Well, we won't bother then.

*Point of view of Mam and Dad watching waiter going off with the
order.*

(*voice over*) They regiment you, don't they? You have to have
what they want. Still. I like these tablecloths. And that
wallpaper's bonny.

Mam and Dad are eating their meal.

MAM It's all right is this, isn't it, Dad?

DAD It's not Welsh Rarebit.

MAM Ay, but it's nice. We're branching out a bit. Italian
restaurants.

DAD We shan't have to be going into cafés now, you know, now
there's nought coming in.

MAM Well, it's a change.

EXT. OUTSIDE ITALIAN RESTAURANT. DAY.

MAM I've got a bit of shopping to do.

DAD I'll just have a walk round, meet you at the shelter.

EXT. MORECAMBE STREETS. DAY.

*Dad wanders away from the front and the tourist part of the town.
A bricklayer is building a wall, mixing cement. Dad watches him for
a bit.*

BRICKLAYER How do you do.

DAD How do you do.

*Dad goes on watching him for a fair while, then touches his cap,
nods and goes on, bricklayer watching him go.*

EXT. MORECAMBE STREETS. DAY.
Dad stops by a man digging his garden, watching him turn over the soil.
DAD You've gotten yourself a right job there.
MAN Aye.
DAD You're making a good job of it.
MAN Aye.
The same. He watches for a while, and then goes on.

INT. SHELTER. DAY.
BORING WOMAN He was three hours on the table. Three hours.
And they still didn't save him. It'd gone to the brain.
*Mam is sat with her postcards, trying to start writing them again,
but having to make a show of listening.*
He died on the table. Twice. Only the first time they
resuscitated him. Well, the doctor came in and said should they
resuscitate him again. They asked me. It was my decision. It
was terrible. I said, 'Well, if it's all the same to you, no, I didn't
want him fetched backwards and forwards.' I think the body
knows best. Oh, here's your hubby.
She moves up to let Dad sit down.
Besides. He wasn't like my husband, not at the finish.

INT. SHELTER, LATER. DAY.
Mam still writing postcards.
DAD There's no need to be sending off postcards every day, you
know. It isn't as if we were on our holidays.
MAM You've got to keep in touch.
DAD We can't run to the stamps. There must be four-bobsworth
in postage there.
MAM Folks expect it.
DAD Not every five minutes they don't.
MAM I don't know why you don't read. You're fast what to do
with yourself, that's your trouble.
DAD I am. Trailing round after you all day. I've gotten right
stalled.
MAM Well, go off by yourself then, if I'm such a burden.
DAD Ay, well, I will.
MAM Ay, well, do.
But he doesn't. Pause.

Come on, let's make tracks.
They go.

INT. BEDROOM. NIGHT.
Mam is getting into bed. Dad is in bed already.
She turns the light off and there is silence.

MAM Dad.

DAD What?

MAM I'm sorry.

DAD We seem to do nothing but trail about, that's all.

MAM It takes time.

DAD We get all dolled up and go out and where is it we're going?
To get a loaf and two tomatoes.

MAM You're not used to it.

DAD I wouldn't care, but this place we're always under each
other's feet. It's like a rabbit hutch.

MAM Nay, it's not. It's just that we're in all day.

DAD Retirement.

MAM Well, it's retirement for me, too.

DAD Nay, it isn't. It's the same for you. This is the way you've
always been. Doing the housework, going down the road. Me, I
had six men under me.

MAM Maybe you could see about trying to get an allotment.

DAD I know one thing, we're going to have to pull our horns in.
We don't want to be putting in for the Supplementary.

MAM It's nothing to be ashamed of.

DAD We shall just have to clamp down a bit. If it wasn't for that
bit from our Bertram we wouldn't be able to manage. I don't
know.

MAM And we'll have to get out more. See more folks. Mix.

DAD You work all your life and this is what it's for, it's all leading
up to this.

MAM (*crying*) Nay, Frank.

DAD What're you roaring about? Give over. We're like these
young folks now. No ties, no place, nowt. Relatives scattered all
over the shop.

MAM You want to think of it as a holiday.

DAD It's not holidays. Holidays you've got to pack it all in, you've
only got a fortnight, then you've got your work to go back to.

53

Us, we've got nothing to go back to. We've got all the time in the world.

MAM Nay, we haven't. We don't know how long we've got.

DAD Now don't start getting morbid.

MAM I think we ought to try and mix a bit more.

DAD Mix.

MAM Anyway, I'm sorry.

DAD Go to sleep.

INT./EXT. GOSPEL HALL. DAY.
It is an old-age pensioners' meeting. Full.
Mam and Dad sat in the middle, Dad looking glum and out of place,
Mam trying half-heartedly to join in.
They are singing.

PENSIONERS We are H-A-P-P-Y, H-A-P-P-Y.
We are H-A-P,
We are H-A-P,
We are H-A-P-P-Y.
Many more women than men in the audience.
A woman bouncing away on the piano, and a man in white flannels
and white shirt, slightly camp, conducting.

CONDUCTOR Come on, sing up. We can show the young 'uns a thing or two, eh?
A rather reedy woman is standing up, witnessing.

MISS VENABLES God wants us to be healthy if only we'll allow ourselves to be. It's we who are standing in his way, thinking wrong, negative thoughts. 'Oh, I do feel poorly today. Oh dear, this headache is getting me down.' Sometimes I think we think ourselves into the grave.
Some murmurs of assent.
Animals don't think, do they? You don't see dogs going about with long faces or worrying where their next meal is coming from.
Camera should be on Mam and Dad in much of this.
Mam is nervous of Dad's reaction, which is very sceptical and embarrassed.
And they're God's creatures just like us.

CONDUCTOR Thank you, Miss Venables. Now, Mrs Liversidge, I believe you have a thought you want to share.

Mrs Liversidge consulting a crumpled bit of paper.

MRS LIVERSIDGE Yes, I have. I think the body is the mind. I think they're both part of the same thing. Just as a tree is part of a wood and wood is part of a tree.

There is an awkward pause.

CONDUCTOR Would you like to take that thought any further, Mrs Liversidge?

MRS LIVERSIDGE (*happily*) No.

CONDUCTOR Now Miss Passmore is going to give us 'Jerusalem' and then we'll adjourn into the Wilberforce Room for some tea.

Miss Passmore starts on 'Jerusalem'. She is rather shaky, both on words and notes, but fills in the missing bits without embarrassment with 'la la la'.

EXT. OUTSIDE HALL.

Sound of pensioners singing 'Tell Me the Old, Old Story' in the hall, with hand-clappings, as Mam and Dad come away.

EXT. SUBURBAN STREETS. NIGHT.

Mam and Dad walking home.

DAD We're not failing. They must think we're dateless.

MAM You've got to make an effort. Join in. That woman next to me was ever so nice.

DAD I don't care. Three months ago I was doing a responsible job and now I'm fit for nowt but clapping my hands with a roomful of daft old lasses.

MAM It wasn't all like that.

DAD I had six men under me. I'm not soft in the head.

MAM It's all right saying that, but how many folks do we speak to in the course of a week?

DAD You were the one that wasn't fond of folks. You were the one who thought soon as we got to Morecambe we'd be invaded with folks.

MAM Well, it hasn't got to the season yet. There'll be all sorts to do.

DAD Anyway, I don't care if I never speak to a flaming soul. I'm not going there again.

They are passing lighted windows, people taking their dogs out. Other lives going on.

55

MAM We never used to fratch, did we? It's being under each
other's feet all day.
DAD I am H-A-P-P-Y. I am not H-A-P-P-Y.
They both laugh.
MAM And she couldn't sing, that woman. I don't know how
she'd the face to stand up.
They are going up the path.
The curtain twitches. They let themselves in.
MRS LONGSTAFF There's a letter for you.
MAM Thank you. Nosey beggar.

INT. FLAT. NIGHT.
MAM Where's my other glasses? (*Mam is finding her reading
glasses.*) They only wrote last week. I hope there's nothing
wrong. These flaming airmail letters. I never know which side
to slit.
Dad is putting the kettle on. She is reading.
Dad. Dad. He's coming home. He's coming here. He's going
to be here for a week.
DAD When, our Bertram?
MAM Nineteenth to the twenty-seventh. On business.
DAD It's nobbut a fortnight. Isn't that lovely? Nay. What're you
worrying for, he's coming home.

INT. LOUNGE. MIDLAND HOTEL, MORECAMBE. DAY.
*They are sat in the lounge having afternoon tea with Bertram, their
son, a man of about forty.*
MAM I've often seen folks come in and wondered what it was like
inside. Mind you, it's only ordinary, isn't it? Is it very
expensive?
BERTRAM It doesn't matter, does it? I'm not here every day.
MAM Here, Dad.
DAD Well, we're only having our tea. We haven't booked in for a
month.
MAM Look at them folks over there. She looks right common.
They aren't better class at all. They don't look any different
from us.
BERTRAM You don't have to be better class. Money's all that
matters.

MAM Look at that frock. I wouldn't go to the closet in that frock.
And see! That kiddie's picking his nose.

BERTRAM Mam.

MAM Are we showing you up?

BERTRAM No.

DAD Behave yourself. She's always staring.

MAM He is brown. You're brown. He's brown, isn't he, Dad?

DAD Ay, well, it'll be the sun.

BERTRAM Yes.

MAM It is grand to see you.

BERTRAM It's grand to see you too.

MAM They have that music. It's everywhere nowadays. They have
it on railway stations now, you know. Do they have it in
Australia?

BERTRAM Oh yes.

MAM I can't do with it. I'd rather have it loud enough to listen to
or not at all. Wouldn't you, Dad?

DAD I don't mind.

MAM No, you wouldn't.

DAD Well, what's the point of discussing it?

MAM You could ask them to turn it off.

BERTRAM Mam.

DAD She's always like this. You see what I have to put up with.

MAM Have another cake, go on.

BERTRAM No, I have to watch my weight.

MAM You're not fat. Is he, Dad? Go on, you can eat another.

BERTRAM No. I've had enough.

MAM Here.

DAD He's had enough.

MAM (*whispering*) Do you think we could ask for some more hot
water? It's getting a bit strong.

BERTRAM Well, ask for some.

MAM (*after trying to catch waiter's eye*) Excuse me, but do you
think we could have a bit more hot water?
*She starts to hand the jug to the waiter, who was going to take it
anyway, and in the confusion knocks over the milk jug.*

DAD Nay, Mam.

MAM Ooh. I am sorry.

WAITER It's nothing, madam.

MAM Whatever must they think?

DAD It's nowt.

BERTRAM Forget it.

MAM Are you going to leave a tip? Nay, Bertram, that's too
much. Tell him, Dad.

BERTRAM It's nothing.

MAM Do you think I could go spend a penny? Look after my
bag. (*She goes.*)

BERTRAM Mam's no different.

DAD No. She revels in it here. Mind you, she always has.

BERTRAM How are you?

DAD Nicely. We're both nicely. Well, you can tell.

BERTRAM You look well. Can you manage?

DAD Oh yes. I mean, we couldn't if you hadn't got us the flat and
everything, but we're all right.
The waiter comes up and Bertram pays the bill.
We don't spend much. Naught much to spend it on. We've got
everything we want, you know. Thanks to you.

BERTRAM Oh no.

DAD Oh yes.

BERTRAM I should think it does you good here, too.

DAD Oh yes. It's clean. There's no muck.
They are waiting for Mam to come out of the Ladies.
Oh come on, Mam. Trouble with your mam is, when she goes
to the toilet she has to have an all-over wash afterwards.
Mam appears.

MAM Come on. It's a lovely lavatory. Are we ready?
Dad gives her her bag. The waiter is passing.
I am sorry about that milk.

BERTRAM Mam.

WAITER It's nothing, madam.

EXT. LAKE DISTRICT. DAY.
Bertram takes them for a drive in the car to the Lake District.
Shots of them sat in a rowing boat, with Bertram rowing.
He takes their photographs sat on a seat.
Voices over shots of them in the Lake District.

MAM In summer it's overrun with cars. They're going to have to
restrict it.

DAD That's one thing we miss. Transport. Fares are shocking.

MAM Wicked.

DAD If we had a little car we could go all over.

BERTRAM You want to learn to drive.

MAM That's what I tell him.

DAD Nay, I'm past that.

MAM Daffodils by Ullswater.
> I wandered lonely as a cloud
> That floats on high o'er vales and hills.
> Then all at once I saw a crowd,
> A host of golden daffodils.
> When oft upon my couch I lie,
> In vacant or in pensive mood . . .

DAD That'll be the day.

MAM I learned that at Green Lane School fifty-five years ago. It's a privilege to be out on a day like this. I bet there's nothing like this in Australia, is there?
Shot of them walking along a road, the three of them, and Mam putting her arm in Bertram's as they walk along, and looking at him, really happy.

EXT. SANDS. DAY/EVENING.
End of Bertram's visit.
Sands. West End of Morecambe, looking over to Grange.
Big sky. Sunset.

MAM Grange is ever so plain.

BERTRAM You know you can always come out, don't you?

DAD Can we? Do you hear that, Mam?

BERTRAM Any time, I mean, for good.

MAM Nay, well . . . we wouldn't know anybody, would we, except you and Gillian?

BERTRAM Well, who do you know here?

DAD That's what I tell her. We know nobody.

MAM It's your dad. He won't branch out. He doesn't even try to strike up new acquaintances.

DAD I'm past the age for striking up new acquaintances. You're not striking up new acquaintances when you're over sixty-five.

MAM You can. There's always time to strike out.

DAD Not in Morecambe.

BERTRAM Anyway, think about it. Gillian would be really pleased.

DAD She's a grand lass. And the kiddies.

MAM I'd be smothered in Australia. I were smothered in Torquay.
Dad shakes his head.
You get some lovely sunsets here. Grandma always said that. The best sunsets she ever saw were at Morecambe, between the wars.

DAD It'll seem quiet when you've gone. It's been grand having a run out. I can't see it makes much difference where we are, the life we lead. Trailing round the shops looking in windows, sitting out on the front. There's no point in any of it.

MAM It's because you won't get down and get used to it. He won't, Bertram. That's what retirement's like.
The conversation should be fading away as they walk back up the sands to the car parked on the promenade.

DAD This is what I've been working for us, this is knocking-off time.

MAM I keep telling him. It's been grand seeing you.

BERTRAM It's been grand seeing you.

INT. FLAT. DAY.
Dad staring out of his window with his hat and coat and scarf on. He is waiting for Mam.

DAD Come on. Be sharp.

MAM We haven't got to be anywhere.

DAD It's always waiting. I've done nothing but wait for you ever since we were married.

MAM Is that letter ready to post?
She is getting a drink of water, going to the lav. She has her hat on.

DAD I'm fast what to say. What is there to tell them?

MAM Tell them Mrs Wainwright's dead.

DAD It's all deaths. That's all we ever tell them. He won't remember who Mrs Wainwright was anyway.

MAM He will. He used to play out with their Derek.

DAD She was a right particular article anyway. What're we doing writing halfway across the world to tell them about Mrs Wainwright for?

MAM She's dead.

DAD You wouldn't have crossed the street for her when she was alive.

MAM You're always going on at me now, you. We never used to have a wrong word.

DAD I can't see the point of it.

MAM Nay, Dad.

DAD Oh, stop pulling your face, and be sharp, we shall miss the film.

MAM I don't want to go.

DAD Well I'm not traipsing about all afternoon. Get yourself ready.

MAM I am ready.

INT. CINEMA FOYER. DAY

MAM I don't like going to the pictures in an afternoon anyway. I don't like coming out when it's light.

DAD Well, you'd better ask them to change the concession. Two, please. Pensioners. Have you got our cards?

INT. CINEMA. DAY.

Almost empty. A few people scattered here and there.

DAD Do you want an ice cream?

MAM I don't want a whole one. (*calling after him*) . . . And not chocolate.

Dad is waiting in front of the usherette. Two children are served.

USHERETTE Fifteen p.

DAD Have they gone up, then?

USHERETTE No.

DAD Give us two spoons, then.

MAM Open me this spoon. I don't know why they have to put it all in bags.

Film starts.

INT. CINEMA FOYER. DAY.

MAM Pictures nowadays, they have right funny endings. You never know where you are. What was he going to do? And they have to put sex in. They're all the same.

DAD It was all right.

MAM Ay, you like all that.

DAD Nay. I never do.

MAM You did. Some of it . . . you don't know where to put yourself.

DAD Let's walk on a bit. It's taken up.

MAM It's got warmer. I bet you it's going to be lovely this summer. Are you all right?

DAD Course I'm all right. It strains your eyes a bit though, when you're not used to it.

EXT. PROMENADE. DAY.

DAD Shall we have a sit-down?

MAM Nay, it's too cold to sit.

DAD Let's sit a bit.

MAM Are you still feeling funny?

DAD I'm all right.

Shot of them walking along the deserted seafront.
They are passing a public lavatory.

I think I'll just shed a tear.

Mam waits. And five minutes go by. She walks up and down
He still doesn't come out. She gets agitated, looks up and down the
front. A man comes along.

MAM Excuse me, I wonder whether . . . it seems funny asking.

Man looks at her, uncomprehending.

My husband's gone into the toilet and he's been in there twenty minutes, well, I mean . . . I don't think he intended to, like, not so long.

MAN You don't know, do you? Anyway there'll be an attendant.

MAM There isn't always, is there, and I can't really go in . . .

MAN Could you not find a policeman?

MAM There isn't one, I've been looking.

MAN What does he look like?

INT. PUBLIC LAVATORY. DAY.

It is empty.

MAN Hello, hello.

He walks down the cubicles. Most of the doors are open. He pushes
one of the doors. Dad is sat there in his clothes, slumped against
the wall.

EXT. PROMENADE. DAY.
Public lavatory.
> *Getting into ambulance. A small crowd watching. Just as the*
> *stretcher is lifted in, Dad moves.*
DAD Alice?
MAM Frank.

INT. CASUALTY WAITING ROOM. DAY/EVENING.
Two young doctors talking together, laughing.
One straightens his face and comes over.
DOCTOR Do you understand what a stroke is, Mrs . . . (*He looks*
   down at his paper.) . . . Palmer?
MAM Is it like a seizure?
DOCTOR What happens is that the blood breaks through into the
   brain and interferes with its functions.
MAM Yes, doctor.
DOCTOR It may only be a small part of the brain, in which case
   there may not be much damage done. We shan't know that
   until he comes round.
MAM I see.
DOCTOR But the longer he stays unconscious, I'm afraid the
   more serious it is.
MAM He's never had anything like this before, he's always
   been . . .
DOCTOR No, well that's . . .
MAM I can't think what would have caused it.
   Doctor waits.
DOCTOR Can we telephone? Is there someone we can ring, who'd
   come to stay with you?
MAM Not really. No.
DOCTOR There must be someone. Neighbours.
MAM We don't have any . . . right . . . neighbours. I'll just wait.
DOCTOR Are you sure?
MAM Yes.
DOCTOR I'll get someone to bring you a cup of tea.
MAM Thank you.
   The doctor is going away.
   Er . . .
DOCTOR Sorry?

MAM Weak tea.
DOCTOR Yes.

INT. HOSPITAL. AN OFFICE. DAY/EVENING.
Nurse filling in a form.
NURSE And who's his next of kin?
MAM Well, I am.
NURSE No, apart from you.
    *Mam looks round the office as the nurse writes out the information.
    She looks at the things on the wall. A busty calendar. Jokey notices:
    'The Buck Stops Here,' 'Danger. Men at Work'. Postcards from
    abroad, etc.*
MAM We've got a son, in Australia. But he wouldn't want him
    fetched back. You see, we've come from Leeds.
NURSE Is there anybody there?
MAM He's got some cousins in Pudsey.
NURSE It's only a formality.
MAM I don't know.
NURSE Anyway, it's only in case the worst comes to the worst.
    The doctor comes in behind Mam, slight shake of head to the nurse.

INT. HOSPITAL. DAY.
*Mam is sat alone on bench against a white ground-glass screen. She
has been crying. Figures are moving behind the screen, blurred by the
frosted glass. Voices half-heard. Occasional remarks. Laughter, distant
noises. A sort of nowhere feeling.*
NURSE Would you like to come in now, Mrs Palmer?

INT. HOSPITAL WARD. DAY/EVENING.
*There are screens round the bed in the ward. The patients are having
their teas. Chattering. Which is stilled as she comes in. Some smile,
apologetically. She comes round the screens. Big glass windows.
Lights. Shot of her against a big window, low down, with Dad on the
pillow, all in bottom of frame.
His watch is still ticking on his wrist. She spits on her handkerchief
and wipes a mark off his face. Subdued sounds of the ward.
She looks at him . . . gets up. Looks back just before she goes round the
screen.
She goes down the ward, passing two porters waiting with a trolley.*

*One gives a slight nod as she goes, and they begin to wheel the trolley
down the ward.*

INT. SUB POST OFFICE. DAY.
Mam has written out a telegram: DAD PASSED AWAY SUDDENLY
MONDAY 3.45 P.M. I WILL WRITE TO YOU, MAM.
WOMAN Shall I put letter follows?
MAM What?
WOMAN Letter follows. It's cheaper.
MAM Oh yes.
WOMAN And it'd be better, 15.45 hours. That'd save you ten p on
    the p.m. You see.
MAM 15.45?
WOMAN That is 3.45 you see.
MAM Will they know that?
WOMAN In Australia? I think so.
MAM No. I'll put the other.
WOMAN All right, love.
    Mam pays.
MAM Oh, and I'd better have an airmail letter thing.

EXT. SEAFRONT. EMPTY DAY.
*Vast empty sands, with the tide out. Mam is walking on the front near
their shelter. As she passes she sees the boring woman sat there, giving
her a little smile. She walks on along the promenade.*
    Fade out.

A Visit from Miss Prothero

CAST AND CREDITS

A Visit from Miss Prothero was first transmitted
by the BBC on 11 January 1978 with the following cast:

MR DODSWORTH	Hugh Lloyd
MISS PROTHERO	Patricia Routledge
Directed by	Stephen Frears
Music	George Fenton

The living room of a semi-detached house. A worn, comfortable, cosy place. Dozing in an armchair and similarly worn, cosy and comfortable is Mr Dodsworth, a man in his sixties. In a cardigan and carpet slippers with the top button of his trousers undone, Mr Dodsworth is retired. He is just having five minutes and, unless one counts the budgie, he is alone.

A few moments pass, sufficient for the tranquillity of the household to be established, then the door-chimes go. Mr Dodsworth does not respond. The chimes go again.

Mr Dodsworth stirs and fastening the top button of his trousers gets up and addresses the budgie.

MR DODSWORTH Who's this then, Millie? Who's this?

He goes out, leaving the living-room door open. The front door opens. (*off*) Is it you, Miss Prothero?

MISS PROTHERO (*off*) It is.

MR DODSWORTH (*off*) I didn't expect to see you.

While Mr Dodsworth hovers in the living-room doorway the visitor comes in boldly. It is a middle-aged woman, who runs a critical eye over the warm, comfortable, cosy room. She is none of these things.

MISS PROTHERO I was beginning to think I'd got the wrong house.

MR DODSWORTH Why? Had you been stood there long?

MISS PROTHERO A minute or two.

MR DODSWORTH No, it's the right house. Number 59. The Dodsworth residence.

MISS PROTHERO I rang twice.

MR DODSWORTH To tell you the truth I was just having five minutes.

MISS PROTHERO I'm surprised. You were the one who couldn't abide a nap.

MR DODSWORTH Was I? You'll take your coat off?

MISS PROTHERO I was waiting to be asked.

He starts to help her off with her coat.

I shan't stop.

MR DODSWORTH No, but . . .

MISS PROTHERO I still have my back, so I'll keep my undercoat on.
Mr Dodsworth is tugging at her cardigan sleeve, trying to take it off.
That's my undercoat.

MR DODSWORTH Sorry. Sorry.

MISS PROTHERO This time of year can be very treacherous.
(*Spring, summer, autumn, winter . . . to Miss Prothero the seasons
are all potential assassins.*) And I'd best keep my hat on as well.
I don't want another sinus do.
*Mr Dodsworth is about to bear away the fainted form of Miss
Prothero's swagger coat when she stops him.*
I'm forgetting my hanky.
*She takes it out of the pocket and blows her nose as Mr Dodsworth
carries her coat out to the hallstand.*
There's half a dozen people I ought to go see only I thought
you might be feeling a bit out of it. I said to Doreen, 'I know
Mr Dodsworth, he'll be wanting to be brought up to date.'

MR DODSWORTH (*off*) What on?

MISS PROTHERO What on? Work! Warburtons!

MR DODSWORTH (*off*) Oh, *work*. No. No.

MISS PROTHERO (*to herself*) I'm sorry I came then.
*She remains standing in one spot, surveying the room as Mr
Dodsworth bustles back.*

MR DODSWORTH What I mean, of course, is I do want to be
brought up to date but to tell you the truth, Peggy, since I've
left I've hardly had time to turn round. What with bowling on
Tuesdays and my Rotary thing on Fridays and Gillian and the
kiddies bobbing in every five minutes, I honestly haven't given
work a thought. Which is amazing when you think I was there
all those years. But you know what they say: retirement, it's a
full-time job. Ha ha.
*Miss Prothero doesn't laugh. She vaguely flinches. Miss Prothero is
one of those people who only see jokes by appointment.*
What about you? Have you taken the day off?

MISS PROTHERO Mr Dodsworth, when did I take a day off? In all
the years we worked together when did I ever take a day off?
Even the day I buried Mother I came in in the afternoon to
do the backlog. It shows you how out of touch you are. What
day is it?

MR DODSWORTH Thursday.

MISS PROTHERO What week? Week 35. The Works Outing.

MR DODSWORTH Are we into Week 35? There you are. It just
shows you how I've lost track. You've not gone, then?

MISS PROTHERO After last year? I haven't.

MR DODSWORTH Is it Bridlington again?

MISS PROTHERO Langdale Pikes.

MR DODSWORTH A beauty spot! That's a departure. It's generally
always Bridlington. Or thereabouts. Langdale Pikes. Quite
scenic.

MISS PROTHERO That's because Design put their spoke in.
Costing and Estimates pulled a long face but it's only fair:
it goes by departments. I dread to think where they'll choose
next year.

MR DODSWORTH Whose turn is it then?

MISS PROTHERO (*ominously*) Maintenance and Equipment.
Mind you, as I said to Mr Butterfield in Projects, with a
coachload of animals the venue is immaterial.

MR DODSWORTH It's only once a year.

MISS PROTHERO That coach, if it stopped once it stopped several
times. Mr Teasdale's never looked me in the eye since. Wendy
Walsh won't even speak to him.

MR DODSWORTH I never thought he had it in him.

MISS PROTHERO He was a wild beast. It's Mrs Teasdale I feel
sorry for. Married to him. And she only has one kidney.
Anyway Mr Skinner soon sized him up. He kept him filling
out 5D forms the whole of the first week: that took the wind
out of his sails. I thought 'Full marks to Mr Skinner.'

MR DODSWORTH Oh yes, Skinner. How is Skinner?

MISS PROTHERO Getting into his stride. I think he'll turn out to
be a bit of a dynamo.

MR DODSWORTH He seemed a nice fellow. Young, but nice.
Aren't you going to sit down?

MISS PROTHERO I was waiting to be asked. (*She settles herself in a
chair by the fire.*) No. Don't you worry about Mr Skinner.

MR DODSWORTH I wasn't.

MISS PROTHERO He wouldn't thank you if you did. He goes his
own way does Mr Skinner. Our new broom! All I wonder is
how someone of his calibre bothers wasting his time at

Warburtons. He could go anywhere, Mr Skinner. Brazil. New York. They'd snap him up. (*On a table by where she is sitting is a wedding photograph.*) Is that Mrs Dodsworth?

MR DODSWORTH Which?

MISS PROTHERO This woman with her arm through yours.

MR DODSWORTH We'd just got married.

MISS PROTHERO Oh. I suppose that's why she's smiling. Funny dress.

MR DODSWORTH Is it? They're coming back now.

MISS PROTHERO Like that? Are they? I haven't seen them. No, I was saying, it's not that I'm short of somewhere to go. I've got one or two people who're always begging me to pop in, one of them a retired chiropodist, but I knew you'd be wanting all the latest gen from Warburtons. I'd have come sooner but it's been a busy time, as you can imagine.

MR DODSWORTH What with?

MISS PROTHERO With the change-over. The new regime. I just bobbed on a bus. With the 23 going right up Gelderd Road it makes it very handy. You can tell; I was coming out of the house at twenty-five to and it's only ten past now.

MR DODSWORTH You must have been lucky.

MISS PROTHERO It's just a matter of pitching it right. Don't think I've ever had to wait for a bus, ever.

MR DODSWORTH I've started pottery classes.

MISS PROTHERO Whatever for?

MR DODSWORTH I made this last week.

MISS PROTHERO Oh. What is it?

MR DODSWORTH It's an ashtray.

MISS PROTHERO I didn't think you smoked. You wouldn't recognise the office now. There's all sorts been happening.

MR DODSWORTH There has to me. I'm starting cooking classes.

MISS PROTHERO Cookery? For men?

MR DODSWORTH For anybody. There's several of us retired people, it's a right nice young lady does the teaching. It's cordon bleu.

MISS PROTHERO Cordon bleu!

MR DODSWORTH I thought it was about time I branched out a bit.

MISS PROTHERO I can see I've come to the wrong place. I thought you'd be busting for news of Warburtons and here you are all

set up with pottery and cookery, out and about every night. We
must seem very dull.

MR DODSWORTH No, Peggy, you're wrong. You don't. But the way
I look at it is this: I spent half my life at Warburtons and apart
from Winnie it was my whole world. I've been retired four
months and I'm beginning to see it's *not* the whole world, not by
a long chalk. I was there thirty years, it's time I branched out.

MISS PROTHERO Well, there you are, you say it's not the whole
world: I got three letters last week from Japan, there was a firm
enquiry from Zambia and Mr Skinner says once we get a
foothold in these oil-producing countries, there's no reason
why the whole of the Middle East shouldn't be banging on the
door.

MR DODSWORTH At Warburtons? Really?

MISS PROTHERO We had a delegation round last week from
Romania.

MR DODSWORTH They'd come a long way.

MISS PROTHERO Mr Skinner introduced me. Considering they
were from behind the Iron Curtain, I found them very
charming.

MR DODSWORTH What do they want coming round from
Romania?

MISS PROTHERO We've got Mr Skinner to thank for that. He's a
leading light in the Chamber of Trade. He says Warburtons is
part of a much wider world picture. Export or die. And he
runs that office with the smoothness of a well-oiled machine.
Not that I'm saying you didn't.

MR DODSWORTH Well, it was friendly.

MISS PROTHERO Yes. He's put a stop to all that.

MR DODSWORTH What?

MISS PROTHERO All that going to the toilet. Mr Teasdale falling
out for a smoke. Pauline Lucas coming down for half an hour
at a stretch. He soon had her taped.

MR DODSWORTH Is she still ginger?

MISS PROTHERO Who?

MR DODSWORTH Pauline. She was blonde. I thought ginger
suited her better.

MISS PROTHERO I thought it was a bit on the common side. And
there's not so much of the Pauline nowadays either. People get

called by their proper titles. It's Miss Prothero, Mrs Lucas. None of this Pauline and Peggying. Status. I like it. (*Suddenly Miss Prothero lunges for the electric fire.*) Could we have a bar off? Miss Cardwell's had her baby.

MR DODSWORTH Who?

MISS PROTHERO Miss Cardwell. In the typing pool.

MR DODSWORTH Maureen? Had a baby? I thought she had rheumatic fever. In Nottingham.

MISS PROTHERO Well, if she did she got it knitting bootees.

MR DODSWORTH Boy?

MISS PROTHERO Girl. The image of him, so I'm told.

MR DODSWORTH Who?

MISS PROTHERO Mr Corkery.

MR DODSWORTH In Despatch?

MISS PROTHERO Costing. He's been transferred.

MR DODSWORTH Poor Maureen.

MISS PROTHERO Poor nothing. She waltzed down with some snaps of it last week. I didn't know where to put myself.

MR DODSWORTH Will she keep it?

MISS PROTHERO She'll keep it all right. Same as Christine Thoseby kept hers. Park it in the day nursery all day and come in dressed up to the nines. Equal pay! They don't deserve it. I ran into her the other day, Christine. Yellow cashmere costume, high boots. That's the trouble these days: people don't know where to draw the line. (*Pause.*) Food in the canteen doesn't get any better, mince three times last week. Somebody's making something on the side, meals that price. You never see that supervisor but what she's got a parcel. Wicked. If I were the fifth floor that's where I'd clamp down.

MR DODSWORTH They always seem to have a smile, that's the main thing.

MISS PROTHERO Of course they have a smile. Something to smile about, the money they make. That supervisor's just gone and got herself a little bungalow at Roundhay.

Mr Dodsworth doesn't want to know about the canteen, mince on the menu or the supervisor's bungalow at Roundhay. He doesn't want to know about Warburtons at all. There are worlds elsewhere. He goes over to the birdcage.

MR DODSWORTH You haven't met Millie, have you? This is Miss
Prothero. Say how do you do.
Millie doesn't oblige.
She's been a bit depressed today.
*But Miss Prothero is not to be turned aside by the state of mind of
an unknown budgie.*
MISS PROTHERO I wasn't aware they got depressed. What've
they got to be depressed about? They don't have to work for
a living. (*Pause.*) I've changed my extension.
MR DODSWORTH Oh yes?
MISS PROTHERO You remember I used to be 216. Now I'm 314.
MR DODSWORTH Going up in the world.
MISS PROTHERO Doreen Glazier's 216 now. Big change for her.
Preston and Fosters rang last week and didn't realise. I saw
Mr Skinner smile. She's still got that nasty eczema.
MR DODSWORTH Doreen? Poor girl.
MISS PROTHERO The doctor thinks it's nerves. I think it's those
tights. Man-made fibres don't do for everybody: I pay if I wear
crimplene. But Doreen's never really been happy since her
transfer. I ran into Miss Brunskill in the lift and she says when
Doreen was in Credit and Settlement she was a different
person. How old do you think she is now?
MR DODSWORTH Doreen?
MISS PROTHERO Miss Brunskill.
MR DODSWORTH Fifty?
MISS PROTHERO Forty-eight, I was surprised. I saw it on her
253. I thought she was nearer sixty. That's with being on the
fifth floor. It takes it out of you.
Mr Dodsworth is restive and bored.
MR DODSWORTH Could you drink a cup of tea?
MISS PROTHERO Tea? With my kidneys?
MR DODSWORTH I forgot.
MISS PROTHERO I wish I could forget. Tea – you might as well
offer me hydrocholoric acid.
MR DODSWORTH Well, coffee?
MISS PROTHERO Only if it's very weak.
Mr Dodsworth gets up and is on his way out.
How are your waterworks?
MR DODSWORTH Sorry?

MISS PROTHERO You were having a spot of trouble with your waterworks, don't you remember?

MR DODSWORTH They're champion now, thanks very much.
Mr Dodsworth thankfully leaves the room to put the kettle on. Miss Prothero bides her time.

MISS PROTHERO (*calling*) And do you still have your appliance?
There is no answer.
Is it still playing you up?

MR DODSWORTH (*off*) I never think about it now.

MISS PROTHERO (*still calling*) Typical of this country. Can't even make a truss. (*She says the dreadful word with a kind of triumph.*)

MR DODSWORTH (*off*) Sugar?

MISS PROTHERO If there is any.
Mr Dodsworth returns.

MR DODSWORTH We're just waiting of the kettle.

MISS PROTHERO In which case, if you don't mind, I think I'll pay a call.

MR DODSWORTH It's up on the landing. Facing you as you go up. (*He listens as she goes upstairs, opens the door of the toilet and bolts it after her.*) Then get off home you bad, boring bitch. (*He goes over to the birdcage.*) What does she want to come on round here for in the first place? We're quite happy, aren't we, Millie? Aren't we? We're quite happy. (*He gets out a little table and two plates as the toilet is flushed. Miss Prothero returns and Mr Dodsworth goes out as she comes in, saying cryptically:*) Kettle.
While he makes coffee in the kitchen Miss Prothero looks critically at the mantelpiece.

MISS PROTHERO Is this your clock?

MR DODSWORTH (*off*) Yes. It's a nice one, don't you think?
Miss Prothero shouts some of this to the kitchen. Other remarks she makes to herself.

MISS PROTHERO Quite honestly I was against that. I spoke up when it was first mooted. Well I felt I had to. Time to give someone a clock is at the start of his career not the end. I said anyway. What do you want to know the time for, sat here? Time dribbling away and nothing to look forward to. Tick-tock tick-tock. It would get on my nerves.

MR DODSWORTH (*off*) It's not got a tick. It's electric.

MISS PROTHERO You've still got the hands going round. It saves winding, I suppose.
Mr Dodsworth returns with a tray, two cups and some cake.
MR DODSWORTH There's more to a clock than time. It's a memento. It makes me think back.
MISS PROTHERO You were saying just now you didn't want to think back.
MR DODSWORTH Well I do and I don't. You know how it is.
MISS PROTHERO My proposal was something useful. An electric blanket.
MR DODSWORTH Yes, only I like the inscription. You couldn't inscribe a blanket.
MISS PROTHERO You were lucky it wasn't a rosebowl. Another useless article.
MR DODSWORTH Cake? It's our Gillian's.
In Miss Prothero's eyes this is no recommendation.
MISS PROTHERO Just a small piece. No. Half that.
MR DODSWORTH Winnie and I were given a canteen of cutlery when we were first married. It's stood us in good stead. See. Cake knives, everything. (*He displays the battery of cutlery and selects her a cake knife.*)
MISS PROTHERO I can manage. They're only to wash up.
Miss Prothero drinks her coffee like medicine, every swallow loud, cavernous and unignorable. Mr Dodsworth flees to the sideboard, then to the birdcage.
What was Millie like?
MR DODSWORTH Millie?
MISS PROTHERO Millie. Mrs Dodsworth.
MR DODSWORTH *Winnie.* Millie's the budgie.
MISS PROTHERO I mean Winnie. (*Pause.*) What was she like?
MR DODSWORTH Well . . . very nice. She was very nice. She was a saint. A real saint. (*Pause.*) Pretty. When she was younger. Full of life. Not very practical.
MISS PROTHERO Women aren't.
MR DODSWORTH Though she rigged this place out. There was nothing here, nothing. She did all this herself, curtains and covers. She could make a place cosy, could Winnie. She used to read a lot. Read all sorts. Naomi Jacob. Leo Walmsley. Phyllis Bentley. The Brontës. She'd read them all.

MISS PROTHERO I suppose it's very nice if you've got the time.
Me, I never open a book from one year's end to the next.
Anyway, it's all escape.

MR DODSWORTH I don't know it was with Win.

MISS PROTHERO Oh yes, travel, romance. The mind's elsewhere.
She'd be a bit lonely here all day, you at Warburtons. She never
went out to work?

MR DODSWORTH Well, she'd got our Gillian to look after. But
she did all sorts. Rugs, crochet. These mats are hers. She never
saw the clock. I'd have liked her to see the clock. What about
your family?

MISS PROTHERO My what?

MR DODSWORTH Family.

MISS PROTHERO Do you mean Father?

MR DODSWORTH Oh yes. I'm sorry. Your mother died.

MISS PROTHERO She didn't die. Father killed her.

MR DODSWORTH Oh?

This is not the response Miss Prothero is after. Pause.
That's news to me.

MISS PROTHERO Over forty-two years of marriage, slowly, day by
day, inch by inch, smiling and smiling in the sight of the whole
world, gently and politely with every appearance of kindness,
he killed her.

There is an endless pause.

MR DODSWORTH What did he do for a living?

MISS PROTHERO He was a gents' outfitter.

MR DODSWORTH Really?

MISS PROTHERO It was Other Women.

MR DODSWORTH Oh ay.

MISS PROTHERO In droves.

*What lives other people led. A gents' outfitter in Leeds with droves of
Other Women. And he had hardly lived at all, thought Mr Dodsworth.*

MR DODSWORTH What was he like?

MISS PROTHERO Tall. Little tash. A limp.

MR DODSWORTH A limp?

MISS PROTHERO Mother always said that helped. They felt safe.

*Women have always felt safe with me, thinks Mr Dodsworth. But
then they were. Miss Prothero obviously feels quite safe. But then
she is.*

MR DODSWORTH Is he still living?

MISS PROTHERO Oh yes. He's had a stroke. He's in a home at
Farnley. Paralysed all down one side. They have to do
everything for him. Sits and sits and sits.

MR DODSWORTH Still. He has his memories.

Yes, Miss Prothero thinks, of Other Women.

MISS PROTHERO Once he got taken for Ronald Colman.

MR DODSWORTH Who?

MISS PROTHERO Father.

MR DODSWORTH Did Ronald Colman limp?

MISS PROTHERO No, but he had a tash.

*Mr Dodsworth thinks of old Mr Prothero, paralysed all down one
side up at Farnley, sat with his memories of droves of Other Women
and once having been taken for Ronald Colman.*

MR DODSWORTH It doesn't paralyse the memory, then, a stroke?

MISS PROTHERO Why?

MR DODSWORTH It leaves you with half your movements.
I wondered whether it left you with half your memories.

MISS PROTHERO Well, you wouldn't know, would you? If you
can't remember it, how do you know you've forgotten it?

*Mr Dodsworth tries to bend his mind round this, fails and falls back
on Art.*

MR DODSWORTH Do you fancy a bit of music?

MISS PROTHERO I don't mind.

MR DODSWORTH Do you not like music?

MISS PROTHERO I don't mind. If it's played I listen to it.

MR DODSWORTH That's something else I might take up. Musical
appreciation. They have classes in that.

MISS PROTHERO I don't care for the violin. Not on its own.

MR DODSWORTH I think you'll like this. I do.

He puts a cassette in the player. It is the theme from Un Homme
et une Femme. *It goes on and on and on. Miss Prothero sits
awkwardly waiting while Mr Dodsworth listens appreciatively. She
gives it a minute or two before deciding it's time to break the spell,
which she does by suddenly getting to her feet.*

MISS PROTHERO They've introduced music in the lifts now. That
was Mr Skinner's suggestion. It's industrial psychology. Is that
clock fast?

MR DODSWORTH No.

MISS PROTHERO I was thinking of catching the twenty past.

MR DODSWORTH Oh yes. (*He turns off the music.*)

MISS PROTHERO But I've a bit yet. (*She sits down again. Pause.*) I like to get back before dark. Two women attacked on the 73 last week. You'd never get me upstairs. It's just asking for it.
Pause.
I don't seem to have told you much news. Mind you, if I told you everything that had been going on I don't suppose you'd thank me.

MR DODSWORTH Well, you have. You've brought me up to date on Maureen's baby. Doreen's skin trouble. It's just put me in the picture a bit. It's all I want.

MISS PROTHERO That's only the half of it.

MR DODSWORTH Perhaps, Peggy. But you see, it's this way. I was with Warburtons thirty years. Thirty years that saw big changes, some, I flatter myself, the work of yours truly. And doubtless the next thirty years will be the same. More changes. Except now it's somebody else's turn. It's time for me to stand aside and let them get on with it. I don't resent that, Peggy. A chapter is closed. A new one begins. The wheel turns. You see, when you get to my age, you accept that, Peggy. I'm not saying I didn't make my mark. I did. In my own way I revolutionised Warburtons. Incidentally, that reminds me. I've got something I want you to take.
Mr Dodsworth goes out into the hall and can be heard rummaging under the stairs.
(*off*) When I left I told Mr Skinner I'd let him have this, when I can find it. You can take it him, if you don't mind. Here we are.
He comes in with a large, flat parcel wrapped in worn brown paper and tied with string. He tears off the brown paper. It is very dusty.
Recognise this?
It is a framed chart of inter-office procedure, chains of authority, Central, District, Sub-District, and so on, drawn up in an elaborate and decorative way, in various colours. It may be more convenient to have it on a roll of paper, rather than in a frame.

MISS PROTHERO I recognise it of course. It's the old revised lay-out.

MR DODSWORTH It's basically the same as the one we have in the office but old Mr Trowbridge in Design – except it wasn't

called Design then, in the Drawing Shop – I got him to make
me a bit fancier one for Winnie really. She used to hear me
talking about the lay-out that much, I had it done for her. It's
a nice thing, I thought it'd go well in Mr Skinner's office. Mind,
it's a bit mucky. I'll get a cloth. (*He goes out.*)

MISS PROTHERO Well! This brings back memories!

*It may only be because the diagram is dirty but Miss Prothero is
looking at it with some disdain. Mr Dodsworth returns with a cloth
and cleans it up whereupon she condescends to look closer and even
seems interested.*

MR DODSWORTH It's only the names that are different . . . and
there's the three new departments but basically it's the same
set-up as we've got today. Fancy (*He points to the date.*) 1947!
It was cold. Bitter cold. We used to be starved stiff. Everybody
in Credit and Settlement used to be sat there in their overcoats.

MISS PROTHERO I remember. The place must have been a
shambles then.

MR DODSWORTH It was, Peggy. It was.

MISS PROTHERO No system at all.

MR DODSWORTH How could there be a system when filing was
on three floors. You'd be running up and down those stairs all
afternoon looking for a voucher and then find it was over at
Dickinson Road all the time. It beats me how we ever got any
payments in at all in them days.

MISS PROTHERO It was old Mr Warburton's fault. Nobody could
do anything with him stuck there.

MR DODSWORTH If you've built a firm up from being one room
then naturally you think you know best.

MISS PROTHERO He was the only one who knew where anything
was. You should delegate. He couldn't delegate.

MR DODSWORTH By, but he was a worker! There till ten every
night.

MISS PROTHERO But there was no system. System is what you
want. It was all hand to mouth.

MR DODSWORTH I tell you, Peggy . . .

*There is no need to tell Peggy anything. She is sitting there, smiling a
distant smile because she knows it all and a great deal more besides.*

. . . when I first took over in Credit and Settlement I did
nothing at all for about a month. I just sat there in that office

in my overcoat trying to fathom it all out. How it functioned. How it should function. How it could be made to function. And eventually I thought, 'Well, Arthur, if you can only get the filing on to a proper footing that'll be a start.' I reckoned that'd maybe take two or three months at the outside. Do you know how long it took? Four years. But I reckon that four years saved Warburtons thousands, hundreds of thousands in the end. Because out of it came – (*He refers to all this on the diagram.*) – direct debiting, inter-departmental docketing, direct directorial access, the marrying of receipts and invoices and really, all the lay-out of the new complex. It's all here. In embryo. Do you know what the turn-round was when I first came into that office?

MISS PROTHERO Ten days.

MR DODSWORTH Three weeks. And you know what it was when I left? Well, you know what it was when I left. Forty-eight hours. And there it is. All I like to think is that when the fifth floor rings up for a 237 and it's there in five minutes there'll be somebody thinking – 'Thank you, Arthur Dodsworth.' Anyway, you take it. Give it Mr Skinner with my compliments. I'm not wanting to rush you off but you don't want to miss your bus. I'll put you some clean paper round it. (*Mr Dodsworth rummages in a drawer.*)

MISS PROTHERO The trouble is Mr Skinner's very particular about anything on the walls. He had Doreen take down all her postcards. And Mr Teasdale's silly notices. 'You don't have to be mad to work here but it helps.' I never thought that was funny. Mr Skinner didn't either. Now the walls are confined to relevant information.

MR DODSWORTH This is relevant information, right enough. The basics are the same as they are today. I took him through it before I left. He soon had the hang of it. Of course that's the beauty of it. Logic and simplicity. (*Mr Dodsworth gets Miss Prothero's coat from the hall.*) Still, if you don't want to take it, I'll pop by with it sometime.

MISS PROTHERO I should hang on to it. It'll be like your clock. A memento.

MR DODSWORTH Peggy. This is a working diagram.

MISS PROTHERO Things have changed.

MR DODSWORTH Not basically. Basically things are the same. (*He stops and looks at her.*) Aren't they?

MISS PROTHERO That's what I've been trying to say. Only you would go on about all the things you were doing, wider worlds than Warburtons.

MR DODSWORTH What things?

MISS PROTHERO Cookery classes, pottery. Cordon bleu.

MR DODSWORTH What things?

MISS PROTHERO I shall miss my bus.

MR DODSWORTH You won't. That clock's fast.

MISS PROTHERO Your presentation clock fast? You've not had it six months.

MR DODSWORTH I didn't like to say. The electric's poor here. I think that affects it. You said things have changed. What things? *Miss Prothero sits down heavily.*

MISS PROTHERO Everything.

MR DODSWORTH *Everything?*

MISS PROTHERO You haven't really left me much time. However. When I think the damage was done was that first Monday. *Miss Prothero is determined to catch her bus. She is also determined to tell Mr Dodsworth everything. Speed is of the essence.*

MR DODSWORTH What first Monday?

MISS PROTHERO Mr Skinner's . . . his first Monday we had a really shocking run of 476s and then to cap it all Costing sent up a couple of 248s . . . I mean, I think they were trying it on.

MR DODSWORTH They would be. You don't get a 248 once in six months and two together, I never had that in thirty-odd years.

MISS PROTHERO Well, that put him wrong side out for a start.

MR DODSWORTH Why didn't he just docket them and get the whole lot carted off to the fifth floor?

MISS PROTHERO What I said to Doreen Glazier. I think he just didn't want to go running upstairs on his first day. It's understandable, but anyway the upshot was we had to go through the whole rigmarole. Those two 248s took all day.

MR DODSWORTH Costing, they want their backsides kicking.

MISS PROTHERO The next thing I hear he's been in to see Mr Skidmore.

MR DODSWORTH Mr Skidmore!

MISS PROTHERO Mr Skidmore. He gives him the green light

and do you know what the first thing he does is? Revamps the entire docketing system.

MR DODSWORTH But there was nothing wrong with the docketing system.

MISS PROTHERO Don't tell me. I thought of you, Mr Dodsworth. I thought, well, I'm glad Mr Dodsworth isn't here to see this. I ran into Mr Butterfield in Accounts. He knew what was happening.

MR DODSWORTH He would.

MISS PROTHERO No, I said to him it would break Mr Dodsworth's heart. It would have broken your heart.

MR DODSWORTH That's a funny way of going on. You can't mess about with docketing while you've got receipts and invoices married up.

MISS PROTHERO Right. A fortnight later they were separated.

MR DODSWORTH But it took me four years to get them together.

MISS PROTHERO It took him two weeks to get them apart. After that it was a short step to direct departmental debiting.

MR DODSWORTH That would have to be entirely restructured.

MISS PROTHERO Scrapped.

MR DODSWORTH Scrapped!

MISS PROTHERO We were knee-deep in 5D forms and you know Maintenance are never there when they're wanted: I was actually taking them downstairs and bundling them into the incinerator myself. And of course who should I run into on one of the trips but Mr Sillitoe, who was with me my first year in C and S, do you remember, and he laughed and he said . . .

MR DODSWORTH But what's happened about filing?

MISS PROTHERO Oh, did I not tell you that? I thought I'd told you that. Filing was all computerised in September anyway. You see, what you have to remember about Mr Skinner is that he was six months at Newport Pagnell. He's got all that at his fingertips.

MR DODSWORTH Well, I don't care what you say, our turn-round was forty-eight hours. You can't get much slicker than that.

MISS PROTHERO Halved.

MR DODSWORTH Halved?

MISS PROTHERO Halved.

MISS PROTHERO Twenty-four hours now, and Mr Skinner says that's only a stage not a target. He envisages something in the range of twelve hours . . . even, you'll laugh at this, even same-day turnover.

MR DODSWORTH You'll kill yourselves.

MISS PROTHERO No. Half-past four and I'm generally just sat there. All done and docketed.

MR DODSWORTH What about that . . . inter-departmental docketing?

MISS PROTHERO Oh, we still do that.

MR DODSWORTH That's something.

MISS PROTHERO Only it's all in alphabetical order now.

MR DODSWORTH Alphabetical order! What kind of a system is that!

MISS PROTHERO Listen, I must go.

MR DODSWORTH I don't see it. What happens . . . what happens if you get a 318 and a 247 on the same sheet? If you don't have direct departmental debit you've got the whole process to go through on two separate dockets.

MISS PROTHERO Can't happen. Not under the Skinner system. You see they couldn't be on the same sheet in the first place.

MR DODSWORTH They could be on separate receipt dockets but on the same 348.

MISS PROTHERO Yes, that happened on Friday. Mr Skinner fed it into the computer and it sorted it out in no time.

MR DODSWORTH I think that's an admission of failure.

MISS PROTHERO It only takes two minutes.

MR DODSWORTH Computers, what are they? Glorified adding machines.

MISS PROTHERO Don't let Mr Skinner hear you say that. He says a computer is an instrument of the imagination. He says that with another computer, me and Miss Glazier, he could run Credit and Settlement single-handed.

MR DODSWORTH That's Newport Pagnell talking.

MISS PROTHERO I didn't want to tell you all this but you would drag it out of me.

MR DODSWORTH I just want to get a pencil and paper.

MISS PROTHERO I must run.

MR DODSWORTH Hang on a sec . . . (*He starts making calculations.*)

MISS PROTHERO It's a waste of time. You won't crack it. We've been going now for nearly four months and, as I say,

Mr Skinner runs that office with the smoothness of a well-oiled machine.

MR DODSWORTH You could catch the ten to, not the twenty past.

MISS PROTHERO I've my supper to get.

MR DODSWORTH You could have your supper here.

MISS PROTHERO It's getting dark. Still, I can call again. I thought you'd be lonely. I said to Doreen, I bet he's lonely. And it's made a nice little outing. You get out of touch.

MR DODSWORTH It's true. I'd not realised.

MISS PROTHERO Tell you what I can do. If I come again . . .

MR DODSWORTH No, you must come.

MISS PROTHERO . . . and that's fetch you some copies of the 114s. Glenda'll run me off one or two if I ask her nicely and then you'll be able to see how the procedure works, and that'll set your mind at rest.

MR DODSWORTH Would you do that? That is good of you. Oh, Peggy, I should be ever so grateful . . .

MISS PROTHERO Well, we always had a soft spot for one another you and me, didn't we? Bye-bye. (*She mouths this silently.*)

MR DODSWORTH (*following her into the hall*) And think on, call round any time. I shall be here. I won't go out. I'll make a point of not going out. Thank you ever so much for coming. Take care.

The front door closes. There is a pause and Mr Dodsworth comes slowly back into the room. He closes the door and picks up the chart, looks at it for a moment or two, then puts it down. He goes over to the birdcage, but without speaking to the bird. Mr Dodsworth stands in his sitting room feeling his whole life has been burgled, the contents of the years ransacked and strewn about the room. Some items he knows have gone and as the days pass he will remember others. Next time Miss Prothero will tell him more; and he will have less. He sits down in his chair.

MR DODSWORTH Oh, Winnie, Winnie.

Me, I'm Afraid of Virginia Woolf

CAST AND CREDITS

Me, I'm Afraid of Virginia Woolf was first transmitted
by London Weekend Television on 2 December 1978.
The cast included:

NARRATOR	Alan Bennett
HOPKINS	Neville Smith
GINGER-HAIRED GIRL	Julie Walters
DOCTOR	Frank Middlemass
WILLARD	Robert Longdon
MRS HOPKINS	Thora Hird
WENDY	Carol Macready
MRS BROADBENT	Margaret Courtenay
MRS TUCKER	Lynne Carol
MISS GIBBONS	Barbara Hicks
SKINNER	Derek Thompson
MR DODDS	Hugh Lloyd
MRS GARLAND	Gillian Martell
MAUREEN	Janine Duvitski
TRICKETT	Bernard Wrigley
BOY IN TRICKETT'S CLASS	Paul Rosebury
ANOTHER BOY	Bernard Strother
BOSWELL	Alan Igbon
WOMAN IN WENDY'S CLASS	Pat Beckett
CARETAKER	Dickie Arnold
Producer and Director	Stephen Frears
Designer	Martin Johnson
Music	George Fenton

PART ONE

INT. DOCTOR'S WAITING ROOM. DAY.
The waiting room is full and the first sequence is on the faces of patients waiting, the bell ringing and one patient going into the surgery as another comes out. Hopkins, a man of about thirty-five, enters the waiting room.

NARRATOR (*voice over*) Hopkins, coming into the waiting room, found only one seat vacant, next to a girl with gingerish hair. He sat down. Time passed. The room emptied. And soon there was only Hopkins, marooned beside the ginger-haired girl.
Hopkins is reading and looking uncomfortable.
(*voice over*) Hopkins's problem was this: there were now so many empty seats that if he went on sitting there the girl would think he wanted to sit next to her. But if he sat somewhere else she would think he didn't. Life, it seemed to Hopkins, was full of such problems and literature was not much help.
Hopkins shuts his book. Gets up. Looks, rather stagily, at a magazine and sits down again one seat away from his previous seat, and so from the ginger-haired girl.

HOPKINS Spread ourselves.

GINGER-HAIRED GIRL What?

HOPKINS No need to bunch up. Take your pick.
He gets up again and sits somewhere else, even farther off. Spreads his arms across the adjacent chairs, expansively. Then he goes back to his book. Pause.

GINGER-HAIRED GIRL I'm before you!

HOPKINS I know.
Pause.

GINGER-HAIRED GIRL They've sent my sputum to Newcastle.
Pause.

HOPKINS Newcastle? What for?

GINGER-HAIRED GIRL These tests.

HOPKINS It seems a long way.

GINGER-HAIRED GIRL Well, they do that now. It's all this decentralisation. Underdeveloped areas. Light industry. The

93

bogey of unemployment. (*Pause.*) It's not a place I've been to personally, Newcastle. I've never fancied it somehow. Have you been?

HOPKINS Newcastle? No.

NARRATOR (*voice over*) This was a lie. Hopkins had been to Newcastle, many times. So why did he not say so? This was what he had come to ask the doctor.

HOPKINS No, I've never been to Newcastle. Nor want to. I've never been anywhere up there. Never been to Middlesbrough. Sunderland.

GINGER-HAIRED GIRL (*scornfully*) You haven't been to Sunderland? You've never been to Sunderland? Well, stroll on. I've got a sister-in-law lives in Sunderland. I must have been there fifty times. Don't try telling me anything about Sunderland. (*The bell rings and she goes into the surgery.*)

HOPKINS I'm always doing that. Putting myself in people's place. Well, I'm going to cut it out.

Time passes. The ginger-haired girl comes out of the surgery.

Listen. You know I said I'd never been to Newcastle? Well, I have been. I've just remembered. I've been there in fact on at least twenty-seven separate occasions.

The ginger-haired girl has completely collapsed. She is on the verge of tears. Hopkins is abashed.

GINGER-HAIRED GIRL He's sending me to a specialist. I've got to go to a specialist.

She exits, leaving Hopkins mortified.

INT. DOCTOR'S SURGERY. DAY.

DOCTOR Come in, Mr Hopkins, sit down. You notice that we have an alien presence. This is Mr Willard. Mr Willard is a medical student sitting in on my surgery. We're just initiating him into the horrors of general practice, ha ha. Eh, Mr Willard?

Mr Willard is an expressionless youth with a pageboy haircut.

I take it you don't have any objections to him just sitting there. And of course if you did you wouldn't dare say so, I know. Ha ha. Now. (*He has got Hopkins's notes.*) Mr Hopkins has been my patient now for some time . . . let's see . . . two years?

HOPKINS Two.

94

DOCTOR (*reading rapidly from notes*) Two years. And in that time
he's made fairly frequent visits to the surgery with a variety of
complaints . . . I see here you first came along complaining of
tightness in the chest. Chest and heart subsequently examined,
quite sound. Then discomfort in the abdomen, sense of . . .
fullness. Our old friend migraine. Even complained of pain . . .
ha ha . . . in the neck, but again without discernible physical
origin. Pain, in short, in various departments, though never
anything we could quite put our fingers on, and I think we
more or less decided last time, didn't we, that Mr Hopkins's
problem is ah . . . psychological . . . even psychosomatic. None
the less real for all that but mental rather than physical. Mr
Hopkins is a lecturer at the Polytechnic in Economics.

HOPKINS English Literature.

DOCTOR English Literature. Our priceless heritage. I can just
about get as far as Agatha Christie. Time, that's the problem.
Where do you find it? He has no financial worries. One of
those fortunate mortals who are tied to the cost of living and
indeed index-linked. He should be laughing . . . but quite
plainly isn't. Now why? Mr Willard, any thoughts?
*Willard remains expressionless, then says something in an undertone
to the doctor.*
Yes. Yes. Mr Willard, with the outspokenness of youth, wonders
if this is a . . . ah . . . sexual problem. But I'm afraid he scores
no points there, does he, Mr Hopkins? Mr Hopkins and I went
into all that pretty thoroughly and it appears that while he is
not married, wise man, Mr Hopkins has a lady friend with
whom he gets on, if not like a house on fire, certainly . . .

HOPKINS Quite well.

DOCTOR Not famously, but quite well. No worries at work,
no worries at home. How would you sum up your situation,
Mr Hopkins?

HOPKINS I'm not happy. I'm uneasy, uncertain of myself. People
make me uneasy.

DOCTOR Do I make you uneasy? (*Hopkins is silent.*) Does Mr
Willard make you uneasy?

HOPKINS (*voice over*) Yes. (*aloud*) No.

DOCTOR Well, I'm surprised to hear it because he scares the
pinstripes off me. Another one of these bright young devils

95

they send us from medical school, Hopkins. Computer diagnosis, tissue type. Brain scan. Technicians, Hopkins, scientists. Run rings round an old quack like me. Me, I just listen and look. Prehistoric.

HOPKINS I don't feel the same as everybody else.

DOCTOR We none of us are the same, are we? You, me, Mr Willard.

HOPKINS I'm always wondering about what people think. That's not healthy, is it?

DOCTOR It is up to a point.

HOPKINS I'm not ill. I've got a good job. Should I be happy? I don't know.

DOCTOR Which of us is happy? I'm not. I don't think friend Willard is happy.

WILLARD (*expressionlessly*) I am, quite.

The Doctor looks intensely disapproving.

DOCTOR I think we'll try you on a different anti-depressant.

Hopkins has gone. The Doctor and Willard are finishing for the day.

DOCTOR Willard. You are young. But in this matter of happiness it has been my experience that we none of us wish to be told of the happiness of others. It does not help, Willard. Confess to misery, say one's life is futile, hail the onset of bankruptcy, yes, Willard, because nothing encourages one's fellows more. They go away smiling. But say, 'I am happy. I am having a good time.' No, Willard. The spirit plummets. (*Pause.*) What is your chosen field in medicine? Your speciality.

WILLARD The inner ear.

DOCTOR Good. Good.

INT. BUS. DAY.

Hopkins gets on the bus. He sits on the seat nearest the platform, so that he is facing the seat opposite, on which is an expressionless man.

NARRATOR (*voice over*) Hopkins was never without a book. It wasn't that he was particularly fond of reading; he just liked to have somewhere to look.

We see Hopkins avoid the gaze of the man by opening his book. The conductress waits for his fare.

CONDUCTRESS What's your book, love?

Hopkins shows it to her as she gives him his ticket.

Any good?

HOPKINS Not really.

CONDUCTRESS You can't win 'em all.

The bus has stopped and a girl has got on. She sits opposite Hopkins.

NARRATOR (*voice over*) A book makes you safe. Shows you're not
out to pick anybody up. Try it on. With a book you're harmless.
Though Hopkins was harmless without a book.

HOPKINS (*aloud*) I know.

The girl opposite sees him speak and smiles.

NARRATOR (*voice over*) Now she thinks he's talking to himself.

Hopkins therefore smiles apologetically at her.

(*voice over*) Now she thinks he's trying to pick her up.

*The girl should be slightly amused so that we know, as he doesn't,
that it wouldn't matter if he were.*

HOPKINS I wasn't smiling at you. I was actually just smiling at
my book. I've just got to a really funny bit. (*Forces a laugh.*) It's
hysterical.

CONDUCTRESS Is it fiction or non-fiction?

HOPKINS Virginia Woolf.

CONDUCTRESS Is she funny?

HOPKINS Killing.

*The girl gets off and a large black lady gets on and sits next to
Hopkins so that he involuntarily moves a bit to give her room.
Shot of Hopkins's anxious face with his large black neighbour.*

I was just thinking: when I made room for you on the seat, did
you notice, I sort of shifted, budged up a bit. Well, that was all
I was doing, making room for you. I mean, I wasn't moving
away because you were bla – I'd have done the same for
anybody, that's what I mean. I was just giving you more room.

LARGE BLACK LADY What's troublin' you there, man?

HOPKINS Nothing. Never mind.

EXT./INT. STREETS/INSTITUTE. DAY.

*Cut to either external shot of Hopkins walking through the streets
towards the Mechanics' Institute or in the building itself. On his way
along corridors towards the municipal cafeteria.*

HOPKINS (*voice over*) Why bother what other people think?
I mean. Why bother? (*aloud*) I am not going to bother.

Someone passing looks sharply.

(*voice over*) Now he thinks I'm talking to myself. (*aloud*) My God.
Someone else looks.
(*voice over*) Now she does too. What's the matter with me?

INT. MUNICIPAL CAFETERIA. DAY.
Hopkins is just sitting down at a table where his mother is already firmly installed.

MRS HOPKINS You want to be like me. I never bother what anybody thinks. You're shy. That's your trouble. You take after me.

HOPKINS What are you doing here?

MRS HOPKINS Is it a crime? To want to see one's own flesh and blood once in a blue moon? Is that a felony? A distant glimpse of one's only son.

HOPKINS I've got a class in a minute.

MRS HOPKINS 'College lecturer spurns mother.' 'I skimped to give him his start.' I know this. You eat the wrong food. (*Takes one of his chips.*) I don't wonder you're constipated. Are you constipated?

HOPKINS No.

MRS HOPKINS Well, I would be. Eating that muck. Mind you, my stomach's on a knife edge. The doctor said, 'Mrs Hopkins. It could just go either way.' (*Pause.*) When did you last go?

HOPKINS I am not constipated.
A woman at the next table looks.

MRS HOPKINS That's right. Show me up. I'm only your mother.

HOPKINS What do you want to be coming down here for?

MRS HOPKINS Because I'm daft, that's why. Because I want my head examining. They've given you a cracked cup. Let's take it back.

HOPKINS No.

MRS HOPKINS I thought that was the latest thing with you people now, the consumer. You've got to stand up for yourself in this take-it-or-leave-it society. Drink out of the other side then.

HOPKINS What're you frightened of me catching? VD?
The woman looks again.

MRS HOPKINS Do you want to humiliate me?

HOPKINS What've you come down here for? What do you want
to see me about?

MRS HOPKINS What do I want to see you about? Do I have to
want to see you about something? I want to see you about
having brought you up single-handed. I want to see you about
having put you in for a scholarship. I want to see you about
being my son.
Pause.

HOPKINS Oh, Mam.

MRS HOPKINS Is that her?

HOPKINS Who?

MRS HOPKINS Your girlfriend.

HOPKINS I haven't got a girlfriend.

MRS HOPKINS Who was it Mrs Goodall saw you with?

HOPKINS She's a girl. She's a friend. She's not a girlfriend. Mrs
Goodall.

MRS HOPKINS I don't know why you patronise this place. They
don't even run to a toasted teacake. I said, 'I want a toasted
teacake.' She said did I mean a cheeseburger! Yorkshire! It's the
home of toasted teacake. You shouldn't have to spell it out. It's
barbarism. And it's not clean. Look at that sauce-bottle top.
It's a Mecca for germs. You'd think they could run to a
dispenser. Hygiene's just gone out of the window. Before you
came in I paid a visit: that toilet's a real hell-hole.

NARRATOR (*optional: voice over*) Life for Hopkins's mother was a
canopy slung between three poles. Dirt, Disease and the
Lavatory.

HOPKINS Mam, can I ask you something? Why did you call me
Trevor? You christened me Trevor. Why?

MRS HOPKINS After thirty-five years you ask me why we called
you Trevor.

HOPKINS Well, why?

MRS HOPKINS Because your dad and me chose it. Because it's
a nice name.

HOPKINS Well, I hate it. I hate my name. I think maybe that's
what's wrong with me. Being called Trevor. I'm not a Trevor,
am I? Couldn't you see that?

MRS HOPKINS At six weeks old?

HOPKINS I'm a James or a Charles. A Martin even. But not Trevor.

MRS HOPKINS You're our Trevor.

NARRATOR (*voice over*) Trevor was what he was called. Trevor was not what he was. In the entire history of the world Hopkins could recall no one of note who had been called Trevor.

HOPKINS You're in the outside lane before even the pistol goes. It's not Trevor Proust, is it? Trevor Strachey. Trevor Sibelius. Lenin, Stalin, where would they be if they'd been called Trevor?

MRS HOPKINS What about Mrs Beaver's son? He's called Trevor and he's the North-Western Area Manager for Kayser Bondor. Trevor hasn't stopped him getting to the top. Trevor.

HOPKINS Don't keep on saying it.

MRS HOPKINS (*looking at the evening paper*) Blaming your name. What if you were called Doris? I am. I see the President of Romania's mother's died. There's always trouble for somebody. How's your work going?

HOPKINS All right.

MRS HOPKINS 'All right.'

HOPKINS Well, you wouldn't understand if I told you.

MRS HOPKINS I might. You underestimate your mother.

HOPKINS Well, I'll tell you. I'm working on an article on 'Culture and Expropriation in the Novels of E. M. Forster'.
Long, long pause.

MRS HOPKINS That woman's just put a sandwich in her handbag. And she's got a fur coat on. I'd have been educated if I could have stopped on at school. The teacher always read out my compositions. You get it all from me. Your dad never opened a book in his life. Bless him.

HOPKINS I'll have to go in a minute.

MRS HOPKINS I just wish it wasn't called polytechnic. Why don't they call it a university? I tell folks you're at the polytechnic and they think you teach woodwork.

NARRATOR (*voice over*) Not married at thirty-five and sat here with his mam. What did it look like? Hopkins knew only too well what it looked like.
A woman coming in gives him a little wave, instantly spotted by Mrs Hopkins, then goes and queues at the cafeteria.

MRS HOPKINS Oh. Is that her?

HOPKINS Where?

MRS HOPKINS Where! The one who's waving at you. *Wave.*
  He waves half-heartedly and Mrs Hopkins smiles graciously.
  How old is she?
HOPKINS I don't know. Thirty.
MRS HOPKINS Is that what she says? Mrs Goodall said she was
  oldish.
HOPKINS Are you satisfied now, now you've seen her?
MRS HOPKINS I had some purchases to make and I was in the
  vicinity. What's her name? Shirley?
HOPKINS Wendy.
MRS HOPKINS Same thing. Why hasn't she got off before now?
HOPKINS Maybe she doesn't want to.
MRS HOPKINS They all want to. Every woman wants to. Unless
  they get thwarted. There'll be something about her, else why's
  she wasting her time teaching yogi. I know one thing. She
  shouldn't wear trousers.
HOPKINS Who?
MRS HOPKINS Your girl.
HOPKINS She's not 'my girl'. I don't have a girl. She's just
  somebody I . . .
MRS HOPKINS Somebody you what?
HOPKINS Somebody I know.
MRS HOPKINS Yes. I know too. Somebody you carry on with.
HOPKINS Mam, I'm thirty-five.
MRS HOPKINS Don't tell me. By the time I was thirty-five I was
  married and two children.
HOPKINS Anyway, they're not trousers. They're ski pants.
MRS HOPKINS Oh, ski pants, is it now? (*Pause.*) She's not one of
  these lesbians, is she?
HOPKINS What do you know about lesbians?
MRS HOPKINS You'd be surprised what I know. More in my head
  than nits. There was a talk on them on *Women's Hour.* I can't
  see what folks make such a fuss about. It's only women and
  other women. Like me and Mrs Goodall.
HOPKINS You and Mrs Goodall?
MRS HOPKINS Friends. Doing things together.
HOPKINS Doing what together?
MRS HOPKINS Having tea in Marshall and Snelgrove's.
HOPKINS Having tea in Marshall and Snelgrove's isn't lesbianism.

MRS HOPKINS It's only liking being with other women.

HOPKINS Not in Marshall and Snelgrove.

MRS HOPKINS Well, where?

HOPKINS Bed. (*Long outraged pause.*) You brought the subject up.

MRS HOPKINS Well? So. Anyway I've been in bed with other women.

HOPKINS Who?

MRS HOPKINS Your Aunty Phyllis for a start.

HOPKINS Aunty Phyllis isn't women. Anyway, when were you in bed with Aunty Phyllis?

MRS HOPKINS During the air raids. When Uncle Bernard was in North Africa.

HOPKINS Where was my dad?

MRS HOPKINS On nights.

HOPKINS That's not lesbianism.

MRS HOPKINS It wasn't for me. It might have been for her.

HOPKINS What did she say it was?

MRS HOPKINS Nerves. Anyroads, you seem to know a lot about it.

HOPKINS Lesbianism? Yes, well, I come across it in literature.

MRS HOPKINS Well, I hope it is in literature and not in Huddersfield. Course it's all right if you're educated. That makes it all *carte blanche*. Well, I was the one that wanted you educated. You want to remember that when you're running your mother down.

HOPKINS I don't.

MRS HOPKINS You're not, are you?

HOPKINS What?

MRS HOPKINS That.

HOPKINS Lesbian?

MRS HOPKINS No. The other.

HOPKINS Mam. I'm nothing, Mam.

MRS HOPKINS I bet they've never seen Zermatt.

HOPKINS What?

MRS HOPKINS Them ski pants. I see Mrs Proctor in them sometimes and she's got a bum like a boiler end. Oh. She's sitting somewhere else.

Wendy has sat down at another table.

I can't be good enough for her.

HOPKINS Mam.

MRS HOPKINS No. I'm going now. I know when I'm not wanted.

HOPKINS Mam. It's all right. Stay.

MRS HOPKINS No. You have your own young lives to lead.

HOPKINS Mam.

MRS HOPKINS Give us a kiss.

> *He lets himself be kissed.*

Oh, I've lipsticked you. (*She rubs the mark off with her hanky, then goes.*)

NARRATOR (*voice over*) Mrs Hopkins had it in mind to pause, for a second, by Wendy's table in order to give her a smile of infinite pain and resignation. A smile which would say, 'Be gentle with him, Wendy. I am his mother.' But Wendy was busy rubbing a bit of yoghurt off her blouse and so the moment passed.

> *Wendy comes over with her muesli and slopping cup of coffee.*

WENDY I couldn't have sat with you, Trevor. I wanted to, but I couldn't. Mother and son. You made such a nice picture. So complete somehow. And such a good, good face, Trevor. It shines out.

HOPKINS You've got yoghurt on your chin.

WENDY Trevor.

NARRATOR (*voice over*) Hating his name, Hopkins had found someone who said it one hundred and three times.

WENDY What was she saying?

HOPKINS Mam? She was just telling me how my Aunty Phyllis and her had this lesbian relationship.

WENDY Trevor. How wonderful. And how wonderful she was able to tell you. You must be very close. It's sad how those nearest to us are in some sense the furthest away. How we see them as *parents*. Mother, capital M. Father, capital F. Not people.

HOPKINS Small p.

WENDY Exactly. And whereas you and I probably assume that so-called deviant relationships are confined to the more intellectual sections of society, there is no reason why they shouldn't occur lower down the social scale where people are more instinctual.

HOPKINS Your hair's in your muesli.

Wendy extracts it and puts her hair in her mouth and sucks the muesli from her hair.

WENDY How did it happen?

HOPKINS They slept together during an air raid and soon they had this relationship roaring along. You know how it is.

WENDY Isn't that marvellous?

HOPKINS I found it all rather sordid.

WENDY No. No, Trevor, it's marvellous.

HOPKINS It's five to seven.

WENDY Trevor, can I tell you something very seriously? You eat the wrong food. I was reading the other day they've done a study of dandruff and do you know what they've traced it back to?

HOPKINS Masturbation?

WENDY Fried foods.

They get up to go, Wendy probably spilling something else in the process.

And as fried foods are the culprit in heart disease as well, it's only a short step to realising that dandruff may be an early warning sign of heart attacks. Nature has a language, you see, if only we'd learn to read it.

INT. HOPKINS'S CLASSROOM. EVENING.

Half a dozen people, mainly in their fifties and sixties, are sitting, waiting.

MRS BROADBENT (*a big masterful woman*) Late again!

MRS TUCKER (*a small vindictive one*) He'll be with that slut from Transcendental Meditation. Having a little tête-à-tête.

MRS BROADBENT In the Corporation's time.

MRS TUCKER Of course.

MRS BROADBENT It all comes out of the rates.

MISS GIBBONS (*a more sympathetic figure*) I see she's brought him his flower again.

Maureen, a wet-looking girl, comes in with a carnation which she puts in a vase on the desk. She cleans the blackboard and gets Hopkins's desk ready.

MRS TUCKER His mother goes to my chiropodist. Smartish-looking woman, pointed glasses, has a fawny Raglan coat. What is it this week?

MISS GIBBONS A carnation.

MRS TUCKER She has quite a nice little semi up at Lawnswood. It was a rose last week. Slipping.

MISS GIBBONS Sir Malcolm Sargent used to have that.

MRS TUCKER What?

MISS GIBBONS Every day of his life. A single blood-red carnation. Didn't matter where he was. Bridlington. Buenos Aires. Six o'clock. Pageboy. Knock, knock. 'Sir Malcolm, your carnation.'

MRS TUCKER And who was it?

MISS GIBBONS He never knew. A Mystery Woman.

MRS TUCKER Save him a lot of money. Carnations are wicked. She'd send it through Interpol.

MRS BROADBENT Multiply this on a national scale and you can see why they're so sceptical at the World Bank. Why should they bail us out? He's seven minutes late.

MRS TUCKER He wouldn't be late if we were in West Germany.
Maureen has started to put up a large photograph. She half-unrolls it, then rolls it up hurriedly again and sits down.
She's not put up the photographs. Maureen. The photographs, love. Are you not putting up the photographs?
Maureen shakes her head and won't look round. They look at each other in wild surmise.

INT. INSTITUTE CORRIDOR. EVENING.
Hopkins and Wendy are walking down a corridor in the Mechanics' Institute.

HOPKINS Am I coming back tonight?

WENDY Do you want to?

HOPKINS That's why I'm saying, 'Am I coming back tonight'! I wouldn't say that if I didn't want to, would I?

WENDY You might. I get the feeling you don't really want to. I get the feeling it's not me you really want. Not the real me, anyway.
Lounging in the corridor outside the classroom is Skinner, a relaxed and good-looking young man.

SKINNER Sir's late.

HOPKINS I'll be right with you. Am I coming back tonight?

WENDY Come if you want to. If you really want to. And it is the real me. The real you wanting the real me. Trevor.

HOPKINS Oh God.

SKINNER Five past, sir.

HOPKINS I'll be right with you.

WENDY You see, it's not what we do, it's the relationship that
matters. I feel anyway.

HOPKINS This is Mr Skinner from my class.

SKINNER Dave, sir.

HOPKINS This is Miss Turnbull.

SKINNER I know. From Judo.

WENDY Yoga. I'm late. I don't know, Trevor. I'm doing deep
meditation with my class tonight and when I go under I
sometimes come out feeling completely different. Sometimes
when I come out I feel it's all irrelevant.

HOPKINS What?

WENDY Sex.

MRS BROADBENT (*overhearing*) Mr Hopkins. You are late.

INT. HOPKINS'S CLASSROOM. EVENING.

*The main speaking members of the class are Mrs Broadbent, Mrs
Tucker, Miss Gibbons and Maureen, whom we have already seen; Mrs
Garland, a rather arty woman; Mr Dodds, a cantankerous self-taught
man of about sixty, and Skinner, who is about twenty-five.*

HOPKINS I'm going to talk tonight about that group of writers,
painters and . . . friends . . . that we call the Bloomsbury
Group. In particular I am going to talk about two novelists,
E. M. Forster and Virginia Woolf. (*He turns to the blackboard
and writes up their names.*) E. M. Forster. Virginia Woolf.
*While his back is turned Mrs Tucker is gesturing to Maureen to pin
up the posters. Maureen won't take any notice.*
Maureen. Did you not put up the photographs this week?

MRS TUCKER I told her.

HOPKINS Maureen.

*Hopkins shrugs and does it himself. He unrolls the picture of
E. M. Forster. It has a moustache drawn on it, a little beard and
a large cigar. He unrolls the picture of Virginia Woolf. This has been
decorated with a large pair of tits.*

PART TWO

INT. HOPKINS'S CLASSROOM. EVENING.

MRS TUCKER It's shocking.

MISS GIBBONS Wicked.

MR DODDS Wicked? It's bloody blasphemy.

HOPKINS Well. I'm sure he wouldn't have minded (*meaning Forster*). Why should we?

MRS BROADBENT Why should we? The point is: these photographs are council property.
Maureen is busy trying to rub out the decorations on the photographs.

MR DODDS They want horsewhipping. They want taking out and horsewhipping.

HOPKINS It's only a joke, probably.

MRS BROADBENT A joke? Is twopence on the rates a joke? Because that's what this sort of thing is costing the local authority. Leaving aside social workers, family service units and all that paraphernalia. A joke is it? Oh. Ha ha.

MR DODDS They want taking out publicly, their trousers taken down and horsewhipping.

MAUREEN Mr Hopkins. Could I borrow a bit of your carnation water? (*She tries to wash the lines off.*)

HOPKINS Never mind, Maureen.

MRS TUCKER Do you know what I blame? These felt-tip pens.

SKINNER Yeah. We should have stuck to stone tablets.

MRS TUCKER Them aerosol things. It only takes a couple of squirts. Squirt, squirt, and it's an obscenity.

SKINNER Squirt, squirt.

MRS TUCKER You stand in the bus shelter and you don't know where to look.

MISS GIBBONS You see all sorts written up in lifts nowadays. I saw a shocking word in Boots.

MR DODDS They want bringing out, their trousers taking down and, in front of assembled civic and religious dignitaries and leaders of community groups, horsewhipping.

HOPKINS Leave it, Maureen.

MISS GIBBONS They vandalised my kiosk.

MRS BROADBENT The Parks Department lay out thousands in geraniums alone.

MRS TUCKER And just try and spend a penny in Horsforth. You can go for miles and not find a single viable toilet.

MR DODDS And when they've been horsewhipped they want parading through the streets to the new complex and made to stand up and apologise for what they've done. They should then have to spend every Saturday doing voluntary work for pensioners and disabled people and then periodically be horsewhipped again.

MRS GARLAND We must look deeper. It's all this urban decay. The inner cities.

SKINNER And her titties.

MRS GARLAND I feel sorry for them, I do.

MRS BROADBENT I don't.

MRS GARLAND I pity them. Finding breasts funny. Are breasts funny? Not in my book. Breasts are beautiful.

SKINNER Seconded.

MRS BROADBENT I prefer the singular. Bust.

MRS GARLAND Why? Bust is such an ugly word. Hard. Unyielding. Bust. Virginia Woolf's bust. No. Breasts. Breast is such a beautiful word. The sound of it. Feel it in your mouth: breast, breast, breast. Say it, everybody. Soft and restful. Nothing to be ashamed of. We all have them.

Maureen looks up, since she plainly hasn't, and goes back to her erasing.

MAUREEN I think I may be able to get his cigar off.

HOPKINS It doesn't *matter*, Maureen.

SKINNER Sir. Sir.

HOPKINS Yes, Skinner.

SKINNER Dave, sir. You sir, me Dave.

MRS BROADBENT Why should he call you Dave? He doesn't call me Pauline.

MRS TUCKER Is that your name?

MRS BROADBENT Yes. Why?

MRS TUCKER Nothing. Mine's Beryl.

MISS GIBBONS Our Gillian has a guinea pig called Beryl.

This gets her a look from Mrs Tucker.

HOPKINS You were saying, Skinner?

SKINNER I reckon our Phantom Scribbler is indulging in a crude form of literary criticism. This basically is a guy who is trying in his simple peasant way to say that the novels of the lady and gentleman in question are deficient in some vital particular.

HOPKINS Hit us again . . . Dave.

SKINNER Take the novels of the lady in question, Virginia Woolf. Sensitive, yes. Poetic, yes. Gutsy? No.

HOPKINS No.

SKINNER And similarly friend Forster.

MRS GARLAND I love Forster.

SKINNER I know, dear, but he wasn't exactly Clint Eastwood, was he?

NARRATOR (*voice over*) Skinner was wearing an earring. Hopkins longed to wear an earring but he knew he could never carry it off. Skinner carried it off beautifully. Hopkins hated Skinner and longed to be him.

HOPKINS Well, what do we think of this point Mr Skinner has made? Anybody? Perhaps instead of feeling outraged and somehow . . . got at, we should use that outrage as a jumping-off point for a discussion of whether these elements, symbolised by the breasts, the moustache and the large cigar are what our two authors lack.

MRS BROADBENT And what about the perpetrators? I suppose we discuss it with them, too?

SKINNER Yeah, why not?

MRS TUCKER It's them youths from the Trigonometry class. They're always in and out, they're the culprits.

HOPKINS I don't think it's important, is it?

MRS BROADBENT Some of us may not have had a university education, Mr Hopkins, but we can teach you a lesson in civic responsibility. If you won't go into the Trigonometry class, I shall.

MAUREEN Please, Mr Hopkins. I've rubbed her nose off.

(*Maureen holds up the photograph of Virginia Woolf minus the nose.*)

INT. TRICKETT'S CLASSROOM. EVENING.
The Mechanical Drawing class, in contrast to the class in Comparative Literature, is very full. Apprentices, eighteen-year-olds, about a third of

them white, the rest Asian or West Indian. They are being addressed by Mr Trickett, a rat. He is at the blackboard.

TRICKETT Page seventeen of your Yarwood. To construct an equilateral triangle given side lengths AB equals BC equals CA equals 75 millimetres. First job anybody?

BOY Draw AB, sir.

Hopkins enters with the mutilated photograph rolled up.

TRICKETT Draw AB, sir. (*Does so.*) Job number two?

ANOTHER BOY Set compasses to 75 millimetres.

TRICKETT Set compasses to 75 millimetres. Having set compasses where do I put them? And wipe that smile off your coal-black jib, Boswell. Where do I put them? I put them where page seventeen of your Yarwood tells me I put them.

BOSWELL Centre A and B, sir.

TRICKETT Centre A and B. Cease your labours for one moment, friends. I spy strangers. Be seated, Boswell. A denizen from the lofty spheres of literature has deigned to grace our humble classroom. Señor Hopkins, what can we do for you? The isosceles triangle, is it? The square on the hypotenuse? I'll come down there to you in a minute, lad.

BOY He's got my T-square, sir.

TRICKETT If I come down there I'll have more than your T-square. Now then, Hopkins.

Hopkins unrolls the photograph so that only Trickett can see it.

HOPKINS I wondered whether any of your class did this.

TRICKETT Oh dear, oh dear, oh dear. Oh dear. Now, lads. Mr Hopkins would like to know whether there is an artist in our midst. Some student of the female anatomy has been embellishing Mr Hopkins's visual aids.

He shows the picture to the class. Great glee. Shining, black glee.

Right. Stand up the Michelangelo. Look at them, Hopkins. Regardez. Innocence written in every cloddish unenlightened line of their features. Draw? This lot? They can hardly hold a pen. Who is the lady in question?

HOPKINS Virginia Woolf.

TRICKETT Virginia Woolf. Virginia Woolf, friends.

BOSWELL Who is she, sir?

TRICKETT Tell us, Hopkins. Expound.

HOPKINS She's a novelist.

TRICKETT She is a novelist, Boswell.

BOSWELL Gormless-looking cow.

TRICKETT Boswell thinks she is a gormless-looking cow. A gormless-looking cow, Boswell, is that what you think?

BOSWELL Yes, sir.

TRICKETT Well, don't. Do you understand me. Why? Because, friend Boswell, that is lip. L-I-P. Lip.

BOSWELL Sometimes it's lip and sometimes it's not lip. I never know.

TRICKETT Exactly, Boswell, exactly. However. You know my class, Hopkins. Deprived products of broken homes, condemned to labour out their days at ordinary common repetitive tasks. Even the best of them are factory fodder, Hopkins. What are you, Boswell?

BOSWELL Factory fodder, sir.

TRICKETT Exactly. If you are lucky. And the rest, Hopkins, Y.U.P.s. Have you come across yups yet? These are they. Young unemployed persons, the latest underprivileged group to be clasped to the dry bosom of the Welfare State. Creatures sunk in the trough of ignorance, lasciviousness, foolishness and despair. And from which there is one thing and one thing only that can deliver them, Hopkins. Literature, Hopkins? No. Virginia Woolf? No. Art? No. The one thing that will deliver them is their Higher National Certificate. But we shall not achieve it like this, my friend. Goodnight.

He pushes Hopkins out into the corridor.

INT. WENDY'S CLASSROOM. EVENING.
Wendy's Yoga class. The class is in full swing, which is to say everyone is motionless, involved in some contemplative exercise.

WENDY Let your skeleton grow heavy but your body light. Take the left side of your face to the left. Take the right side of your face to the right. Take the back of your head to the front of your head. And, in your own time . . . let the silence in. Let your eyes become heavy. Slowly open your eyes and let the peace in.

A woman opens her eyes not to let the peace in but to watch Mrs Broadbent and Hopkins, who have come in with the damaged poster. She gives them a shy, embarrassed smile. Almost a wink.

Open your eyes to the utmost. Open your ears to the utmost.
Your skeleton grow heavy.

MRS BROADBENT Could I have your full attention just for one
moment? Did anyone here do this? Speak up. No? Right. As
you were. Carry on.

She goes briskly out, leaving utter confusion in the Yoga class.

WOMAN Bugger it. I was just going under.

INT. HOPKINS'S CLASSROOM. EVENING.

Hopkins is lecturing.

HOPKINS . . . and a good deal has been written and continues to
be written about this small circle of friends around Virginia
Woolf, the circle we call the . . .(*Maureen has her hand up.*)
Yes, Maureen?

MAUREEN Bloomsbury Group.

General looks of distrust from the class.

HOPKINS It wasn't a formal group. No membership cards. No
subscriptions. They didn't have meetings at set times. It wasn't
like this meeting here. We couldn't be the Bloomsbury Group.

*Mrs Broadbent's expression indicates 'I don't see why not.' Mrs
Garland shakes her head implying 'Of course not.'*

Just a few like-minded people who kept running into one
another, dining together, gossiping. Common interests,
common assumptions, talking the same language, laughing
at the same jokes. But as a group ill-defined, vague and
amorphous.

He writes it up on the board. Skinner has his hand up.

No, I know you know. Maureen, our dictionary lady.

*Maureen looks up 'amorphous' in a dictionary, which she has
backed in brown paper.*

(*lecturing, voice under*) Virginia Woolf. Her husband Leonard.
Vanessa Bell, Virginia's sister. Clive Bell. The painter Duncan
Grant. Lytton Strachey. E. M. Forster. These are what you
might call hard-core Bloomsbury.

NARRATOR (*voice over*) Hopkins saw what vicars must feel like
Sunday after Sunday. The same people. The same sort of
people. Single ladies. Widows. Sad men. Refugees from life.
Except Skinner. Skinner had an earring and one of those
thong things round his neck. Skinner was not a refugee.

HOPKINS Yes, Maureen?

MAUREEN 'Amorphous: shapeless, unorganised. Greek, *Morphos.*
Form.'

MR DODDS I've got a better dictionary than that at home. It has
wine lists.

MRS BROADBENT Wine lists? In a dictionary?

MR DODDS Vintage years. Plus the time in various parts of the
world and the names of all the emergent countries.

HOPKINS And at the centre of this circle, this coterie . . . Yes, if
you want, Maureen . . .

Maureen goes for the dictionary like a mad thing.

. . . Virginia Woolf herself. (*the now somewhat battered picture of
Virginia Woolf*) A sad lady. Nervous, highly strung . . .

MRS TUCKER (*to Miss Gibbons*) Like you.

HOPKINS . . . who must always be asking, 'What is it like to be
me here now?'

Skinner puts his head down on his desk.

But it is ironical that a writer who struggled to pin down the
moment in words and make it free of time and circumstances
should be remembered chiefly as part of that time and these
circumstances, the centre of that circle of friends . . . that
coterie . . . yes, Maureen?

MAUREEN 'Set of persons associated by exclusive interests.'

HOPKINS So what I'd like to do if I could is to try and steer us
back from her life to her work.

Mrs Garland nods sagely.

(*voice over*) Don't nod, sweetheart, you've never read a word.
(*aloud*) It has been said that the novel widens experience and
poetry depends on it.

SKINNER Who by?

HOPKINS In this sense Mrs Woolf's work is nearer poetry . . .
I think it was Harold Nicolson.

SKINNER Christ.

HOPKINS Why?

SKINNER Nothing. I pass.

MRS GARLAND Excuse me.

HOPKINS (*voice over*) Oh hell.

MRS GARLAND . . . but didn't Harold Nicolson's wife Vita
Sackville-West have a very intimate relationship with Virginia?

HOPKINS (*voice over*) Virginia! Mrs Woolf to you, you art-struck cow. (*aloud*) Yes, she did.

MRS GARLAND A relationship that was in part at least physical.

HOPKINS That's open to debate.

SKINNER Let's debate it then.

HOPKINS Would there be any point? I don't think any of us have precise information. (*voice over*) Or were you crouching in your Leavisite underpants in the wardrobe at the time? (*aloud*) But while the facts of her life are not irrelevant to her work, I think I ought to . . . yes, Maureen?

MAUREEN (*who has her hand up*) Litotes. 'Not irrelevant.'

HOPKINS Yes, Maureen. I think we ought to try and get back to the permanent record of her books.

MR DODDS There's no tale to them, is there? That's where she leaves me. I like a good tale. Kipling, you see, he's different.

MRS TUCKER Here we go again. He always tries and gets it on to Kipling.

MR DODDS Well, I know about Kipling.

MRS BROADBENT So do we now. We had him all last week.

MRS TUCKER Whenever anybody suffers from nerves, which is what she suffered from, I say, 'What's the hubby like?'

MISS GIBBONS Yes. They're generally at the bottom of it.

MRS TUCKER You see, she never had any children. If you've not had children you don't know what life's all about.

MISS GIBBONS Yes. Except I haven't had children.

MAUREEN Nor have I.

MRS GARLAND She did have children. Her novels were her children.

MR DODDS Then she's better off than me. I wish I'd had novels not daughters.

SKINNER Why?

MR DODDS Because novels don't have fifteen-year-old boy-friends. Novels don't come in with teeth marks on their neck. Novels don't hang around the bus station half the night waiting for the coach to come in from Catterick. Novels don't get pregnant.

MRS TUCKER How is she?

MR DODDS I don't want to talk about it.

Later in the lecture.

HOPKINS In general her books are very decorous. They're concerned with feelings, impressions rather than actions. In the novels of Virginia Woolf we do not expect to come across a scantily clad blonde standing over a body with a smoking gun in her hand. Any more than in the novels of E. M. Forster do we follow a trail of discarded undies towards the bedroom. Undies do not lead to bedrooms or marriage to mayhem. But supposing they did would this be any more Life than a middle-aged lady sitting reading in a garden? (*voice over*) Yes. Yes. It would. (*aloud*) So if in the novels of Virginia Woolf and E. M. Forster there is not enough of what we call euphemistically life . . .

Maureen reaches for the dictionary.

No, Maureen. Are you looking up 'euphemistically'? Don't. Look up 'life'.

MRS BROADBENT Life? We all know what that means.

HOPKINS She didn't. That was what she was always asking. What is life like?

SKINNER Listen. If Virginia Woolf had been born in Brighouse she'd never have got off the ground.

MRS GARLAND Is Brighouse the yardstick, I ask myself?

SKINNER It is for me.

MRS BROADBENT Well, some of us have wider horizons. We were in London only last week. And I have a son in Sutton Coldfield. Environment? Given a car and a good train service one transcends it.

SKINNER Yeah. What need of art?

MR DODDS A lot of these authors . . . and her in particular . . . I get the feeling they would have despised me. I mean, I'm doing them a favour, I think, reading their books. I know jolly well she'd have really looked down her snitch at me. Whereas it's funny I never get that feeling with Kipling.

HOPKINS I think that's true. We go to literature for different reasons. Entertainment. Enlightenment. For inspiration. Consolation. A book can be a window on the world. It can also be a lens, to focus or magnify. But there is a sense too, as you say, in which the process works in reverse. Books are a window on ourselves. A lens under which we, not the world, are examined. Can we live up to them? Are we worthy of them? We feel got at by books. Disturbed. Our lives are called into question. In that sense we not only read books. Books read us. Yes, Maureen?

MAUREEN (*reading in her flat frightened voice*) 'One. Life. State of functional activity and continual change peculiar to organised matter. Being alive. Two. Energy, liveliness, vivacity, animation. Three. Period from birth to death. Phrases as: True to . . . As large as . . . Get the fright of one's . . . The . . . and soul of the party. This is the . . . What a . . . Not on your . . . The time of one's . . . '

MRS HOPKINS Never mind.

MAUREEN It goes on.

SKINNER You bet.

MRS HOPKINS Forget it.

INT. HOPKINS'S CLASSROOM. EVENING.
The lecture is over. Hopkins is just clearing up.
Skinner continues to sit there, although everyone else has gone. This makes Hopkins uneasy.

HOPKINS Do you want anything?

SKINNER If I was to ask you out for a drink, would you come?

HOPKINS Yes.

SKINNER What? Like tonight?

HOPKINS No, I can't. I mean, I'd have liked to, but . . .

SKINNER Skip it.
Skinner gets up and gets ready to go. He looks at the mutilated poster of Virginia Woolf.
I came across a story about her once. Your friend. She was caught short on a train and it didn't have a corridor. So she made this elaborate funnel out of *The Times* and did it out of the window. (*He indicates how.*)

HOPKINS I don't know why you come. You run rings round this lot. You know all the answers. Are you married?
Skinner says nothing.
I don't mean to imply . . . that you're . . . oh Christ. What?

HOPKINS Nothing.

SKINNER You don't mean what?

HOPKINS Nothing. Never mind.

SKINNER That's right. Never mind. Relax. I am married. Got one kid. And it's either this or watching colour TV. I think I prefer this.

HOPKINS Do you?

SKINNER Yes.

Skinner has begun to clear up. He picks up the battered pictures.

HOPKINS Tear that up.

SKINNER You reckon?

HOPKINS Yes.

SKINNER It's council property. Well, love. Was it worth it? Look at the figures. Ten novels, five nervous breakdowns, no kids, one suicide. And this is where it's landed you, sweetheart: a further education class in the Mechanics' Institute, Halifax, on a wet Tuesday night in 1978. Let me introduce you, Virginia, old love. Here it is. Posterity. (*Puts her in the wastepaper basket.*) You're sure you don't fancy that pint?

HOPKINS Oh yes. I do.

SKINNER Ditch her.

HOPKINS I can't.

SKINNER Let's all go. Have a threesome.

HOPKINS No, that wouldn't be a good idea.

The caretaker comes in and starts straightening up the room and grumbling.

Maybe we could go next week?

SKINNER Sure. If you fancy. Next week. Week after. I don't have a tight schedule.

CARETAKER Comparative Literature. Comparative pigsty. Look at all this. I don't know. You'd think it'd be Yoga what would turn the place upside down. You go in the Fortescue Room and it's a palace compared to this. What do you do?

SKINNER What do we do, Mr Hopkins? Well, we tend to kick off with some fairly generalised sex-play, after which one of the pensioners in the class is chased round the room and violated by the rest. We then get down to some serious E. M. Forster. What do you think we do?

CARETAKER Don't you speak to me like that.

HOPKINS Sorry.

SKINNER No. Not sorry. With you it's too much sorry. Not sorry at all. Look. This is a lecturer in Comparative Literature. His job is throwing ideas about. You are a caretaker. Your job is straightening up the chairs afterwards. That's his work, this is your work. So stop chuntering because if we each one of us does our work and rejoices in it we shall all achieve salvation. Correct?

The caretaker is left open-mouthed.

HOPKINS Sorry.

Hopkins and Skinner go.

INT. CORRIDOR OUTSIDE HOPKINS'S CLASSROOM. EVENING.

SKINNER I can't tempt you then?

Wendy is coming along the corridor.

HOPKINS Too late.

As he passes her, Skinner winks.

SKINNER Tonight's the night.

Wendy takes Hopkins's arm.

WENDY I don't like him. Don't you like me having my arm through yours?

HOPKINS Yes, only . . .

WENDY What?

HOPKINS I'm busting.

WENDY Well, go then.

HOPKINS I can't here. It's a madhouse.

INT. GENTLEMEN'S LAVATORY. EVENING.

Hopkins stands against an abstract background of tiles.

NARRATOR (*voice over*) Hopkins ought to have ditched Wendy and gone with Skinner, instead of doing the right thing. He did not know it but he now loved Skinner. Doing the right thing is not always the right thing to do. Still, at least the lavatory was empty. Hopkins was one of those people who finds solitude in this department a *sine qua non*.

Hopkins moves over and stands in a stall. The door of the lavatory opens and a well-to-do middle-aged man comes in. He stands next to Hopkins.

(*voice over*) Too late. With anybody there he could not go. While his neighbour discharged in a confident Niagara . . .

We hear the sound of an assured piss.

. . . all Hopkins could do was wait. In one stall the mighty Zambesi; in the other the Aswan Dam. And so Hopkins waited.

*The man finishes pissing and washes his hands. He dries his hands
with Hopkins still waiting in the stall unable to discharge. The man
comes up behind Hopkins and speaks into his ear.*

MAN This toilet is only a stone's throw from the West Yorkshire
Constabulary. You're playing with fire.

*The man goes. Hopkins heaves a sigh of relief and we hear him
begin to piss.*

PART THREE

INT. WENDY'S FLAT. NIGHT.
Hopkins and Wendy are sitting in silence.

WENDY Trevor. Am I boring you?

HOPKINS No. No. Why.

WENDY I just thought you seemed a bit bored, that's all. Are you?

HOPKINS No. I'm not bored. Are you bored?

WENDY Me? No.

HOPKINS That's good.
   Long pause.

WENDY Trevor.

HOPKINS What?

WENDY It's good when you feel you don't have to talk.

HOPKINS When?

WENDY When you feel you understand one another so well you
   don't need to say anything.

HOPKINS Say what?

WENDY Anything.

HOPKINS Why, what do you want to say?

WENDY Nothing. (*Pause.*) My parents had that.

HOPKINS What?

WENDY This unspoken understanding. They could sit with each
   other in utter silence and each know what the other was
   thinking. (*Pause.*) So there was no point in saying it. Of course
   they spoke sometimes. I'm not saying that. Factual
   information.

HOPKINS Yes. I suppose if the cistern was overflowing somebody
   would have to speak. Or the cat had been sick in the piano.

WENDY You stamp on poetry, Trevor.

Later.

WENDY Trevor.

HOPKINS What?

WENDY I think when one is married . . .

NARRATOR (*voice over*) She meant 'we'.

120

WENDY And I don't mean 'we', I think when one is married it is terrifically important that one's children should see one naked. Don't you think so?

NARRATOR No.

HOPKINS Up to a point.

WENDY One of the saddest things in my childhood was that I never saw my father naked. And now it's too late.

HOPKINS He's not dead.

WENDY No, but he's got a plastic hip. One ought to be able to see that the body has its own special beauty at every age. Not merely the bodies of the young. The middle-aged body, that has a beauty. The aged body. One of the most beautiful people I've ever seen was . . . you won't believe this . . . Gandhi.

HOPKINS Yes. He wasn't exactly sexy though, was he?

WENDY Have you ever seen your mother bare?

HOPKINS I don't want to think about it.

WENDY Poor Trevor. (*She goes into the kitchen.*)

HOPKINS That flaming name again.

NARRATOR (*voice over*) Did he say he couldn't stay all night now or afterwards? Afterwards.

HOPKINS I can't stay all night.

Wendy comes back.

WENDY What did you say?

HOPKINS Nothing.

WENDY Why?

HOPKINS I have to teach first thing.

WENDY So have I.

HOPKINS I've got my laundry to get ready.

WENDY Why don't you say, 'To hell with my laundry'? Live, Trevor.

HOPKINS Live! This!

WENDY What I'd like is if we were both to take our clothes off and just sit. Not do anything. Just be. I like your way of being, Trevor. I think one is a different person with one's clothes off. A more natural person. More real. I am anyway. You are too.

HOPKINS Yes.

NARRATOR (*voice over*) On the contrary. This was the real him. The one in the shirt, pullover and nasty Terylene trousers. Get all that off and he didn't know who he was.

WENDY As I see it the body is the basic syntax in the grammar of humanism.

NARRATOR (*voice over*) Why did they have to wade through this every time? Other people got foreplay. All he got was *The Joys of Yoga*.

WENDY Where are you going?

HOPKINS The lav.

INT. WENDY'S BEDROOM. NIGHT.

Wendy is in bed. The bedside light is on. Hopkins begins to undress and, as he does so, turns off the light. As he is getting his shirt over his head Wendy leans over and switches it on again. He leaves the light on for a moment or two but just before taking off his trousers switches it off again. And so on. And off. And on. But when Hopkins finally makes it into bed the light is off.

WENDY Why can't we have the light on? I can't see my hand in front of my face.

HOPKINS It's not in front of your face, is it?

WENDY I want to see you, Trevor.

HOPKINS I don't want to see myself.

WENDY I want you to see me.

HOPKINS What for?

WENDY Trevor. I want to see you seeing me.

HOPKINS Well, I wouldn't anyway, would I, light or no light. I've not got my glasses on.

WENDY Trevor.

Pause.

HOPKINS Wendy.

WENDY What, Trevor?

HOPKINS Do you mind not saying my name so much.

WENDY Why, Trevor?

HOPKINS There, that. Trevor. Like that. Try not to say it so much.

WENDY Why, darling?

Pause.

HOPKINS Not really 'darling', either.

WENDY What am I to call you?

HOPKINS You. That's fine. Call me you.

WENDY Oh, Trevor.

NARRATOR (*voice over*) A yoga instructress and supple as an eel.
She would do anything. Some people would give their right
arm to be here.

WENDY What's the matter?

HOPKINS You're lying on my right arm.

WENDY Sorry.

NARRATOR (*voice over*) What Hopkins wanted . . . it was only part
of his problem . . . but what he wanted was someone who
didn't want him. He had such a low opinion of himself that if
someone wanted him that must mean they weren't worth
having.

HOPKINS Why?

WENDY Why what?

HOPKINS Nothing. I was just being cosmic.

WENDY Oh Trevor. Trevor?

HOPKINS What?

WENDY I couldn't put on some Bruckner, could I?

HOPKINS Yes. Anything.

WENDY I'll slip my kimono on. I want to stay warm for you,
Trevor.
Wendy goes to the record player.

NARRATOR (*voice over*) Hopkins wondered if Hemingway had
ever had to go through this rigmarole. Or Kafka. Or Leonard
Woolf, the poor, frustrated sod. 'Oh shut it, Virginia. This is the
only lighthouse you're going to.'

WENDY What are you thinking about?

HOPKINS Virginia Woolf.

WENDY You're a true scholar, Trevor. I can't find Bruckner.
You've no objection to Mahler?
She puts on Das Lied von der Erde. *Fade out on her advancing
towards the bed.*

*Afterwards. Wendy is in bed. Hopkins is dressing by the light of the gas
fire.*

HOPKINS Night, night.
But she is asleep. He turns the gas fire off.

EXT. DESERTED STREET. NIGHT.
Hopkins is waiting at a bus stop.

HOPKINS That's it. Temporary membership of the human race.
    For half an hour, maybe, I join. Get a green card. Am like
    everybody else. We have seen the Lions of Longleat. O my pale
    life.

A bus comes. He gets on.

INT. BUS. NIGHT.
*Hopkins sits downstairs, just inside the door on the seat nearest the
conductor. There is nobody opposite. Book on his lap. The West Indian
conductor takes the fare. The bus stops. A boy and girl get on. Sit
opposite him. The boy with his arm round the girl.*
*The boy and girl begin to kiss passionately. Hopkins opens his book.
Deep devouring unashamed passion. He looks up from his book and
catches the girl's open eyes looking over the boy's shoulder as he kisses
her neck. Looks away. He looks at his book. The girl whispers to the boy
while kissing his ear. The boy looks across at him. He kisses her again.
Looking while he kisses. Hopkins does not look up. He reads. The bus is
stopping. The boy and girl lurch to their feet.*

BOY You want to watch it, you.

HOPKINS Me?

BOY Just watch it.

GIRL Yeah.

BOY You want to watch what you're watching. Creep.
    *The boy hits him hard in the face. The bus stops. They get off.
    Hopkins's book has dropped on the floor. The conductor, impassive
    throughout, picks up the book.*

CONDUCTOR Your nose be real bleeding, man.
    Hopkins feels his nose.
    De bus gone go past the Infirmary. Gone drop you in the
    Infirmary, man?
    Hopkins nods. The conductor rings a ticket.
    'Nother five p.

EXT. STREET. NIGHT.
*The bus stops and Hopkins gets off. Waiting at the bus stop to get on
is Skinner.*

SKINNER Hello. What's been happening to you, then?

Skinner turns back with Hopkins and they walk towards the Infirmary.

INT. THE INFIRMARY. NIGHT.
Hopkins and Skinner are sitting in the out-patients' clinic. A woman sits beside Hopkins and opposite another woman weeps helplessly.
SKINNER Do you fancy a coffee?
HOPKINS Yes. Do you?
SKINNER Do you take sugar?
HOPKINS No.
Skinner goes off for some coffee. The woman opposite continues to weep and in order not to look at her Hopkins, his nose bleeding still, opens his book. He reads for a while or tries to, but an out-patients' in Halifax is not the best place to read Virginia Woolf, particularly with a bloody nose. The woman beside him looks at him curiously.
WOMAN Love. Love. Your blood's going all over your book. Blood, love. It's all over your book.
Hopkins closes his book.
NARRATOR (*voice over*) Hopkins felt sick. He had a headache and his nose hurt. The woman crying embarrassed him. The evening had not been a success. He put away his book.
Skinner appears at the end of the corridor bringing coffee.
(*voice over*) It would be months before he opened it again, but when he did and saw the blood blotted on the pages he found he looked back to that night as a happy one. Without believing in corners that night he had turned one.
SKINNER What's up with her, do you think?
HOPKINS I don't know.
NARRATOR (*voice over*) Something had happened.
SKINNER 'Never mind.' (*Raises his cup and smiles.*) Cheers . . . Trev.
Hopkins smiles too.
HOPKINS Cheers . . . Dave.
We freeze frame on the bloody but smiling face of Hopkins as the music from South Pacific *swells. In the final credits sequence, Hopkins shares the frozen frame with Skinner, who is also smiling. But it is Hopkins whose smile is wicked. Skinner looks rather fond. The words of the song make it plain that this has been a love story.*

ALAN BENNETT

I'm not ashamed to reveal
The world-famous feeling I feel.

I'm as corny as Kansas in August,
I'm as normal as blueberry pie,
No more a smart little girl with no heart,
I have found me a wonderful guy!

I am in a conventional dither
With a conventional star in my eye.
And you will note there's a lump in my throat
When I speak of that wonderful guy!

I'm as trite and as gay as a daisy in May,
A cliché coming true!
I'm bromidic and bright as a moon-happy night,
Pouring light on the dew!

I'm as corny as Kansas in August,
High as a flag on the Fourth of July!
If you'll excuse an expression I use,
I'm in love, I'm in love, I'm in love, I'm in love,
I'm in love with a wonderful guy!

Green Forms

CAST AND CREDITS

Green Forms was first transmitted under the title *Doris and Doreen*
by London Weekend Television on 16 December 1978
with the following cast:

DOREEN	Patricia Routledge
DORIS	Prunella Scales
MR LOMAX	Peter Postlethwaite
DOROTHY BINNS	Joan Sanderson
Directed by	Stephen Frears

*An office. Plants on the window ledge and postcards on the wall imply
that though this is a place of work that is not the be-all and end-all. So
the office is cosy if a little run-down: in one of the interior windows a
pane of glass is broken; one lamp wants a shade, another a bulb; the
Venetian blind lacks several slats and the rubber plant is plainly on
its last legs. These dilapidations are precise and will turn out to be
important. In this office are three desks, one occupied by Doreen, a
married lady in her thirties, another by Doris, an unmarried lady in
her forties; the third is empty and plainly unused. There are two doors,
one to the corridor and the other to a passage, at the far end of which
is an unseen toilet and washbasin. The desks are furnished with the
usual office clutter and there is an In/Out tray by the corridor door for
incoming/outgoing mail. Shelves are lined with buff folders containing
papers, some so fat they are tied up with string. Other folders are piled
on chairs, in dusty brown paper parcels on the tops of tin office
cupboards and some have accumulated on the floor round the desks.
There is a mass of miscellaneous information here which a computer
would put paid to in five minutes. However, there is no computer, just
Doris, who is reading the newspaper and Doreen, who is contemplating
her desk.*

DOREEN Are green forms still going through Mrs Henstridge?
    Pause.
DORIS Newcastle.
DOREEN Newcastle?
DORIS Newcastle.
DOREEN You don't mean Manchester, Fordyce Road?
DORIS No. I mean Newcastle, Triad House.
DOREEN Then where's Mrs Henstridge? (*Pause.*) She was green
    forms for as long as I can remember. And now you say it's
    Newcastle.
    Pause.
    Newcastle?
DORIS Staff appointments and changes in personnel: Newcastle.

The green form is inside an inter-office envelope. One look inside the envelope tells Doreen the form is green and therefore not their pigeon. If she does take the form out of the envelope she should not read it.

DOREEN Newcastle. Not Mrs Henstridge. Thin-faced woman. Blonde-ish. She had a son that wasn't right. Lived in Whingate.

DORIS I don't know where people live.

DOREEN Well, where's she gone and got to if she's not doing green forms?

DORIS Search me.

DOREEN I can remember when it used to be Southport.

DORIS It isn't Southport.

DOREEN I'm not saying it is Southport. Southport is being wound down.

DORIS Up.

DOREEN Up what?

DORIS Wound up.

DOREEN Wound down. Wound up. Phrased out anyway. I hope she hasn't been made . . . you know . . .

DORIS What?

DOREEN Well . . . redundant. I wouldn't like to think she's been made redundant; she was very nicely spoken.

DORIS I haven't had the pleasure.

DOREEN Mrs Henstridge? Oh yes. You'll have gone up in the lift with her many a time. Smartish, oldish woman. Check costume. Brown swagger coat. (*Pause.*) Fancy them phrasing out Southport. I never thought they'd phrase Southport out.
Pause.

DORIS Phasing, not phrasing.

DOREEN Come again?

DORIS Phasing. The phrase is 'phase'. Not phrase.

DOREEN What did I say?

DORIS Phrasing.

DOREEN Oh. Well. If you'd come up to me ten years ago and said, 'They're going to phase out Southport,' I'd have laughed in your face.

DORIS You wouldn't.

DOREEN I would.

DORIS You wouldn't. If someone had come up to you ten years ago and said, 'They're phasing out Southport,' you wouldn't have known what they were talking about: you didn't work here then.
Pause.

DOREEN How's Mother?

DORIS Naught clever.

DOREEN No. I didn't think so, somehow.

DORIS Anyway, why single out Southport? I ran into Mr Butterfield in Planning and he says a question mark definitely hangs over Ipswich.

DOREEN Ipswich! That's only been going five years.

DORIS Four. She was on the commode half the night again.

DOREEN Poor lamb.

DORIS I think she must have eaten something. You can't turn your back. Last time it was the vicar. I just caught him doling her out the Milk Tray, else that would have been another three-o'clock-in-the-morning do. She's on a knife edge. People don't realise. One coffee cream and it's three months devoted nursing down the drain. I'm trying to build her up.

DOREEN What I'm wondering is . . . where will the axe fall next?

DORIS Axe? What axe? This isn't an axe. These are scheduled cutbacks. Selective redeployment as set out in the '78 report. Axe! I know one thing. It won't fall on yours truly.

DOREEN Why not?

DORIS Because I'm Grade 3, that's why.

DOREEN Well, I'm substantively Grade 3. Technically I'm Grade 4 but I'm holding down a Grade 3 job. If Central hadn't gone and frozen gradings I'd have been made up months since. Wouldn't I?

DORIS They won't unfreeze gradings while differentials are depressed. Even in this cock-eyed group.

DOREEN No. I know.

DORIS I don't think people *are* out of work anyway. I was reading in the paper yesterday a firm in Warrington is sending £50,000 of seersucker slipovers to Finland. Does that sound like out of work?

DOREEN I can't see myself in seersucker somehow. Even in Finland. Anyway, I'm not going to worry: I've got Clifford.

DORIS Oh, Clifford.

DOREEN That's the thing about marriage, there's always the two of you.

DORIS There's two of Mother and me.

DOREEN We've talked it over and Cliff says that in the event of a real downturn in the economic climate he could fall back on the smallholding and me do my home hairdressing. People are always going to want their hair done, inflation or no inflation, and there's always a demand for rhubarb.

DORIS Yes. Well. I hope it keeps fine for you.

DOREEN 'Which twin has the Toni?' Remember? It's stood me in good stead has that. You don't catch me in a salon. Only you think it's Newcastle? This green form.

DORIS Newcastle.

DOREEN (*as she addresses it and to herself*) Not . . . Mrs . . . Henstridge. Off you go to Newcastle. (*She takes it to the Out tray by the door.*) We are getting on this morning. Proper little beavers. Oh, the *Bulletin*'s come. (*It is in the tray.*) You didn't tell me the *Bulletin* had come. (*reading from the* Bulletin) 'It's goodbye to Leeds, Cardigan Road. Smiles and sadness at simple ceremony.' Fancy shutting down Cardigan Road. That would have been unthinkable five years ago. It has its own canteen.

DORIS What am I talking about? (*She goes over to the Out tray and takes out the envelope with the green form.*) Doris Rutter, you want your head examining. Newcastle?

DOREEN Oh, little Brenda Horsfall's dead. 'Death will leave gap at Goole.' You remember Brenda?

DORIS Doreen.

DOREEN You called.

DORIS Smack me.

Doreen smacks her outstretched hand without looking up from the Bulletin.

This isn't Newcastle.

DOREEN I never thought it was. I said all along it was Mrs Henstridge.

DORIS It's not, though. That's what confused me, you introducing her. Mrs Henstridge has got nothing to do with it.

DOREEN Better smack me then.

Doreen gets smacked too.

DORIS Under the new procedure this belongs on the second floor. It has to go through Staff and Appointments.

DOREEN Oh, nice Mr Titmuss.

DORIS After that it goes to Newcastle. Hearken to the book of words. (*Doris reads from a procedural manual.*) 'Selection and Appointments, North Western Area. Newcastle, Triad House. PO Box 230. Local and District Documentation:' (i.e. us) 'all communications on a district level to be routed through Area Staff and Selection with contingency copies to Records and relevant departments concerned.' We're not a relevant department concerned. Somebody on the second floor is living in the past. Docket it 'misrouted' and bung it straight back to Staff Selection.

DOREEN Mr Titmuss.

DORIS The very same. No, let me. I want to append a note.

DOREEN (*still glued to the* Bulletin) 'Thirty-five years at Bristol, Hotwells Road: veteran Reg punches his last clock.'

DORIS (*typing*) 'Dear Stanley, don't I have troubles enough? What goes on down there on the second floor, or has your triumph in the badminton semi-finals gone to your head? Definitely your baby. Hard Cheddar, Doris.' (*She staples it to the green form and puts it in the Out tray by the door.*) When were these pink forms due back in Personnel?

DOREEN Last Monday.

DORIS I suppose I ought to look through them. Though I don't see why we should break our backs for Mr Cunliffe. What have Personnel ever done for us? Except make our lives a misery.

DOREEN (*reading from the* Bulletin) 'Say Jack and Nanette, "Any kindred spirit passing through Rugeley, Staffs., and wanting a natter about the old prehistoric days at Bebington Road, remember, folks, coffee time is from 9 a.m. to 11 p.m."' People are nice.

DORIS Oh, Blood and Sand!

DOREEN Language.

DORIS That puts paid to Mr Cunliffe. No pink forms today. (*She holds up some forms.*) One PS 104. Two PS 104s. Three PS 104s.

DOREEN I don't believe it. What do they think we are?

DORIS That's three hours' solid work. Three PS 104s. I think a cigarette is called for.

The telephone rings. Doreen answers it.

DOREEN 3507 Precepts and Invoices, Mrs Bidmead speaking. One moment, Mr Cunliffe. I'll see if she's in.

Doris shakes her head.

She appears to have slipped out. Can I be of any assistance? Well, if we have any pink forms, and at this moment in time I'm not sure that we have, one thing I do know: we are not sitting on them. At a guess I should say they're somewhere in the pipeline. (*putting her hand over the receiver*) He's talking about shortfall.

DORIS He wasn't talking about shortfall when Mr Parry had shingles.

DOREEN You weren't talking about shortfall when Mr Parry had shingles. I seem to remember some of us working round the clock. (*hand over the receiver*) What does he tell the computer?

DORIS That's his problem. He's been to Newport Pagnell.

DOREEN Didn't they teach you that at Newport Pagnell? (*hand over receiver*) He says there's going to be an alteration. We'll be laughing on the other side of our faces. We won't know what's hit us. (*shaken*) He's put the phone down. Doris.

DORIS What?

DOREEN What does he mean?

DORIS It means he wants these pink forms. I was going to do them but I'm not now. People will just have to learn to be polite. Personnel. Let them wait. I can find something else to do. These 104s. No. I can't face them. If only we didn't have to bother with these silly, faffing forms we could get on with some real work. (*She picks up the* Bulletin, *which Doreen has discarded.*)

DOREEN Has it gone cold? It feels to me to have gone right cold.

DORIS Something about Newport Pagnell here. 'Newport Pagnell comes of age. Smiling graduates of the twenty-first computer course at Roker Park gather round C.I.S.S.I.E. (Computer Instructor for Senior Staffs In Electronics).' Cissie! (*She reads the item scornfully.*) 'Cissie is now a rather battered old lady and is soon to be replaced by a more sophisticated

model. By the time you read this the old girl will have done her
last print-out. Sorry, Cis, but it happens to us all. Ed.'

DOREEN I don't know why you don't go on a course or two.

DORIS And where am I supposed to put Mother in the meantime?

DOREEN Send her to that place at Bispham.

DORIS I don't want to go on a course. You just want me out of
the way.

DOREEN It would improve your prospects.

DORIS I don't want prospects. Prospects is what I don't want.
Prospects means you get woken up in the middle of the night
and asked to fly with Mr Swithinbank to Saudi Arabia. Why?
Because you've got prospects and you've been on the Far East
course. Though when you come in on a morning and find
three PS 104s on your desk maybe it's preferable.

DOREEN What?

DORIS Saudi Arabia. PS 104, 104, 104. Office stinking precept
forms. Who bothers with precept forms these days?

DOREEN I hope she's not dead.

DORIS Who?

DOREEN Mrs Henstridge. I don't think she is. I seem to
remember something about the Wirral.

DORIS She's probably been sacked. What grade was she? Wasn't
she your grade?

DOREEN I don't know. Remind me to get Clifford some chops.
He loves chops.

DORIS When we say redundancy we mean you, Mrs Henstridge.

DOREEN Tina's not on heat again, is she?

DORIS No. Why?

DOREEN You just seem a bit bitter today somehow.

DORIS You'd be bitter if you'd got a shovelful of 104s on your
desk. One for a lampshade. One, would you believe it, for
an electric light bulb. And the other. (*She looks for it.*) Where
is it? . . . Why don't they get stuff direct from Stores like
everybody else? Precepting for individual items. A gross of
light bulbs, yes. That's worth a 104. But *one*. It's procedurally
correct, but it's insanity. If everybody started putting in a 104
whenever they wanted a light bulb we should be swamped.
One of them is for a washbasin plug. When I can find it.
A *washbasin* plug! Then people say you're looking older!

DOREEN Listen. Tell me again. Mother. Which of her hips is the plastic one?

DORIS It depends which way you look at her. Left if you're looking at her. Right if she's looking at you. Why?

DOREEN It's just that Clifford's sister-in-law's had one fitted and I thought they might have a bit of something in common.

DORIS Why? Which side is hers?

DOREEN I don't know. I shall have to ask. Anyway, who says you're looking older?

DORIS I do. Where is it?

DOREEN What?

DORIS This other 104.

DOREEN What do you want it for?

DORIS I don't want it. I just want to know where it is for when I do want it.

DOREEN I wish I had your system.

DORIS All this rigmarole. They cost five p to buy. And just think what our time's costing.

DOREEN We could apply for a washbasin plug if we wanted. We've lost ours.

DORIS We haven't lost it. It was pinched.

DOREEN It disappeared.

DORIS Nicked. By Personnel.

DOREEN Are you sure?

DORIS Positive. What sort of a mentality is it pinches a plug from a washbasin? Several of them have degrees.

DOREEN How do you know it was Personnel?

DORIS I saw it.

DOREEN Saw what?

DORIS I saw our plug.

DOREEN Where?

DORIS In the toilet in Personnel.

DOREEN On the fourth floor? What were you doing there?

DORIS Looking for our plug.

DOREEN How do you know it was ours?

DORIS Because I recognised it.

DOREEN They're standard issue.

DORIS Listen. When it disappeared last time it was the third time in six months, so I thought 'Right, Doris. We'll settle these buggers.' So I got a new one and cut a little nick in it. Then a fortnight later it went again. Nicked.

DOREEN You mean the one you'd nicked?

DORIS I didn't nick it. I put a nick in it. The one I'd put a nick in was nicked. Right?

DOREEN I see.

DORIS Well, when they had everybody down in the canteen for the efficiency drive, I took the opportunity to do a little fact-finding survey of the departmental toilets.

DOREEN Doris!

DORIS And guess where Doris found it? Personnel.

DOREEN Never.

DORIS Positive. Little nick in it. It must have been. Nobody else in their right mind is going to put a nick in their washbasin plug, are they?

DOREEN So why didn't you confront them with it? Lay it before Mr Skidmore.

DORIS Do you remember Miss Batty of Costing?

DOREEN Shy woman, a bit on the grey side. Wore a little blue coatee.

DORIS Well, she'd keep missing their toilet seat: she'd go down to Stores to put in for a replacement, it'd last about a fortnight then it would get pinched. She'd put in for another. Same thing. It got so that she daren't go into Stores.

DOREEN I can imagine. She was a very refined woman.

DORIS Eventually when she got to her sixth replacement Miss Batty got a red-hot poker and burnt her name on the underside. Unfortunately they had somebody down from the sixth floor to do with industrial psychology. He was in Costing talking about incentives and said could he use the toilet? Well, I suppose, being from the sixth floor he lifted the seat and the upshot was Miss Batty got sent on three months' unpaid leave and lost her grading. Hypertension. She now looks after her brother in Rhyl.

DOREEN Tragic.

DORIS So don't ask me why I didn't take it up with Mr Skidmore. Only I know. And Personnel know I know.

DOREEN Yes. We still haven't got a washbasin plug, though, have we?

DORIS No problem. When I want to fill the basin, like when I do my foot, I use one of the issue paperweights. What do you want a plug for?

DOREEN Same reason you want a rubber plant.

DORIS What rubber plant?

DOREEN I've got one now. A PS 104. For a rubber plant.

DORIS A PS 104 for a rubber plant. Who puts in a PS 104 for a rubber plant? (*Pause, as Doris compares documents.*) The same person who puts in a PS 104 for a washbasin plug. What's the personnel number on yours?

DOREEN R13/57/212/X.

DORIS (*reading out another document*) R13/57/212/X.

DOREEN (*reading out another document*) R13/57/212/X.

DORIS (*reading out another document*) R13/57/212/X.

DOREEN Doris.

DORIS Doreen?

DOREEN They're all from the same person. (*Pause*) Don't you feel chilly?

DORIS (*slowly*) Somebody's going mad.

Someone comes along the corridor talking and the door opens with difficulty. This is because the door handle is broken. It is also because Lomax, the office messenger, has only one arm. Another messenger, Boswell, who is silent and black, remains propped in the doorway while Lomax unloads the incoming files from the trolley. It is to Boswell all Lomax's conversation is addressed. Doris and Doreen are ignored and they endeavour to ignore him too.

LOMAX I said, 'ASTMS?' He said, 'Yes.' I said, 'I've always assumed I was Transport and General Workers. 'A common mistake,' he said. Nice-looking feller. Bit of a beard. Only young. I said, 'ASTMS? That's Scientific, Technical and Managerial.' 'Mr Lomax,' he said (he knew my name), 'Full marks.' I said, 'Well, for a kick-off I'm not Scientific. Furthermore I am not Technical, and in addition I am not Managerial.' He said, 'Excuse me, friend, but haven't I seen you adjusting the thermostat for the central heating?' I said, 'That is one of my functions.' 'Right,' he said, 'you're Scientific. Don't you on occasions man the lift?' 'Manually operated in cases of emergency, yes I do.' 'Right,' he said, 'you're Technical. Do you have access to a telephone?' I said, 'Yes.' 'Right,' he

said, 'you're Managerial. Frank,' he said (he knew my name),
'you shouldn't be in the TGWU, you. You, Frank, are hard-
core ASTMS. You are what we call an ancillary worker.' I said,
'Naturally, I shall want time to study this one out. You're
probably a political person. I vote, but that's about as far as
it goes. Furthermore,' I said (I put my cards on the table),
'furthermore, I've frequently had occasion to vote Conservative.'
'Don't apologise, Frank,' he said. 'It's a free country.' 'Whereas
you,' I said, 'I don't know, but I imagine, just looking at you
(and I don't mean the earring; my eldest lad wears one,
married with a nice little milk round in Doncaster) you are . . .
probably a militant.' 'Up to a point, Frank,' he said. 'Yes.' So
I said, 'Well let's get it quite straight at the outset, I have no
sympathy for that at all. I fought in the Western Desert and
I have no sympathy for that at all.' He went very quiet. He said,
'Frank. Let me ask you one question. Pay and Conditions.
Satisfied or not satisfied?' 'Not satisfied,' I said. 'Nor are we,'
he said! '*Nor are we*. Can I ask you another question? Are you
index-linked?' 'Alas,' I said, 'no.' 'Top of the agenda, Frank,'
he said. 'Our number one priority.' So I said, 'What about
comparable facilities? TGWU has a very nice holiday home
at Cleveleys.' He said, 'Have you ever been to Mablethorpe?'
No. 'Frank,' he said, 'you've got a treat in store.'
*Doris and Doreen have been steadfastly ignoring this conversation
while attending to every word. Lomax has been bringing in more
and more work from the trolley. There is only one item on the Out
tray, the green form.*
Is this all there is to go? A green form. Staff and Appointments.
Misrouted. Right hive of bloody industry this is. (*They ignore
him.*) 'Anyway,' he said, 'I don't want to twist your arm, but
there's a difficult time coming. There are storm clouds ahead,
Frank. Big, black storm clouds. Putting it in simple economic
terms, it's going to rain, Frank. It's not merely going to rain.
It's going to piss it down. And some people, some people, are
going to get wet.'
*Doreen is plainly agitated by this conversation to which she is
steadfastly not listening.*
'They are going to get so wet that they are going to be washed
clean away. Washed down the drain. So if it's raining, Frank,

what's the first thing you do? You get yourself an umbrella. And the ASTMS is that umbrella, the umbrella tailored to your needs. (*Lomax is going.*) I see you have only one arm, Frank,' he said. 'One of the less publicised aspects of ASTMS activity is the provision of more facilities for the disabled. We've been pulling a lot of strings on that. What happened to your arm?' he said. 'Rommel,' I said. 'Who?' he said. 'Before your time,' I said. 'Tobruk. You probably saw the film.' 'Sorry, Frank,' he said, 'the film was before my time too . . .'

Lomax goes out, followed by Boswell. The door closes. Opens again. Doreen gets up and closes it.

DOREEN You'd think having one arm would make somebody nicer.

Doris is consulting various manuals, looking for the reference number.

Blind people are nice. Nine times out of ten. And look at Mr Goldthorpe with the funny foot, he's lovely. But I wouldn't thank you for a union. Me and Cliff, that's the only union I'm interested in.

DORIS RB/57/212/X. RB is what? East Anglia?

DOREEN (*looking through the newly arrived post, etc.*) Thames Valley. Postcard here from Pauline Lucas.

DORIS Thames Valley.

DOREEN 'Dear Girls, journey to Luton uneventful but a nice crowd on the plane. We are staying at this big new hotel on an unspoiled part of the Spanish coast. We have palled on with a couple from Birmingham.' (Or is it Billingham?) 'He is a comptometer operator and she is in fabrics. Tell Mr Cunliffe I miss him, I don't think. Vince sends his love but only a bit because in my present mood' (underlined) 'there isn't much to spare.' Exclamation mark. 'P. S. I think it's the garlic.' (*She pins it up.*) Good old Pauline. Always has a nice time.

DORIS Fifty-seven is year of entry. Joined Thames Valley in 1957.

DOREEN You don't think it's just somebody trying it on?

DORIS Trying what on?

DOREEN Well, once upon a time when we were still in the old annexe I had ten 476s in the same day. I nearly went mad. Then I thought it might be somebody in Records, flirting.

DORIS Funny way of flirting, 476s. 203s you could understand it.

DOREEN You never know with Records, forms are all the same to them. They don't have the sweat of filling them out.
DORIS And was it?
DOREEN Was it what?
DORIS Somebody flirting.
DOREEN No. A bottleneck at Cardiff.
DORIS It's somebody who was taken on in 1957 at Thames Valley. Now what's 212?
DOREEN Doris.
DORIS What?
DOREEN There is an easier way. If that's her Personnel number, why not ring Personnel?
Pause.
DORIS Pick up the phone. Pick it up, Doreen. Ring. 'Hello, Personnel. Precepts and Invoices. Doreen Bidmead speaking. I wanted you to be the first to know: I have just plunged a knife into Doris Rutter's heart.' How can we ring Personnel? You may, Doreen, but I couldn't. It would stick in my throat.
DOREEN What?
DORIS The washbasin plug. They stole it, remember?
DOREEN I was only thinking aloud.
Awkward pause. Doris is all this time going through documents trying to decipher the Personnel number.
I still wonder about Mrs Henstridge. Didn't she have a daughter that was in an accident? I've a feeling the hat came round.
DORIS They wouldn't send the hat round for her daughter. Her daughter never worked here.
DOREEN They send the hat round for the famine victims. They don't work here.
DORIS They send the hat round for all sorts these days. I hope they send the hat round for me when my turn comes. If it's not a wedding it's a famine. Earthquakes practically twice a week nowadays. Never stops. Ethiopia. What have we got to do with Ethiopia?
DOREEN I just have this feeling I chipped in for a spray.
DORIS Here we are. (*She finds the reference.*)
DOREEN It's not called Ethiopia now, is it? It's something else. All the names have changed. Africa. Ceylon. You don't know

where you are. Why can't everything stay exactly the same all the time, that's my philosophy?

DORIS Diana Bunce. Angela Barltrop. Deirdre Barnes. Dorcas Burns. Betty Brookes. (*Pause.*) Dorothy Binns. Dorothy Binns.

DOREEN Dorothy Binns.

DORIS Dorothy Binns. RB/57/212/X is Dorothy Binns.

DOREEN Do you know, I'm going to have to put my cardigan on.

The lights fade slowly down to indicate a brief passage of time.
Up again.

DORIS Dorothy Binns. (*Pause.*) Dorothy Binns. (*Pause.*) Dorothy Binns.

DOREEN I wish you wouldn't keep saying 'Dorothy Binns'. Saying 'Dorothy Binns' isn't going to get us any further.
Pause.

DORIS Dorothy Binns. I've seen her name somewhere. I've seen it today. Dorothy Binns.

DOREEN Can't we try and get some more gen instead of just sitting there saying her name? Saying her name. It gets on my nerves. Dorothy Binns.
Doris looks through the forms.

DORIS R13/57/212/X. Dorothy Binns.

DOREEN Oh, shut up about her. What's it matter anyway? I'm not going to just sit here all day saying Dorothy Binns. I'm getting on with some work. (*Pause, while Doreen starts to go through some of the papers Lomax has delivered.*) Doris.

DORIS What?

DOREEN I hardly like to say this.

DORIS What?

DOREEN I seem to have got some 104s too.

DORIS How many?

DOREEN Three.

DORIS That makes six. I'm going mad. What's the Personnel number?

DOREEN Same. The mystery woman.

DORIS Dorothy Binns. Who is she?
Pause.

DOREEN Doris.

DORIS What?

DOREEN Why do we want to know all about her? (*Pause.*) We could just fill in the forms and have done with it. It won't take all that long.
Pause.

DORIS You used to be such a bright girl. When I pulled you out of the typing pool. So *bright.* Only then you were just plain Doreen Allnatt. It's the Bidmead that's done it. You and Clifford stuck there all night. Nothing to talk about except forced rhubarb. Since when did that hone the mind? Winter-sprouting broccoli. Course we want to know who it is, you silly article. This Miss Binns has suddenly landed us with a fistful of 104s. Who is she? Why's she doing it? Nobody bothers with 104s these days unless they're going by the book. If everybody started going by the book we'd be swamped. It's a change in work patterns, an increase in workload. I'm not having it. If you can't understand that, Mrs Bidmead, then you'd better stick to rhubarb.
Pause.

DOREEN Doris.

DORIS What?

DOREEN I know.

DORIS Know what?

DOREEN How we can find out about Dorothy Binns.

DORIS How? And if you say try Personnel I'll staple your tits together.

DOREEN (*shocked*) Doris.

DORIS I don't care. There's something happening here and I want to know what it is.

DOREEN You might at least say 'Pardon my French.'

DORIS When?

DOREEN If you say anything like that. Pardon my French.

DORIS It isn't French.

DOREEN Clifford says 'Pardon my French' if he even says 'bloody'. (Pardon my French.)

DORIS Good for Clifford. Well? You said you knew? How? How do we get the magic information? (*Pause.*) All right. Pardon my French.
Pause.

DOREEN It's a bit late now. (*Pause.*) Try Tanya.

DORIS Tanya who?

DOREEN You never know anybody, do you? It's the sixth floor. 'Work has a human face.' Tanya Lockwood. At Garstang. The computer centre. Tall willowy girl. Them big glasses. Won a candlelit dinner for two in the productivity bonus scheme. (*She is telephoning.*) Hello, Garstang? Harrogate speaking. Precepts and Invoices. Mrs Bidmead. Tanya Lockwood, please. Computer Centre. Oh? (She's been transferred.) To whom am I speaking? I don't believe it. I do not believe it. Is it really? Well isn't that *funny*. And then they say there isn't a God! (It's Mrs Henstridge.) How are you? We were just wondering where you'd got to. We're champion, you know, trundling along. Things don't change, do they? Tobago! Goodness. That's a far cry. (Her daughter's gone to the Solomon Islands.) And do you like it there? No, not the Solomon Islands, Garstang. (She loves it.) I imagine it is clean, yes, but I think I'd miss people, you know. People. *People.* (She says she knits a lot.) We were only saying this morning how you used to have sole responsibility for green forms. Do you remember when green forms went through you? They did go through you, didn't they? Oh, Newcastle. Not you. Oh well. Something went through you, because I remember. I was thinking it was going to be Tanya Lockwood. Tanya Lockwood. Thin girl. Big glasses. I wonder where she's gone. Listen, I'll tell you why I'm ringing. We've got a little problem-ette here. Doris is saying to give you her love. (*Doris isn't at all.*) Doris. Doris Rutter. Her mother had that bad hip. Lives at Meanwood. She has a little Jack Russell, you remember. She sends her love. (She sends it back.) We've got a little problem-ette here *vis à vis* some PS 104s. You can well laugh. We're not laughing I can tell you. (*She is in fact.*) They all seem to emanate from someone by the name of Dorothy Binns. We're trying to get some gen on her. Dorothy Binns. We've got her Personnel Registration Number. We thought of asking Mr Cunliffe in Personnel – yes, he can be charming when it suits him but we have a little demarcation dispute with Personnel at the moment to do with toilet requisites. What we wondered was if you could just slip the name of this Miss Binns . . . well I'm saying Miss, she might

be Mrs . . . into the computer and see what it comes up with
in the way of her history with the group, present-day location,
and so on. Yes. (*Long pause.*) Yes. Yes. I do see that, yes. (It's
fully programmed for the next fortnight.) Yes. Yes. Couldn't
you perhaps slip it in during the lunch hour? No. I know it
doesn't have a lunch hour, but you do presumably. Unless
Garstang's a very different place from Harrogate. Ha Ha. No.
(*Long pause.*) No. No. Well never mind. We'll explore other
avenues. Nice to have come across you again. No. Don't work
too hard. (*End of phone call. Long silence.*) I can't believe it's
the same woman. As soon as I mentioned the computer she
went right hard. Machines change people, I think. Thin-faced
woman. Blonde-ish. Had one of these poncho affairs.

DORIS   She reckoned to be your friend.

DOREEN   Oh no. I saw her in the lift once or twice, that's all.
Sharpish face. Now I think of it, her hair was probably dyed.
Never mind.

Pause.

DORIS   Dorothy Binns. (*Pause.*) Dorothy Binns. (*Pause.*) Dorothy
Binns.

DOREEN   I think I'll just pay a visit.

DORIS   I've seen it somewhere today, I know.

DOREEN   (*off*) What's that?

DORIS   I said I've seen it somewhere.

DOREEN   (*off*) What?

DORIS   Dorothy *Binns.* (*She gets all the PS 104s together.*) What did
I do this morning? (*shouting to Doreen*) What did I do this
morning? I came in. I had some coffee.

DOREEN   (*off*) You had some coffee.

DORIS   I looked through the post.

DOREEN   (*off*) Telephoned Hazel about badminton.

DORIS   Telephoned Hazel about badminton. Cleared my In tray.

DOREEN   (*off*) Read the paper.

DORIS   (*slightly irritated that of all the things Doreen remembers none
are work*) Read the paper. Stopped you sending that green
Personnel form to Newcastle.

DOREEN   (*off*) What?

DORIS   Was that it? The green Personnel form? No. Can't have
been. I never even looked at it. I don't know. (*She starts going*

through the list of PS 104s.) One lampshade. One light bulb. One carpet runner. One waste-paper basket. One washbasin plug. One soap dispenser. One towel rail.

Doreen appears at the door drying her hands.

DOREEN What were those last ones again?

DORIS One towel rail. One soap dispenser. One washbasin plug.

Doreen looks back down the corridor to the toilet.

DOREEN Go on with the list.

DORIS One lampshade. One light bulb. One carpet runner.

Doreen wanders about the office, locating each item as Doris mentions it.

DOREEN Doris.

Doris says nothing.

Doris.

DORIS What?

DOREEN There's something funny about those 104s.

DORIS We know that, closet. Otherwise why would I be sitting here, racking my brains? They all emanate from the same person. Dorothy Bloody Pardon-my-French Binns.

DOREEN No. Besides that. Listen. One washbasin plug. One carpet runner. One waste-paper basket.

DORIS Well.

DOREEN Don't you see. One lampshade. One carpet runner. One light bulb. They're all items *we're* short of.

DORIS They're all items any office in the North Western Area is short of.

Doreen takes Doris by the hand. Conducts her round the office pointing out the deficiencies.

DOREEN (*scornfully*) One lampshade.

DORIS One lampshade.

DOREEN (*scornfully*) One light bulb.

DORIS One light bulb.

DOREEN One door handle.

The door opens of its own accord and Doris absent-mindedly closes it. One rubber plant. One carpet runner.

DORIS One rubber plant. One carpet runner. No, no. Offices, they're all the same.

DOREEN One pane of glass.

DORIS Well, one pane of glass . . .

One pane of glass is missing.

DOREEN Three venetian-blind slats.

DORIS And three venetian bl . . . Let me look at those. No.
Three venetian-blind slats are missing from the blind.
No.

DOREEN It is, it is. Somebody's wanting to do up our office. Our office. Somebody else.

DORIS No. I don't believe it.

DOREEN It is.

DORIS Why would anybody want to do that?

DOREEN It's not anybody, is it? It's the mystery woman. Dorothy Binns. Has it gone hot in here? I'm boiling. Where did you see the name, Doris? Think, Doris, think. (*She flings off her cardigan.*)

DORIS I am thinking.

DOREEN Nobody's ever been interested in us before, have they? The annual inspection, that's all. Otherwise you'd hardly know we were here.

DORIS She knows we're here.

DOREEN Why? Why?

DORIS Doreen. Doreen.

DOREEN I know why. I know. It's redundancy, Doris. It's the cutbacks. Like in the *Bulletin.* 'Goodbye to Leeds, Cardigan Road. Smiles and sadness at simple ceremony.'

DORIS That's it, the *Bulletin.* That's where I saw her name. I saw her name in the *Bulletin.* Dorothy Binns. Where is the bloody *Bulletin*?

DOREEN Oh yes, yes. It doesn't matter about Pardon my French. Where is it?
They search frantically all over the office, scattering files on the floor, until eventually Doreen, with a cry of discovery, runs the Bulletin *to earth in the waste-paper basket.*

DORIS 'Newport Pagnell comes of age. Smiling graduates of the twenty-first computer course at Roker Park . . . Left to right. Gillian Smallbone (Portsmouth). Brian Priestly (Croydon, London Rd). Betty Butterfield (Stoke). R. Jack Fieldhouse (Sheffield). Dorothy Binns (Southport).'

DOREEN And it says smiling. If that's her smiling what's the other like?

DORIS Southport. Southport.

DOREEN Southport's being wound down.

DORIS Up. We still have those pink Personnel forms. Southport'll be in among them somewhere.

DOREEN She has that hair I don't like either. I've never liked that sort of hair.

DORIS Stockport, Stalybridge, Southampton. (*working through the pink forms*) Wolverhampton. What's Wolverhampton doing here?

DOREEN It's because of Solihull.

DORIS Stanmore, Southsea, Southport. Southport. (*She opens the folder.*) Bast, Barker, Barnett, Banerjee, Binns. Binns! I can't see. We need another light in this room.
Doreen moans.

DOREEN I know. And a carpet and a plant, and a washbasin plug and . . .

DORIS Doreen. Get a grip. Look. Look at her credits. She's been all over. Sheffield, Huddersfield, Norwich, Crewe.

DOREEN All those have been wound up.

DORIS Down.

DOREEN Everywhere she's been, Doris, a trail of redundancy.

DORIS Look at the courses. Manpower Services Course, Tewkesbury. Personnel Selection Course, Basingstoke. Time and Motion Study Course, Winchester . . . Manpower Services Computerisation Course, Andover. Time and Motion, Computerisation, they're all different ways of spelling the same word. Redundancy.

DOREEN Doris!

DORIS Doreen!

DOREEN And she's coming here. Here. And not only here. *Here.* There (*the empty desk*).

DORIS We don't know for certain.

DOREEN Those three venetian-blind slats tell a different story.

DORIS Why here? This is a highly qualified, go-ahead, ambitious woman.

DOREEN I know, I know. I'm sweltering! (*She takes off her scarf.*)

DORIS A woman with a long string of qualifications. Middle-management material. Sights set on higher echelons. Fifth-floor fodder. No. Not here. Except . . .

DOREEN Except what?

DORIS Maybe that's how she likes to work. Under cover. Sussing
the place out. Worming herself in . . . then suddenly, ruthlessly
. . . the *knife*.
Doreen shrieks and rushes into the lavatory.
I don't know why you're crying, you wet lettuce. You're
married. You've got Clifford. I've only got Mother. She doesn't
bring much in.

DOREEN (*from the loo*) They must redeploy us. They redeployed
people at Southport.

DORIS Did they hell! Where do they redeploy people at
Southport? What do they redeploy them as? Deck-chair
attendants? Donkey men? Rubbish.

DOREEN What?

DORIS Rubbish. It's the SACK. Henceforth we'll just have to
plan on redeploying ourselves down to the Labour Exchange.
*Doreen emerges. To find Doris has calmed down and is preparing to
start work.*

DOREEN Oh, Doris, thank God for Clifford's smallholding.

DORIS Just what I was thinking.

DOREEN Why?

DORIS Well, I imagine the lay-offs will be selective.

DOREEN Selective?

DORIS The usual principle. Last in, first out. Done by grades.

DOREEN Grades. Me?
Pause.

DORIS Yes.

DOREEN You?

DORIS No.
Doris begins to work at her desk. Pause.

DOREEN What are you doing, Doris?

DORIS Oh, I just thought I'd get on with these pink forms for Mr
Cunliffe. I don't seem to have made much progress with them
somehow today.

DOREEN *Quelle bonne idée.* Bung me a few over. I'll do one or
two. Many hands!

DORIS No trouble honestly. Old Doris can manage. Eazy peazy.
I hope the day hasn't dawned when Doris Rutter can't cope
with a few measly old Personnel forms.

DOREEN Don't think little Doreen's casting any nasturtiums, but as the proverb has it, every little helps. I can do pink forms with the old eyes closed.

DORIS I know that. Who can't?

DOREEN The sooner we're finished, the sooner we're done.

DORIS You could straighten up.

DOREEN Doreen? Straighten up? I don't think it was Doreen made the mess, was it? (*She addresses the chaos.*) Was it, papers? Was it Doreen pulled you all out and threw you on the floor? No, it wasn't, was it? Who was it, then? Who was it made such a mess? Was it her? Yes.

DORIS Better not let the sixth floor hear you talking like that or you'll end up like Miss Batty. Looking after your brother in Rhyl.

DOREEN I don't have a brother in Rhyl. I don't have a brother. You won't let me do pink forms. I've got to do something.

DORIS Tidy up. Ready for Miss Binns.

DOREEN Yes. That would suit you, wouldn't it? My tidying up, you typing. I'm not one of these ancillary workers. I'm skilled.

DORIS Semi-skilled.

DOREEN Skilled.

DORIS Grade 4.

DOREEN Grade 3.

DORIS Only substantively.

DOREEN Gradings can alter.

DORIS Not when they're frozen. You are Grade 4, semi-skilled, ancillary, so clear up that mess, Mrs Bidmead, before Miss Binns comes and finds the place a pigsty.

Doreen starts tidying up.

DOREEN Don't Mrs Bidmead me. I don't wonder you've never got married. Domineering. You'd domineer Goering, you would. Mother! Mother! Mother's just an excuse. Somebody look twice at you, you'd soon cart her off to the gerry ward.

DORIS And she knitted you those dishcloths!

DOREEN It's you I'm talking about, not her.

DORIS I got you on to her list. She's got several people waiting for them. You got preferential treatment. Does that sound like Goering?

DOREEN I've nothing against your mother.

DORIS I should think not. You've never met her.

DOREEN I feel as if I had. I never hear about anybody else.

DORIS I don't talk about Mother.

DOREEN You do.

DORIS I don't.

DOREEN Listen. She spent half the night on the commode. How do I know that? It wasn't in the *Yorkshire Post*. You think you've got a mother monopoly, you. Other people have mothers. Clifford has a mother.

DORIS Clifford's mother hasn't got a plastic hip.

DOREEN He wouldn't broadcast it if she had. Anyway, what are plastic hips these day? There's all sorts with plastic hips. Cabinet ministers. Disc jockeys. Even proper jockeys. It's not a handicap any more. People who've had experience of them prefer them to real ones. And what about me? I'm not strong. But of course we never talk about that. Because I'm a Grade 4, semi-skilled, ancillary worker. Semi-skilfully clearing up all this skilful Grade 3 mess. You've done it on me, Doris.

DORIS I haven't done it on you, Doreen. It's Personnel. They've done it on both of us. It's Mr Cunliffe that's done it on us. The nasty little tripehound. Dorothy Binns!

DOREEN I shall be redundant. Surplus to requirements. Little Doreen Allnatt. All those years ago. Pulled out of the typing pool. For what? Redeployment. Redundancy. The scrap heap.

DORIS Oh, Doreen, I'm sorry.

DOREEN Don't touch me. Don't even speak to me. (*She weeps.*)

DORIS Oh, Doreen. Doreen.

Enter Lomax. Doris's manner instantly changes, whereas Doreen remains the same, still tidying up, crying as she does it.

LOMAX What's up with her? What's the matter, love?

DORIS It's nothing. Her mother-in-law's poorly.

DOREEN (*stops instantly*) She never is.

LOMAX Boadicea been giving you the treatment?

DOREEN No. I'm upset.

LOMAX What about?

DORIS Don't expose yourself, Doreen. That will be all.

LOMAX Personnel want those pink forms.

DORIS Give Mr Cunliffe my compliments and tell him Miss Rutter will let him have the forms by four o'clock at the latest.

DOREEN And Mrs Bidmead.

DORIS Just say Miss Rutter is completing them now.

DOREEN And Mrs Bidmead. Say Mrs Bidmead. Else this new Miss Binns will think I'm just another ancillary worker. She won't let me near a typewriter even.

LOMAX Nothing wrong with being an ancillary worker. I'm an ancillary worker. I'm laughing.

DOREEN Why?

LOMAX I've just got under the umbrella. The ASTMS.

DOREEN I'm not in the union at all.

LOMAX Then come on under quick.

DORIS Doreen.

DOREEN Why not?

DORIS We've always been opposed to unionisation.

DOREEN We! We. I'm an ancillary worker. I'm Grade 4. You're Grade 3.

DORIS Remember the Tolpuddle Martyrs.

LOMAX What grade were they?

DOREEN My grading's frozen.

LOMAX No problem. Object No. 1 of the ASTMS, index-linking. Objective No. 2, thawing gradings. I'll give my friend a tinkle. He'll be round like a shot. You'll like him. Very gentle. Soft-spoken. Little beard.

DORIS Little beard!

LOMAX Shall I?

DOREEN Yes. Yes, ring him. Tell him I'm interested.

DORIS Doreen. Don't lower yourself.

DOREEN Damn you, Doris.

Lomax is going.

LOMAX Girls, girls, girls. Who is it supposed to be coming? Miss who?

DOREEN Binns. Dorothy Binns.

LOMAX Never heard of her. No Miss Binns here. (*He looks at his clipboard.*)

DOREEN She's in the offing.

LOMAX No.

DOREEN She is.

DORIS Doreen.

LOMAX Listen. We've got a Miss Bird coming into Costing and
Estimates. Mr Bottomley into Accounts and Mr Sharples into
Maintenance but no Miss Binns.

DOREEN Are you sure?

LOMAX Do I know everything that goes on in this group or don't
I? There is no Miss Binns. Anyway, I'll telephone my friend.

DOREEN (*uncertainly*) Well, perhaps –

LOMAX You want to get in, girl. Get in while there's still room
under the umbrella.

Lomax goes. Silence.

DORIS I think you'll live to regret that, Doreen.

DOREEN You forced me into it. Ancillary worker. I'm not an
ancillary worker. Only technically, anyway. (*Pause.*) He'd never
heard of Miss Binns, had he?

DORIS No.

DOREEN Doris. Are there some of those 5D forms left?

DORIS One or two.

DOREEN Could I do them?

DORIS If you like.

DOREEN Oh, Doris. (*Pause.*) I'm sorry I said that about Mother.

DORIS What?

DOREEN About Goering and the dishcloths.

DORIS It was nothing. Doreen.

DOREEN Doris.

DORIS You won't be seeing this union person?

DOREEN Nothing to see him about really, is there, Doris? If this
Binns woman's not coming.

DORIS Oh, she's not coming. I know that for certain. It came
to me when our friend was here. Of course he hasn't heard of
her. If this Dorothy Binns was coming here, to our little office,
what would be the first thing we would get?

Doris picks up the manual as Doreen shakes her head.

Look at the procedure. Selection and Appointments, North
Western Area. Newcastle, Triad House. All communication on
a district level to be routed through Area Staff and Selection
with contingency copies to records and *relevant departments
concerned,* i.e. us. If this lady were headed in our direction we
would have been notified of the fact by a green form. We haven't

had a green form. Therefore she is not coming. Procedure, you
see, Doreen, it can be a tyrant. It can set you free. So *relaxez
vous*, Doreen. Let it all hang out. We haven't had a green
Personnel form. She is not coming. So much for Miss Dorothy
Binns!

Pause. Then Doreen slowly puts her cardigan on.

DOREEN Doris.

DORIS What?

DOREEN We have.

DORIS Have what?

DOREEN Had a green form. We had one first thing. The one
I thought went through Mrs Henstridge. Only you said it had
nothing to do with us because we weren't a relevant department
concerned. You sent it down to Staff and Appointments,
Mr Titmuss.

DORIS Doreen. If we were the relevant department concerned,
Mr Titmuss would have sent it straight back. He hasn't, has
he?

DOREEN No. Sorry, Doris.

*At this point the door opens, Lomax pops his head round and puts a
form in the correspondence tray.*

LOMAX ASTMS. Doesn't stop you being a bloody yo-yo.

He goes. Silence.

DORIS Doreen.

DOREEN Yes, Doris.

DORIS Is that from Staff and Appointments?

DOREEN Yes, Doris.

DORIS Is it a green form?

DOREEN Yes, Doris.

DORIS Is there a note from Mr Titmuss?

DOREEN Yes, Doris.

DORIS Read it, Doreen.

DOREEN 'Doris, pet. Somebody up there in Precepts and
Invoices wants their bottom smacking. This isn't our baby at
all. Phew, exclamation mark! You gave us quite a turn. Don't *do*
that sort of thing. We like to sleep in the mornings. Stan.'

DORIS Open it. What's the Personnel number?

DOREEN RB/57 –

DORIS (*joins in*) – /212/X.

DORIS Dorothy Binns.

DOREEN Ms Dorothy Binns. Ms. She's one of them, too. Still, she may not stay long.

DORIS She didn't stay anywhere long. Crewe, Chesterfield, Lytham, Southport. All wound up.

DOREEN Down.

DORIS Out. Personnel. They're the ones. They've done it on us, Doreen.

DOREEN This will be her desk.

DORIS She probably sat at it this morning. Before we came in. What time did we come in?

DOREEN Half past nine-ish.

DORIS That'll stop.

DOREEN I'm so cold.

DORIS It's locked. That means she's brought her stuff already. The nerve. Locking her desk. The cheeky cow. She's never even met us and already she doesn't trust us. I don't lock my desk.

DOREEN I don't lock mine.

DORIS We've got nothing to hide.

DOREEN We trust each other.

DORIS She doesn't.

DOREEN What has she got to hide?

DORIS We'll soon find out. I'm having this open.

DOREEN How?

DORIS The usual way. (*She cuts a slat from the already depleted venetian blind and uses it to insert in the crack in the desk drawer and pick the lock.*) It's all very neat.

DOREEN An apple.

DORIS That means she doesn't have lunch.

DOREEN Oh, Doris, I'm frightened. Look at the point on those pencils!

DORIS A nameplate. Yes. Dorothy Binns.

Doreen has picked out a framed document, which she reads.

DOREEN Listen to this:
'I am the foundation of all business.
I am the source of all prosperity.
I am the parent of genius.
I am the salt that gives life its savour.

ALAN BENNETT

I am the foundation of every fortune.
I do more to advance youth than parents, be they never
    so wealthy.
I must be loved before I can bestow my greatest blessings,
    and achieve my greatest ends.
Loved I can make life sweet, purposeful and fruitful.
I am represented in the most limited savings, the largest body
    of investments.
All progress springs from me.
What am I?'
*An ominous figure stands in the doorway casting a black shadow
across the stage.*
MS BINNS   I am Work. I am Work.

The Old Crowd

AN INTRODUCTION

Lindsay Anderson

The English are proud of their sense of humour: it is what distinguishes them from foreigners. And the mark of a sense of humour, we all know, is the ability to laugh at oneself. The English like to think they like to laugh at themselves. This may have been true once, when there was no apprehension that the Sun might one day Set. But it is not true today.

This is one truth I learned from the experience of *The Old Crowd*. Another, less disputable, is that television is the most conformist of the media, a powerful and pernicious stifler of originality, a bastion of the status quo. I am not thinking in strictly 'social' terms: another connection that *The Old Crowd* made clear was that between social and artistic conformism. The almost universally apoplectic reception it received from the television critics – it was significant that the only one who understood and appreciated it was American – reminds us that the press, whether professedly left or right, is essentially an Establishment body. The highest ambition of a *Time Out* writer in the 1980s will be to get regular employment on *The Sunday Times* or *The Observer*. Protest is a commodity. The good ship *Britannia* is waterlogged in a shark-infested sea. Don't rock the boat!

Another national characteristic: the Anglo-Saxons do not favour art that claims relevance to *actuality*. By which I mean relevance to the contemporary social or political situation, whether at home or out in the world. This explains the fashionable predilection for the plays of Harold Pinter or Tom Stoppard (two authors who flatter their audiences without disturbing them), for the non-disruptive humour of Monty *Python* or *Not the Nine O'Clock News* (facetiousness masquerading as satire), for the novels of Anthony Powell or Martin Amis, the television plays of Dennis Potter. The English conception of 'committed' art is *naïf*, essentially because the English intellectuals shrink from the abrasion of reality. They claim to find significance 'boring' in order to disguise their fear of ideas.

These, as I say, are some ideas brought home to me by the experience of *The Old Crowd* – such a rich experience, even though it was a mere television play, written and made with a great deal of thought, fun and care. Shown once and savaged by the press with a humourless hostility as astonishing as it was suggestive. How on earth did it come to be made at all?

The responsibility must be shouldered first by Stephen Frears, and I shall always be grateful to him for it. Stephen had already directed, with great success, a number of plays written for television by Alan Bennett. When London Weekend Television invited him to make another series of six, he decided that he would direct only some of them himself. The rest he would produce. He paid me the compliment of inviting me to take one on, and sent me three scripts to choose from. I had always admired Alan's writing, for its rare combination of wit and feeling, the way it so precisely catches the poignancy as well as the comedy of existence, which we habitually express in the banal or grotesque clichés of everyday conversation. Also, sometimes hidden beneath the surface triviality of his style, I sensed strong currents of sadness and disturbance.

I liked one of these plays particularly. It happened to be the one furthest from completion. It presented the situation of a moneyed, middle-aged couple who had moved into a London house and were giving a house-warming party for a small group of their oldest and best friends. Their only problem was the loss of their furniture, misrouted on the road from Horsham and ending up in remote Carlisle. They decide to hold their party all the same, with dinner provided by caterers and served by two ambiguous waiters, who may (or may not) be out-of-work actors. As far as I remember, the piece did not have a clearly defined ending. It was called *The Old Crowd*.

This script appealed to me because it was bizarre as well as comic. Its situation struck me as more poetic than anecdotal, very apt to image certain obsessive aspects of contemporary English life: strain, menace, disintegration. And it was unfinished, which meant that there was still room in it for a director to make a creative contribution. All the same, I found that I did not call Stephen back or take the matter further. Partly this was due to an instinctive reluctance (not in the end unjustified) to enter the alien and wasteful world of television, in which one may labour long over a work that will only ever be shown once. Partly it was sheer laziness, a weariness at the thought of starting once again the long travail, the inevitable frictions and painful expense of spirit that is inseparable from any creative, collaborative undertaking. But most of all I drew back because I knew that television was traditionally and emphatically a writer's rather than a director's medium. This was a series of 'Six Plays by Alan Bennett': the directors would be required simply to stage them. My formation in cinema would, I knew, impel me in quite another direction. The stage belongs to the writer and the actors: I have never cared for 'director's theatre'. But the cinema at its best and purest belongs to the director. Television drama is a bastard form. I could approach it only as I would approach the making of a film – personally and subjectively. And that, I felt, might well (and reasonably) be unacceptable. This was essentially why I did not call Stephen back.

He, thank goodness, called me. I told him I liked *The Old Crowd*, and that if it had been a film I was being asked to undertake, I would certainly have enjoyed working on it with the author. But a collaboration for television would work only if that was truly what our relationship could be – as long, in other words, as we could both feel we were making something we could both sign. I didn't want to start anything I felt might not be harmoniously finished. And such harmony is rare.

Stephen understood what I was talking about: directors usually make the most understanding producers. He said he would talk to Alan Bennett. The next day he reported that there was no problem: Alan would be happy to collaborate. So he came round and we started work.

As is the case with every successful collaboration, it would be impossible to separate contributions: at least I could not. Alan's original script provided, of course, the starting point and the basis, the characters and the dialogue. I must take responsibility for the disruptive elements that eventually made our work so resented. I felt that I had never seen anything in television drama quite so exciting, quite so amusing or *real* as those occasional glimpses of sound equipment, even of whole camera crews, that would suddenly flash before one's eyes when television plays had to be recorded 'live'. Without quite knowing why, I suggested we incorporate a series of such glimpses as a developing theme. The idea intrigued Alan and he agreed. Hence the repeated appearances of the camera and crew, observing the dramatic action with detached concentration, extending even to a shot in the gallery with multiple images on the monitors and Stephen Frears, in the role of director, picking his shots while the Old Crowd line up to sing 'Goodnight, Ladies'.

'Alienation' is the Brechtian term – a translation of his *Verfremdungseffekt* – usually applied to such a style, but I have always thought this a heavy word and not a very accurate one. The real purpose of such devices, which can include songs, titles between scenes, etc., is not to *alienate* the audience from the drama, but rather to *focus* their attention on its essential – not its superficial or naturalistic – import. Of course this is almost impossible to achieve with an audience either too unsophisticated to understand the language of art, or too wedded to the aesthetic and social status quo to accept anything that hints at the subversive. For some reason, Anglo-Saxons cannot bear the idea of being taught anything: teaching implies learning, which implies development, change, growing up. Hence their violent resistance to Brecht – whom Bernard Levin once credited with the intelligence of a six-year-old child – until his work could be safely enshrined as an elaborate but meaningless art object at the National Theatre.

Probably the most anarchic ideas in *The Old Crowd* were mine – the homage to Buñuel under the dinner table – the sexual savagery behind the television set . . . but I never felt these developments were inorganic to Alan's original conception, and nor did he. Anyway, the script as he had originally imagined it always seemed to me to carry mysterious suggestions of catastrophe and threat. Our work merely continued along these lines. We had some arguments, of course, as good collaborators must. I would object to some of the jokes with which Alan, being so good at them, would compulsively pepper his dialogue. And he would check me when my inventions became indulgent. He wanted the Lady Entertainer to sing 'Pedro the Fisherman', which I thought too jokey: we settled on 'Because'. I wanted the Old Crowd to sing 'My Old Kentucky Home'; Alan disliked the Fordian echo and specified 'Goodnight, Ladies', which was, of course, the perfect choice. Fortunately both Alan and Stephen were so highly regarded by London Weekend that we were able to develop our script with complete imaginative freedom. Which is the only enjoyable way to work.

I would think that the 'cinematic' as opposed to the 'TV literary' style of *The Old Crowd* would make it difficult to read.

Many sequences are not dialogued at all, depending entirely on the expressiveness of the action and the performers. We were tremendously lucky in our cast. Diana Parry, the very experienced and long-suffering casting director at London Weekend, clearly thought my prejudices were as unreasonable as my ambitions were high, but by great good fortune many friends and colleagues with whom I had worked before in film and theatre were free and even eager to take part. My preference for working with actors with whom I have already collaborated happily and successfully always seems to astonish journalists. I find this strange. There is certainly nothing new about it either in theatre or film tradition. The players in *The Old Crowd* mostly knew each other and knew me from films like *This Sporting Life, If . . .* and *O Lucky Man!* (Rachel Roberts, Peter Jeffrey, Philip Stone), as well as from the Royal Court in the great old days and, more recently, from the Lyric Theatre Company (Jill Bennett, Frank Grimes, Valentine Dyall, James Ottaway). I had known Peter Bennett ever since I'd directed him as one of the Merry Men in the classic television *Robin Hood* series; and I had known Isabel Dean so long as a friend that it felt as though we had worked together. So the Old Crowd were not strangers to me or to each other, and this helped a lot. Elspeth March as the magnificent Totty, Cathleen Nesbitt (repeatedly insisting that she had no idea what was going on, which no doubt helped her to perform with such contained acerbity), Adèle Leigh as the sweet-voiced Lady Entertainer, and David King as her accompanist – all these were cast in the usual way, from memory, suggestion and inspiration. Jenny Quayle and Martyn Jacobs, the 'children', were chosen from the many talented young people whom Diana Parry produced from her long lists. Like latecomers to a party, they at first found the convivial, allusive atmosphere strange; but after three weeks' rehearsal they were each one of a seamless company.

I have emphasised the closeness and the particularity of the players in *The Old Crowd*, because I think the importance of the 'chemistry' of a well-chosen cast often passes unremarked, even unperceived by critics and public alike. So how much more by the reader of a script? It is the actors, after all, who give the human feature and personality to the *idea* of the character, which is all that the writer can provide. You can tell a director's personality by the actors he likes to work with – or by whether he likes to work with actors at all. (Many don't; as many don't too much care whom.) It is a human choice, not just a question of ability, nor just a question of physical rightness. What does he see in her? What does she see in him? These questions can never be answered. But they are all-important.

Nor will readers of *The Old Crowd* be able to hear the witty and emotive music written for it by George Fenton: and how can the arrival of Totty resonate fully without the broad Elgarian theme that elevates her to mythic status? They will not see the spacious and atmospheric décor provided by Jim Weatherup, nor the images lit and composed by John Fyfe and his cameramen. The script really is a blueprint, and less easy to visualise, even to the expert, than the plans for a house, an aeroplane or a food-mixer.

I used to think that I was a reasonably fast, at any rate not a wastefully slow worker; but shooting *The Old Crowd* took much longer than I anticipated. The result, unarguably, of my way of working: it certainly was not due in any way to the technicians of London Weekend. The crew operated, in fact, with extraordinary commitment – somewhat mystified, but intrigued, amused and buoyed up by a feeling that they were taking part in something extraordinary. To some extent, I'm sure, this was because I spent most of my time on the floor (cinema-style) in contact with actors and technicians, while Stephen Frears was in the control room, calling the shots. The chilling effect of reducing the director during shooting to a depersonalised voice, usually communicating with his actors only through the earphoned floor manager, is something I dislike intensely. I have no doubt that the sense of communal enterprise that resulted from having the director on the floor was largely responsible for the technicians' readiness to extend our last day's shooting to four o'clock in the morning. And the actors' too. Expensive, of course.

The Old Crowd took a long time to edit. There were two reasons for this. First, a strike of production secretaries (I think) meant that nothing we shot could be 'time-coded'. In other words, no shots could be numbered or catalogued for identification. This naturally slowed the process; but at least I could take the tapes home with me and play them until I was familiar with the coverage and the variations between takes. We spent some days in Wardour Street doing 'off-line' editing. Where or how this term originates I could never discover: it meant doing a preliminary edit from a transfer of the material before making a final cut version from the original tapes. (Of course you do not 'cut' tape as you do film. You transfer the exact section you want from any shot to a 'master' tape, and so build up, shot by shot, your edited version. It is not easy to explain.) For some reason, also connected with the union, this process had to be kept secret. So when we finally came to edit the final version from the original tapes at London Weekend, my first edit had to be kept on a video machine in an office some distance away from the editing suite. Whenever I needed to refer to it, I had to run down the passage, hurriedly check the off-line version and then run back. Andrew Vere, who did the original cut with me, had to receive a credit as 'Special Assistant to the Director'. Anything more accurate, I was told, would have precipitated another strike.

This whole process took nearly a year. Not of continuous work, of course. The London Weekend editors were busy on weekly sitcoms, the sports reports and current affairs. It was not until a show date was set that I was given enough continuous time to finish the work in a few concentrated days. The technological potential of video is probably limitless; but the elaboration of equipment and the expense of using it impose huge limitations. And I shall always prefer a medium whose material I can touch, inspect against the light, run through my hand.

I was in Sri Lanka when *The Old Crowd* was shown on ITV, nearly a year after we had shot it. I was returning from a theatrical production in Australia with Rachel Roberts, and had mistaken the day of the Singapore Airlines departure for London. When I returned to my hosts, they showed me a clipping from the *Observer* which their friend Arthur C. Clarke, the famous science-fiction writer, had sent over to them. It was a review of *The Old Crowd,* as scathing as it was shallow, by their popular television critic Clive James. Its tone did not surprise me. On the cutting Arthur Clarke had written, 'Poor Lindsay!' Why doesn't he write, 'Poor Clive James!' I wondered.

I really was not surprised. Indeed, Alan Bennett recalls that I had warned him that we'd be told that I had ruined his work and this certainly came true. But it would have been hard to anticipate the barrage of outrage that rained down on *The Old Crowd*, reminiscent of famous philistine explosions of long ago, hardly to be expected in this age of enlightenment. Indeed, speaking personally, the reception of this piece signalled the end of the acceptance which had seemed to make the sixties and early seventies at least a time of promise. The mood had changed: geniality and intelligence were out; the cat-calls came as from a single voice. 'Rubbish!' (*Sunday Telegraph*). 'Tosh' (*Observer*). 'Meaningless' (*Sunday Express*). 'Inexplicable' (*Daily Telegraph*). 'Nonsensical farrago' (*Spectator*). 'Raucous travesty' (*New Statesman*). The *Guardian,* the self-proclaiming defender of cultural as well as political liberality, seemed particularly incensed. Their television critic had remained comparatively calm, noting only that the piece 'wasn't funny' and mourning that Alan Bennett's 'absolutely unique talent' had been 'crowded out'. But the *Guardian's* literary editor, Richard Gott, was so infuriated – perhaps particularly because a few days earlier his paper had devoted a whole page to a friendly account by Tom Sutcliffe of the shooting of *The Old Crowd* – that he wrote a special article, putting his feelings on record. 'Miserably slender . . . insufferably pretentious . . . drivel . . . what does it all mean?' Gott's 'towering rage' (his phrase) provoked a series of letters on the *Guardian*'s correspondence page that mostly echoed his indignation – 'Surely an hour-long TV programme costing £250,000 cannot help in these days of pay restraint!' (K. A. Spencer, Hull) – and culminated in finely rhetorical protests from Lady Gaitskell ('Disgraceful expense . . . an intellectual and artistic "confidence trick" . . . laced with snippets of sly, obscure pornography') and the veteran documentary director and film historian Paul Rotha ('A pretentious load of old cabbage').

Much of the criticism of *The Old Crowd* was interesting for the way it exemplified that old, unchanging philistinism which is insulted by any suggestion that an original work may deserve or require effort for appreciation, and which almost congratulates itself on its cultural ignorance. Two critics in the 'quality press' imagined that the piece was derived from or influenced by Pinter: 'just a protracted send-up of the works of Harold Pinter' (*Sunday Telegraph*), 'full-length parody of a Harold Pinter play' (*Spectator*). The *Daily Express,* on the other hand, thought it was done 'in the manner of the French cinema'. *Time Out* found it 'a mosaic of concerns rooted in Brecht's dramatic theory' (and failing because it was not Marxist). The *Evening News* described it as 'a piece of surrealism'. Richard Gott quoted a friend who thought that Frank Grimes 'biting' Jill Bennett's toe was 'just silly', and the *Evening News* critic asked, 'What was the point of that disreputable and surly waiter getting under the table and cutting off the toes of Jill Bennett's stockings *without her objecting*?' (my italics). Really there are still a surprising number of clean-limbed English gentlemen around who cannot tell a suck from a bite – and are charmingly perplexed when confronted by the perverse pleasures of rough trade.

Behind or beneath this dismissive indignation, there certainly smouldered something much more interesting. A sense of affront and a defensiveness only intermittently acknowledged. The *Guardian*'s features editor (who probably thinks of himself as an anti-Establishment man) had to rationalise his bourgeois resentment with a disingenuousness typically 'liberal'. 'Perhaps it was about the emptiness that lies at the heart of bourgeois society – in itself an excellent *though threadbare* theme.' My italics again: for a theme cannot be 'threadbare' and 'excellent' at the same time. A *Guardian* writer who thinks that 'bourgeois emptiness' is neither a valid nor a present subject must be capable of self-deception indeed. Elsewhere Gott fell back on the reactions of anonymous colleagues – 'Alan Bennett's observation of middle-class manners and speech really isn't that accurate' and 'Poking fun at the middle classes is not enough any more.' Others were less guarded. In the *Daily Express* James Murray protested at 'the brutal pillory of a class the audience were invited to despise'. The *Sunday Telegraph*'s commentator on economic affairs took up the cause of the 'long-suffering middle classes' and justified the status quo by quoting a new Nuffield study ('published in last week's *New Society*') which discredited the idea of a 'crumbling middle class'. The *Observer* critic managed another facing-both-ways jeer at Anderson's presumed conviction that 'Bourgeois Society is crumbling'. The determination to discredit a subversive voice was unmistakable. It was certainly significant, as I have said, that the only intelligent, restrained response to *The Old Crowd* came from the American writer Herbert Kretzmer, at that time reviewing television for the *Daily Mail*. 'An unsettling production,' he called it, 'which said more about the state of Britain than a dozen hectoring *Panoramas*,' and which 'reflected, with superb skill and timing, our current mood of impotent rage and resigned despair . . . none of us, in other words, can look forward to relief and respite.' Precisely (and regrettably) so.

'These days you are on your own,' says Rufus grimly to George and Betty and Pauline. 'Wartime.' It does not seem such an extravagant comment on Britain in the eighties, in which seven hundred 'pickets' mass daily against policemen with truncheons and riot shields to prevent one man going to work – emotion on both sides inflamed by omnipresent television cameras . . . In which the robbing, battering and raping of old ladies as they totter home through inner-city streets, their pensions in their purses, has become commonplace . . . In which masked sexual criminals terrorise whole counties . . . In which ambulances fail to arrive, trains fail to run, 'essential services' prove a luxury. * Our Old Crowd are keeping their eyes closed and their little flags flying in a country that presents a reality no more distorted than a cartoon by Rowlandson, a horror comic by Kafka, a satirical extravaganza by Buñuel. (I am talking of genre, of course, not of achievement.) Resolute, however, remains the resolution *not* to see, *not* to acknowledge, *not* to act. I am reminded of a notice some ten years ago of *O Lucky Man!* in the intellectual review *Encounter,* in which an academic from Oxford, John Weightman, dismissed the film because an England in which nuclear power stations exploded, policemen were corrupt and an industrial colossus was shown to be in profitable league with a reactionary African government 'doesn't seem to be England at all'. ('It hasn't settled for a coherent stylisation . . . uninterestingly cynical.') Truly there are none so blind as those who choose not to see.

One stylistic feature of *The Old Crowd* that was not approved by Herbert Kretzmer – though it did not provoke him to the scorn and outrage of his English colleagues – was our intermittent cutaways to the studio, camera, etc. He felt that these intrusions of studio reality into the reality of the dramatic situation let the audience, so to speak, off the hook. 'It's only television,' they could think, and therefore evade uncomfortable implications. My own feeling is exactly the opposite. As long as the world of the drama remains

* Here Lindsay and I differ. I didn't intend *The Old Crowd* as a tract for the times, though the fact that it went out during a lorry drivers' strike led some people to think so.   A.B.

an enclosed one, a self-contained fiction, the audience can regard it as 'only a play'. And I find the interplay or clash of 'realities' stimulating rather than anodyne. Perhaps this is a matter of temperament. And anyway, one would be optimistic indeed to imagine that one could make a contemporary audience *think* with a television or any other kind of play.

Yet the English critics continue to defend the cause of naturalism with vehemence, even with fury. They dealt with the reality-juggling in *The Old Crowd* either by professing befuddlement, or by contemptuous dismissal. 'Any trainee director doing that sort of thing would have been immediately sent back to training school' (*Evening News*). 'Possibly a rather desperate reminder that this was a TV piece, since nearly everything – particularly acting and direction – wore a decidedly stagey air' (*Daily Telegraph*). 'Stale old device . . . this tedious alienating technique . . . this drab device' (*New Statesman*).

Just why, one cannot help asking, this insistence that naturalism is the only valid style in television or cinema? Why this demand that the fiction remain enclosed, this assumption that any reminder of the author's presence is a callow solecism, 'obvious', 'tedious', 'old hat'? (Except perhaps when excused by a foreign accent – Pirandello, Brecht, Buñuel . . .) The *Observer* critic begged the whole question in familiar, cocksure style: 'By such means a few television directors built short-lived reputations back in the fifties. Nowadays the tyro director is expected to get over that sort of thing in training school. Like good directors in any medium, the good TV directors . . . rarely draw attention to their technique.' Critically this is primitive thinking: as no one should need reminding, technique and style are two different things. (The technique of *The Old Crowd* is in fact very simple.) But the prejudice behind the bluster is significant.

In an important sense, a naturalistic work accepts the world as it is. That is to say, it can criticise or expostulate only in terms of the status quo. A dissident or subversive vision demands a style that rejects the terms in which the conforming world presents itself: this is the only way it can offer a version of reality in essentially different, critical terms. The dissenting artist must hack away the props that hold up the status quo, in style as well as theme. So if, in the middle of an apparently 'real' conversation between a group of confident characters, the camera pans away to show *another* camera and technicians (are they technicians or are they actors?) observing them, their reality and confidence is called in question. The effect – like any sudden deflation – may also be comic.

Of course anyone watching and identifying with the characters rather than with the dissenting author will likely find this procedure disturbing. They may resent it to the point of outrage. If they are artistically *naïf*, and if it has never occurred to them that the world can be seen in any perspective other than theirs – then they may really find the whole thing 'incomprehensible', 'meaningless', 'gratuitous'. The dismissive epithets are legion. None of them, as commonly used by critics, signifies anything at all except a determination to discredit the work. And the critics who are likely to be most venomous are those who habitually pass for 'satirical' or 'non-conformist'. The *Observer* critic, Clive James (Television Critic of the Year in 1978 and runner-up in 1979, chat-show presenter and highbrow reviewer) is a splendid representative of such licensed jesters of conformity, read because they are 'amusing', not because their perceptions are either useful or correct.

To be amusing is not necessarily to be humorous. *The Old Crowd* is, of course, a comedy (however 'disturbing') and, of course, there is a comic ambiguity about its stylistic departures from the norm: they are tongue-in-cheek as well as significant. I only wish that it could be seen as well as read. Perhaps one day it will be.

We almost made a film of it. In 1979 I was asked by Jorn Dormer, the Finnish director then in charge of the Swedish Film Institute, to make a film for him. Neither Alan Bennett nor I felt that we had exhausted the potential of *The Old Crowd*, so I suggested a new, expanded film version. The idea was accepted. Alan and I worked on a script: we found that it would be possible to use a set already standing in the Film Institute studio: a young Polish cameraman agreed to come from Warsaw to shoot it. Then, a few weeks before we were due to shoot, the project collapsed. Donner had miscalculated his finances and neglected to secure the approval of his Board. And the unions objected.

It was a big disappointment. But of course the script is still there. And the Old Crowd are still around, or most of them. Any offers?

16 August 1984

CAST AND CREDITS

The Old Crowd was first transmitted by London Weekend Television
on 27 January 1979. The cast was as follows:

GEORGE	John Moffatt
BETTY	Isabel Dean
HAROLD	Philip Stone
GLYN	Frank Grimes
PIANO TUNER	James Ottaway
RUFUS	Peter Jeffrey
PAULINE	Rachel Roberts
STELLA	Jill Bennett
DICKIE	Peter Bennett
OSCAR	Valentine Dyall
PETER	Martyn Jacobs
SUE	Jenny Quayle
FEMALE ENTERTAINER	Adèle Leigh
MALE ENTERTAINER	David King
TOTTY	Elspeth March
OLD LADY	Cathleen Nesbitt
Producer	Stephen Frears
Director	Lindsay Anderson
Designer	James Weatherup
Music	George Fenton

PART ONE

INT. HALL/STAIRS. NIGHT.
*Abstract shot of the top corner of a room near the ceiling, where walls
and ceiling meet. It isn't immediately obvious where or what this shot
is and over it is the sound of the single notes from a piano being tuned.
A small crack appears in the wall, spreads a little, then stops. The sound
of a little plaster falling.
Camera pulls back and we are in an empty London house. The house is
large, roomy and built in the Edwardian period. Newly done up and
decorated, but empty. The whole house should be in either white or off-
white, and very bright. All the lights are on. Through an open door, we
see the end of a grand piano and an Alsatian dog, and the tuner's
back, or half of it.*

INT. UPSTAIRS CORRIDOR. NIGHT.
*Track along an upstairs corridor. Similarly empty and newly decorated.
The door towards the end of the corridor is open and we hear, or half-
hear, the murmur of conversation.*
GEORGE *(out of vision)* Where was this?
BETTY *(out of vision)* This afternoon. On the phone.
GEORGE *(out of vision)* You've not seen her?
BETTY *(out of vision)* No. Not since last week. Why?

INT. BEDROOM. NIGHT.
*Camera comes through the door and we see the middle-aged couple
in the process of getting changed for a dinner party. Two camp beds,
sleeping bags on them, open suitcases, travelling clock. The bathroom
gives off the bedroom.*
GEORGE Nothing. I just wondered what she looked like.
BETTY Looks like? She looks what she always looks like.
    *All the lights are on here too, with newspapers pinned across the
    windows.*
GEORGE She say anything else?
BETTY Who?
GEORGE Totty.

BETTY No.

GEORGE She upset?

BETTY Not that one could tell. (*Pause.*) Then she asked me about our loose covers. Said there was a sofa she'd been meaning to have done.

GEORGE A sofa?

BETTY Did I want to help choose some material? I couldn't exactly say no. Somebody's been given six months to live, you can't very well say, 'Choose your own loose covers.' I slightly felt she was using me. (*Goes into the bathroom.*) Anyway, I said I'd go with her. Next Tuesday. (*She turns tap on briskly.*)

GEORGE Poor old Totty.

INT. BATHROOM. NIGHT.

Betty turns the tap off to hear him.

BETTY What?

GEORGE (*out of vision*) I said, 'Poor old Totty.'

BETTY Oh. Yes. (*She turns the tap on again, but more slowly – quickly would indicate callousness, as slowly does tact and consideration. She is looking at herself in a tiny bit of broken mirror.*)

GEORGE (*out of vision*) Three months puts us in Scotland.

BETTY I don't know if I feel like Scotland this year. Do you feel like Scotland?

GEORGE (*out of vision*) You never feel like Scotland till it comes to the point. Our age, I suppose.

BETTY What?

GEORGE (*out of vision*) Our age, I suppose. About.

BETTY Older than us.

GEORGE (*out of vision*) She could have come tonight.

INT. BEDROOM. NIGHT.

Betty comes out of the bathroom.

BETTY No.

GEORGE No?

BETTY It would have meant Percy.

GEORGE Percy's in Dubai.

The doorbell goes. A double chime.

BETTY Bell.

GEORGE Yes.

INT. HALL/STAIRS. NIGHT.
George comes downstairs. He is still not completely dressed. The bell goes
again. Two notes.

INT. MUSIC ROOM. NIGHT.
Cut to the piano tuner, who is blind. He strikes the same two notes on
the piano as comprise the door chime. George looks in at the door as he
passes. The piano tuner turns his head slightly to indicate he knows he
is there, but doesn't strike any more notes.

INT. HALL/STAIRS. NIGHT.
George opens the door to two men. One in his fifties, the other in his
twenties. Both carrying large suitcases.

HAROLD Mr Nelson?
GEORGE Who are you?
HAROLD The slaves.
GEORGE The slaves! Of course. Enter. Enter. By all means.
    George makes a point of closing the door, looking out first, then
    double-locking it.
HAROLD Harold.
GEORGE Harold.
HAROLD Glyn.
GEORGE Glyn. (*George has put out his hand but somehow it is not*
    seen and he puts it away again.) Notice we have only the barest
    essentials, pending the arrival of our furniture . . . one's bits
    and pieces. Still I think you'll find we have gas, water and
    electricity. All mains services.
    They go through the house to the kitchen at the back of the house.

INT. KITCHEN. NIGHT.
There is a large crate in the middle of the empty floor.
GEORGE They've brought your gear. Do you do this full-time?
HAROLD We're actors. We act.
GEORGE Acting! That is exciting. Are you 'resting'?
HAROLD Excuse me?
GEORGE That's what it's called, isn't it, when you're out of work?
    Resting?
HAROLD I call it out of work.
GEORGE What sort of parts do you play?

HAROLD Glyn frequently plays policeman's parts, don't you, Glyn?
Glyn smiles.

GEORGE He's a bit slight for a policeman.

HAROLD That's the sort of policeman he plays. The sensitive one who cracks under the strain of the constant brutality.

GEORGE And what do you play?

GLYN (*unheard or whispered*) Where is the toilet?

HAROLD I also play policemen. At a more senior level.

GEORGE Well, it's all acting, isn't it?

GLYN Where's the toilet?

HAROLD Where's the toilet?

GEORGE Are you desperate?

GLYN I am.

GEORGE Well, we have a slight problem. Typical story. Workmen here going on six months – floors up, ceilings down. Nightmare. Job completed. Workmen depart. We come to use the toilet and it doesn't work. Four toilets and three don't work.

HAROLD He had every intention of going at the station only the vandals had got there first.

GEORGE Follow me.

INT. HALL/STAIRS. NIGHT.
They go upstairs, leaving Harold alone in the kitchen.

INT. KITCHEN. NIGHT.
As they go upstairs, cut back to Harold alone in the kitchen. Having hung up his dress suit, he is brushing it down.

INT. BEDROOM. NIGHT.
Cut to bedroom where Betty is still getting ready. George enters followed by Glyn.

GEORGE Glyn here is just going to use the bathroom.
Glyn goes into the bathroom and closes the door. A wide smile from George to forestall criticism from his wife, who isn't pleased.

INT. HALL/STAIRS. NIGHT.
George and Betty are going downstairs.

BETTY All I am saying is one doesn't ask to use the loo before one has barely set foot in the house.

GEORGE They're only human.

BETTY One leaves a decent interval.

INT. MUSIC ROOM. NIGHT.

The tuner is finishing tuning the piano. As George and Betty come in
he stops and brings off a vast flourish. This pleases them. He then
strikes up a rather grand waltz, and as they begin to dance, we see the
camera and crew in passing. During the dancing Glyn passes the door,
or looks in but does not come in, goes away again. Suddenly the tuner
stops abruptly in the middle of a phrase and resumes striking his single
notes. Betty and George are brought up short and stop dancing.

GEORGE It's a mystery to me.

The tuner turns his head.

Music.

TUNER I came to it quite late. I used to be a policeman.

BETTY Before you lost your sight?

TUNER Naturally. (*He closes the lid.*)

GEORGE All done.

The tuner gets up and begins to find his way about.

TUNER My coat?

GEORGE Yes. Now. Where are we? Ah, *coat.* You didn't have a
stick?

George raises his eyes and meemoes to Betty indicating 'Should I tip
him?' She nods confirmation. George takes a note out of his pocket
and tries to give it to the blind man. He has some difficulty getting it
into his hand.

TUNER What's this?

GEORGE It's . . . it's . . . it's just a little something.

TUNER Is it a tip?

GEORGE Yes. Is that all right?

TUNER It's not enough for my fee. But as a tip it's quite
generous.

GEORGE That's what it is. The tip. Thank you.

TUNER Thank you.

The tuner has taken out his folded-up white stick, which he begins to
unfold.

GEORGE I say, that's handy.

They watch him unfold the stick in silence. The dog should also be
the focus of some interest. There is a distant silence at this point, to

which the blind man and the dog hearken first, then George and
Betty. Fractional pause before the action resumes. The doorbell goes.

INT. HALL/STAIRS. NIGHT.
In the hall, Glyn is just approaching the door to answer it. He is dressed
in a very ill-fitting waiter's costume, which he is still trying to adjust as
he approaches the door. Glyn opens the door to Rufus and Pauline,
lined up on the doorstep. Rufus, a big hearty man, Pauline, his assertive
wife. The blind man moves forward with his dog.

RUFUS Greetings, greetings. As we enter these portals for the first
time . . . greetings.
The blind man's way is barred.

GEORGE Be right with you.
Pauline falls over the dog. She picks herself up.

PAULINE What a large dog!

GEORGE One step up. Three steps down. One. Two. Three.
George doesn't go down the steps with him.
You'll be all right now? (*George closes the door – George makes a*
point of closing the door: even when Glyn or Harold has closed it he
will make sure it actually is closed.) Sorry about that. Blind.

RUFUS Blind? And venturing through the streets?

GEORGE Yes. He's been a policeman.

BETTY (*as it were beginning the ceremony of welcome afresh*) Well!
You got here.

GEORGE No problems?
Rufus takes out a large truncheon-like torch.

RUFUS No problems at all.

BETTY Oh, my goodness.

RUFUS It's perfectly simple. You just have to walk as though
you've got somewhere to go to. Somewhere you'll be missed
if you don't turn up. Walk as if you meant business.

GEORGE March.

RUFUS Exactly.

PAULINE But what do you do if you're a woman? What do you do
if you're by yourself? Two's the minimum, I think.
Glyn has stepped forward for their coats.

RUFUS Ah. He has the look of a man wanting to take my coat.
Well, there it is. Plus the coat belonging to my good lady.

PAULINE I'm afraid it's otter. I got it ages ago, long before there was any fuss. I don't think that matters, do you?

RUFUS Matters to me. It's practically the only material evidence that I have spent twenty-five years up to my neck in the sewers of commerce.

Betty kisses Rufus and is about to kiss Pauline.

PAULINE You haven't been in contact with this virus?

BETTY What virus?

PAULINE Nobody knows. It's supposed to be Syrian but they're not sure. Apparently you just feel vaguely ill, slight fever, sweating. Like ordinary flu. Two hours later it's all over.

GEORGE Better?

PAULINE No. Dead.

BETTY I hadn't heard about it. Had you heard about it?

George shakes his head.

PAULINE It's everywhere. Vienna is a ghost city.

GEORGE And are they doing anything about it?

RUFUS What can they do about it?

PAULINE The point is that the thing, whatever it is, thrives on antibiotics. They're its breeding ground. So of course the first places to be hit are hospitals. Don't go to hospital whatever you do.

RUFUS Typical of this cockeyed world. The experts bring out this cure-all, before you know where you are it's killing everybody off.

BETTY How awful.

The news about the virus depresses George and Betty while cheering up Rufus and Pauline because they have been able to impart it.

PAULINE I think germs must communicate. I think it's the only rational explanation. What a super house! (*Whirls round.*) Whee! The space! No things. No clutter. Lovely!

GEORGE Yes, well, I ought to explain about the absence of furniture.

RUFUS Really?

PAULINE It's meant. Surely it's meant. Betty. Tell me it's meant. It's the style. Simple. Scandinavian? No?

BETTY No. Not exactly.

GEORGE Thing was, we'd invited everybody. Stella and Dickie, Oscar, Peter and Sue

BETTY You and Rufus.

GEORGE Rufus and you. Just the old crowd. Invitations all sent out on the fairly reasonable assumption we should be pretty well settled in by now. Horsham to here takes what? A couple of hours?

RUFUS At the most.

GEORGE We know there may be extraordinary circumstances, particularly these days, but say forty-eight hours.

RUFUS At the outside.

GEORGE Now ten days. Still hasn't arrived.

RUFUS Isn't that typical?

GEORGE And not merely is our stuff not here, it's apparently somewhere in Carlisle.
During this conversation they progress into the drawing room.

INT. DRAWING ROOM. NIGHT.
There are some hired gilt chairs and a trestle table folded up against the wall. Here too there is newspaper covering the windows. It is so in every room.

PAULINE Carlisle. Oh, Betty! (*She embraces Betty in elaborate sympathy.*)

BETTY I know!

PAULINE I'm surprised.

RUFUS I wish I was.

BETTY Naturally our first thought was cancel. George was poised at the telephone . . .

GEORGE Then we thought no . . .

BETTY To hell with it.

GEORGE Just because some dreary little lorry driver is trying to notch up some buckshee overtime by ferrying our precious possessions to Barrow-in-Furness, why should that stop us having a nice time? Why not *camp out*?

RUFUS Camp out?

GEORGE *Squat.*

BETTY So we're squatting.

GEORGE Living out of a suitcase and loving every minute of it.
Harold approaches with a tray of drinks. Champagne, etc.

RUFUS But isn't that typical? Isn't that absolutely straight down the line what we have come to expect in this God-forsaken country of ours?

This outburst occurs just as he is taking drinks from Harold and is directed point-blank at Harold, without being to him.
This piss-stained ammoniacal little island. This floating urinal. Where you can't wipe your bottom without filling a form in first. And you can't transport your worldly goods from point A to point B without them getting lost in the process. Horsham to London. Two hours. Ten days. I hope you got on the phone.

GEORGE Quite hard. The Post Office hasn't seen fit to connect us yet.

RUFUS . . . I know, though you applied six months ago . . .

BETTY There is a box on the corner, only . . .

RUFUS Don't tell me.

GEORGE . . . vandalised.

RUFUS It's like me. Went into the office one morning. Place a shambles. Paint all over the place.

BETTY Paint?

RUFUS Paint, glue. Sand.

PAULINE And that was only the half of it.

RUFUS Soiled clothing.

BETTY Oh, how frightful.

RUFUS Oh, yes. It's the same everywhere.

GEORGE It's all round here.

PAULINE They never catch them.

RUFUS These days you are on your own. Wartime.

A pause – interrupted by the doorbell.

INT. HALL/STAIRS. NIGHT.
Cut to hall as Glyn opens the door. Stella enters. George and Betty come to greet her, followed by Pauline. Stella is a stylish lady with a dull husband.

GEORGE Stella!

BETTY Stella! Thank God! Thank God!

STELLA Thank God! What a trip! I'm dead. Are we late?

GEORGE Not a bit.

STELLA We got so lost, loster and loster. What's happened to the street lights?

BETTY There were *some*.

STELLA There aren't now. Then Dickie would insist on looking for a policeman.

GEORGE A policeman!

STELLA Of course there weren't any.

PAULINE Stella!

STELLA Pauline!

They embrace.

GEORGE Where's Dickie? Come on, Dickie, hurry up. Let's get the door closed.

STELLA Dickie!

Glyn has taken Stella's coat. In removing it from her shoulders his hand rests momentarily but purposely on her breast.

Oh, thank you very much.

INT. DRAWING ROOM. NIGHT.

Rufus is left alone with Harold. We hear a reprise of the dialogue about the absence of furniture, such as occurred when Rufus and Pauline came in.

GEORGE (*out of vision*) Carlisle.

STELLA (*out of vision*) Carlisle!

BETTY (*out of vision*) It was just going to be the old crowd, you and Dickie, Rufus and Pauline . . .

GEORGE (*out of vision*) Oscar, Peter, Sue.

BETTY (*out of vision*) Thinking of course we'd be all settled in. I mean, it ought to have been here in two hours. To date it's taken ten days.

Rufus wanders round the room. Goes up to take his empty glass to put on Harold's tray. Takes a full one. Looks at Harold full in the face without saying anything, as the vaguely heard dialogue continues.

RUFUS I've seen you before. Haven't I?

HAROLD (*expressionlessly*) It's conceivable.

RUFUS I know you. Why?

Enter Stella, followed by George, Betty and Pauline.

GEORGE (*finishing off his account*) . . . just because some dreary little lorry driver is trying to notch up some buckshee overtime.

STELLA How exciting. How courageous. Don't you think it's courageous? I think it's *heroic*. Rufus!

RUFUS You're thinner.

STELLA A bit.

PAULINE Not anorexia?

STELLA No. Just dry white wine.

PAULINE I love it like this. Bare. Empty. No things. We have too
many things. We all have too many things. I feel I can breathe
here, Betty. Be . . .

RUFUS Where's Dickie?

STELLA Where is Dickie? I'm sure I brought him with me.

RUFUS (*to Glyn*) You haven't put this lady's husband with the
coats, have you?

STELLA Dickie.

DICKIE (*out of vision*) Coming. (*He enters. A very mild and mousy
man.*)

RUFUS Where've you been, Dickie?

DICKIE Valparaiso.

RUFUS Really. Old Dickie's been in Valparaiso. Why?

STELLA Why do you think?

PAULINE He goes all over, don't you, Dickie?

DICKIE Is there somewhere to sit?

GEORGE 'Fraid not.

DICKIE Oh. Why's that?

The doorbell goes.

INT. HALL/STAIRS. NIGHT.
*Cut to Glyn answering the door as the dialogue off continues as before
with choruses of 'Carlisle.' 'Carlisle?' 'Carlisle.' Glyn opens the door.
There is nobody to be seen. He steps outside and, unseen by Glyn,
Oscar slips behind him into the hall. He is in a broad black hat, with
his coat slung over his shoulders, arms not in the sleeves. Glyn comes
back, and is slightly startled to see Oscar there already. George and
Betty come out.*

GEORGE Oscar!

BETTY (*reprovingly*) Oscar!

*Oscar sweeps off his hat in an extravagant gesture, then gives it, less
extravagantly, to Glyn.*

INT. CLOAKROOM. NIGHT.
*Cut to Glyn going into the room where the coats are. He tries on the
hat before setting it down beside the other coats.*

INT. DRAWING ROOM. NIGHT.

Oscar is brought into the drawing room. There is less of an outburst of welcome than with the others. He goes round and kisses each of the ladies on a different part, the back of the neck, the upper arm, the neck. Very discreetly, and to nobody's surprise, except they each murmur 'Oscar.' He squeezes the men's hands, but doesn't shake them.

OSCAR And how is Stella?

STELLA Stella is rather well. How is Oscar?

OSCAR Oscar is all the better for seeing Stella. Pauline. (*Holds her hand.*) You are in pain.

PAULINE No.

OSCAR Yes. There is pain. I am never mistaken.

PAULINE I don't think so.

OSCAR Your back, Pauline. I feel pain in your back.

PAULINE You're right. He's right. I am in pain. My back. I'm so used to it.

OSCAR Let it go, Pauline. Relax. Flow. Let it go, let the pain go, flow out, down, away.

PAULINE Oh, Oscar.

OSCAR And what has Dickie been doing? Making lots of money in clever-Dickie fashion?

PAULINE He made me go into commodities, didn't you, Dickie?

DICKIE Did I?

PAULINE Coffee. I had to buy coffee in the forward market. And a forest. We bought a forest.

BETTY Where?

PAULINE Where, Rufus?

RUFUS Sussex somewhere. Someone was telling me if you'd gone into wine you couldn't lose. At the right time, of course.

PAULINE What is the right time, Dickie?

DICKIE Not now.

GEORGE Somebody told me the thing to do now is sell money.

PAULINE I hope commodities are still all right. There's nothing wrong with commodities, is there, Dickie? Should I go into money? Should I be selling money? It's all in coffee. And this forest.

DICKIE Everybody seems to be selling money. I'm now more inclined to buy it.

PAULINE Should I sell the forest?

DICKIE No point in selling the forest.

RUFUS What about the coffee?

DICKIE It's hard to get a true picture. If we were in South
America I could tell you exactly what to do. Brazil. Paraguay.
During the preceding conversation, Stella promenades with Oscar.

STELLA Paraguay! Isn't he brilliant?
Glyn comes round with drinks.
What an ill-fitting suit. (*Shrieks with laughter.*) It's bizarre.
Glyn says nothing.

RUFUS Now, everybody. A toast. A toast to this house. To its
warmth and its welcome: the house.

GEORGE What about a conducted tour?

PAULINE Yes, please. I love houses.
They begin to troop out.

OSCAR Dare one ask what it cost?

BETTY They were asking sixty-five.

GEORGE Sixty-eight. They started off at sixty-eight . . .
*They go out, Glyn eyeing Stella as they go, Stella still amused by his
suit. Dickie is left looking at a piece of newspaper pinned over the
window, watched impassively by Harold. He is about to tear a piece
off when Harold coughs, so therefore he writes it down.*

STELLA (*out of vision, calling*) Dickie.
He leaves, as Glyn begins to set up the table.

INT. HALL/STAIRS. NIGHT.
*The party is trooping upstairs. There should be separate conversations
going on, parts of which we catch as they go in and out of rooms which
are chiefly along the upstairs corridor.*

INT. UPSTAIRS CORRIDOR. NIGHT.

GEORGE We put in an offer of fifty-six, no, fifty-four. Fifty-four.

BETTY Subject to contract.

PAULINE You always have to say that. Subject to contract.
Everything's always subject to contract.

GEORGE Fifty-four was just a feeler. We never expected to get it
for anything like that. Fifty-four was absurd really.

PAULINE But that's part of the game, isn't it?

GEORGE They then came back with sixty-four. We said fifty-six.
They said sixty-two. We said fifty-eight. Then there was a

terrible silence. Six weeks in which we never heard a thing. So naturally we thought, 'We've lost it.'

PAULINE You weren't *gazumped?*

BETTY I think they had someone else interested.

PAULINE So much gazumping now, few people seem to end up in the house they first started with.

GEORGE Anyway nine o'clock one night, I'd just got into the bath when out of the blue the telephone rings and it's their solicitor to say our offer has been accepted. So we shook hands at fifty-eight and I think we were very lucky, very lucky indeed. It would have been reasonable at sixty-eight. At fifty-eight it's a snip. The nice thing is that they got more or less what they wanted, and we got it for rather less than we'd expected so everybody's happy. That's the main thing. One doesn't like to feel one's put one over on somebody.

INT. DRESSING ROOM. NIGHT.

BETTY It's not a particularly safe area, of course.

RUFUS Where is nowadays? Nowhere. Nowhere's safe. And the country's worse than the town. An elderly cousin of mine was on a bus the other day . . .

STELLA On a bus?

RUFUS Bus . . . night-time, nine o'clock. Quite full, one of these jobs where the driver takes the fares.

STELLA They're all like that now. It's the wages.

RUFUS . . . she was on the bus opposite this young chap, nineteen, quite well dressed, not a *lout* anyway, sitting there *moaning.*

STELLA Moaning?

RUFUS Hugging himself, coat wrapped round him, rocking to and fro, moaning. Naturally she thought drugs . . . (as one would) . . . I say, this is a nice room . . .

As they pass into the next room we see the intervening wall is plainly scenery.

. . . but she watched him out of the corner of her eye for a bit and she decided, 'No. This young man is ill. Really ill.' So she went and had a word with the driver. He's a bit reluctant to stop, nine o'clock at night, middle of nowhere, but eventually he pulls up and comes back down the bus to investigate. And as they look at this youth they see that just where he's hugging himself there's a great patch of blood. Blood soaked right through his coat. (*opening a door*) What's in here? Ah. So the bus driver gets this young lad to let him open his coat so they can see where he's hurt. He opens his coat and out falls a hand. A human hand.

STELLA His hand?

RUFUS No, somebody else's. With a ring on it.

STELLA What sort of ring?

RUFUS Gold. Or something. He must have cut off the hand to get the ring.

STELLA And what happened then?

RUFUS I don't know what happened then.

BETTY And where did you say this was – New York?

RUFUS Horsham.

INT. CORRIDOR. NIGHT.
They pass in and out of various rooms, appearing in the corridor from time to time as they leave rooms and enter others. Dickie is always lagging behind.

STELLA I keep thinking could one go somewhere else?

GEORGE Emigrate?

RUFUS Why not?

BETTY But where?

OSCAR Quite. One almost found oneself thinking of New York.

PAULINE *New York?*

STELLA The thing about New York is that they will let one work.

RUFUS Not officially. Officially one can't work. Officially one needs a green card.

GEORGE A green card?

OSCAR People will do anything to get a green card.

PAULINE Does everyone have a green card?

BETTY No. That's the point. Enormous numbers of people work in New York illegally. The Chinese. New York is full of Chinese, working, saving, going home to China, coming back. And the authorities turn a blind eye.

PAULINE Communist China?

OSCAR Communist China.

STELLA How extraordinary.

BETTY Without them the restaurant business would fall apart.
GEORGE That couldn't happen here.
PAULINE What?
STELLA People working illegally.
RUFUS Oh, no. People don't *work* here anyway, do they? Can't work legally, never mind illegally. That's the trouble.

INT. OLD LADY'S ROOM. NIGHT.
They file into a room where an old lady is watching television. It is a programme about diseases of the eye. She is obviously enjoying it and resents being disturbed.
GEORGE We won't disturb you, Mother. We've given this room to Mother. It's all right . . . she's not one for social occasions. Are you, Mother?
PAULINE It's so spacious. I long to see it furnished.
OSCAR I imagine there'll be a good view?
GEORGE Oh, a splendid view . . . the whole of London.
OSCAR The whole of London? That's handy.
At which point we see that one of the walls is missing and there is a group of technicians watching.
PAULINE You're not overlooked?
GEORGE We have neighbours, but we've never seen them.
OSCAR Probably foreigners. Only people who can afford to live here these days.
PAULINE You had it rewired, of course?
GEORGE Top to bottom.
PAULINE It's best.
OSCAR Cheapest in the long run.
PAULINE Are you oil-fired?
GEORGE Gas.
OSCAR Safest in the long run.
PAULINE Oh, much.
GEORGE Thank you, Mother.
Mother gives no sign of having heard, other than wincing with irritation.

INT. DRAWING ROOM. NIGHT.
Glyn has laid the cutlery. Harold looks and sees the knives and forks are the wrong way round. He wordlessly corrects them. He looks up

as Glyn lifts a large mirror which is on the floor by the wall to hang
above the table, or prop it on the mantelpiece. As he staggers across with
this mirror, helped by Harold, we see in it reflected the studio, cameras
and lights. As they finish placing the mirror the doorbell goes.

INT. HALL/STAIRS. NIGHT.
Glyn opens the door as George and Betty appear at the top of the stairs
at the conclusion of the tour of the house.
BETTY Darlings. Look who's here.
PETER Hi.
SUE *(lifting her visor)* Hi. We're not late, are we?
BETTY It's the children.
GEORGE Not late a bit. Anyway, what's late these days?
    They begin to take off their gear.
PETER We thought we'd never make it.
PAULINE Oh, look. It's Peter and Sue. Come on, everybody. The
    young people are here.
PETER Hello, Auntie Pauline!
SUE Hello!
PAULINE Sue! Peter!
BETTY We were beginning to think something had happened.
RUFUS No fear, they can take care of themselves.
BETTY Hugs, hugs, hugs.
PETER Hello, Auntie Betty. Auntie Pauline. Hope we haven't held
    things up?
GEORGE Not a bit. Not a bit.
    During all this there is a lot of kissing and shaking hands.
PETER How are you, sir?
RUFUS Hello again.
PETER Hello, sir.
RUFUS Hello again.
PETER Hello, sir.
STELLA Peter, darling.
PETER Hello, Auntie Stella. We had a couple of close shaves, but
    we pressed on.
GEORGE That's the spirit.
OSCAR Sue, my precious.
PAULINE Let me kiss you again. Aren't you pretty? And you,
    dear. You're pretty too. Aren't they pretty?

GEORGE Well. Here we all are.

Glyn has taken the coats and put them in the cloakroom. Harold passes through with a tray and dish cover, sidestepping the hubbub of greetings. Betty now goes up to Glyn.

BETTY Would you announce dinner now?

Glyn slouches up three steps of the staircase.

GLYN (*loudly*) Dinner is served.

Peal of laughter from Stella as they go in.

INT. DRAWING ROOM. NIGHT.

As the party comes in Harold is stirring a large tureen of soup with a ladle. He finds a foreign object in the tureen and fishes it out. It is a rubber glove. He secretes it about his person but Betty has seen it. She scarcely turns a hair.

GEORGE Right. Stella here. Pauline there. Rufus, now, don't want you sitting next to your wife, do we? You sit here. Oscar there. Peter and Sue.

STELLA Did you do all this yourself?

BETTY No, we've had it sent in.

STELLA How clever. Who by?

GEORGE This girl. She's built up a vast organisation virtually from scratch and now they cater for practically everybody. The City, the Palace, government ministries. Everybody. Down to the last detail. And she started off with nothing. Now she's got an absolute fleet of vans.

RUFUS There you are, you see. It can still be done. Provided you're prepared to work.

Betty has been putting some food on a plate, while Harold waits with a tray.

INT. HALL/STAIRS. NIGHT.

Dickie is coming down the stairs, listening to his radio. The door opens and Betty comes out, followed by Harold with the loaded tray. Dickie stands aside. Betty and Harold go upstairs.

INT. UPSTAIRS CORRIDOR. NIGHT.

They go into a room. Betty first.

INT. OLD LADY'S ROOM. NIGHT.

Mother is still watching television, and as avidly as before. It is a film in which some young people in a car are being pursued. Harold brings in the tray, sets it up on the table beside her and puts it in front of her. The old lady's attention remains primarily on the television. Betty watches the film for a moment, then goes. The old lady's eyes glitter with pleasure and excitement as on the film the car containing the young people plunges over a cliff, dives on to some rocks and disappears into the boiling sea.

PART TWO

INT. DRAWING ROOM. NIGHT.
The meal is in its late stages. Pudding has been served, which most
people have finished. Dickie is still eating.

RUFUS No – to tell the unpleasing truth, I don't see any light at
the end of our particular tunnel. Talking to a man yesterday,
managing director of a small family firm in the Midlands.
Making electrical components for use in heart-support
machines. Main customer, the Health Service. Employed
about 250 people – mainstay of a small community. Opens
his post one morning, letter from the Department of Health:
'Dear Sir' and so on. New marketing developments cause
cancellation of all forward orders. Components can now be
obtained at a third of the price. Where? Taiwan. Come Friday
night this chap locks up, puts key in an envelope, puts it
through his bank manager's door. That firm is now dead.
I mean, what is the point?

GEORGE It's the same all over the country.

RUFUS An entire community now on Social Security. Cost that in
economic terms.

GEORGE Exactly.

RUFUS Life is poorer.

PAULINE (*looking at Peter and Sue*) Aren't they pretty? Every time
I look at you I just think, 'How pretty.'
Peter's mouth is full, so he doesn't speak.

SUE Lovely pudding.

PAULINE (*to Peter*) Sweet.

GEORGE A toast. Absent friends.

ALL Absent friends.

RUFUS Absent friends . . . wherever they may be.
Pause.

GEORGE Sorry. Didn't mean to put a damper on the
proceedings.

PAULINE I keep thinking about Totty.

BETTY Yes. Poor old Totty.

OSCAR Poor dear Totty.

PAULINE It's not the same without Totty.

SUE (*who never stops smiling*) I wish I'd met her. I've heard so much about her. I thought she might be here.

STELLA It's her blood. Something wrong with her blood.

OSCAR Thinning.

SUE How awful.

STELLA How long do they think it's going to take?

OSCAR Three months.

GEORGE That can mean anything.

BETTY We seem to have known Totty for ever.

OSCAR Longer.

SUE Does she know?

BETTY She knows.

OSCAR I think she's always known.

PAULINE Peter was her special favourite, weren't you, Peter?

PETER Well, Auntie, she is my godmother.

PAULINE Peter's no stranger to sadness either, are you, Peter? When you've lost both your parents in two separate air crashes, you understand pain. Don't you, Peter?

PETER I don't know, Auntie, one does one's best.

PAULINE (*to Stella*) He calls me Auntie, but I'm not really. He just wants someone to hold on to. I think that's why he married so young. Aren't they pretty? (*to Sue*) You're pretty too, my dear. (*to Stella*) Isn't she?

STELLA Yes. I gather you're also an accomplished clarinettist.

SUE (*smiling*) Oh, I'm not much good really.

OSCAR Is there money? Totty.

GEORGE I take it there is.

OSCAR (*talking to Dickie as if to a child*) Is there money, Dickie? Totty. Money?

DICKIE There's some money.

RUFUS What sort of money, though? There's money and money.

BETTY I don't think anybody's going to starve.

RUFUS Oh, I don't think anybody's going to starve.

BETTY Talking of starving, George, look after people.

GEORGE More pudding, anybody? More pudding, Pauline?

PAULINE It's delicious.

GEORGE Stella?

STELLA I won't, if you don't mind.
RUFUS Have you heard about these holes?
BETTY Holes? What holes?
RUFUS These holes that keep appearing. There are these holes
that keep appearing. Opening up in places. One in Camberwell
yesterday apparently. A couple last week near Peterborough.
Happening all over. Bristol. Dundee.
BETTY How big?
RUFUS Varies. Cardiff, one was 200 feet across.
GEORGE Cardiff? I know Cardiff.
RUFUS Cardiff. Everywhere. Being hushed up apparently.
GEORGE They hush everything up if they can. It must be the
drought, mustn't it?
RUFUS Or the rain. One or the other. I think there may be more
to it than that.
*During this conversation Stella drops her napkin, fairly obviously,
and Glyn, watching her, sees it fall. He gets down on the floor and
there is a shot of underneath the table, Glyn crawling between the
legs of the guests to Stella's foot. He hands her up the napkin, then
takes one of her shoes and puts it in his pocket. She is aware of this,
but does not react. Taking a small pair of scissors from his pocket he
cuts a hole in Stella's stocking and sucks her big toe. The doorbell
goes.*

INT. HALL/STAIRS. NIGHT.
*Harold answers the front door. A couple stand there, muffled up. They
are wearing tin hats (air-raid-warden type), but the scene is in long
shot so that we are not quite certain. They take them off as Harold
brings them to the music room.*

INT. DRAWING ROOM. NIGHT.
OSCAR That's another thing they've hushed up . . . rabies in
Burgess Hill.
GEORGE Rabies in Burgess Hill? I find that hard to credit.
STELLA Oscar, you're such a liar.
OSCAR Four cases in the past week.
BETTY Oh, how *depressing*.
GEORGE No matter, life goes on.
Harold whispers to George.

Ah. We thought we'd have coffee across the hall, so if you could all bring your chairs. Follow me.

Stella follows him, still with one shoe off.

Follow me, everybody.

PAULINE (*to Peter*) I'll bring your chair, shall I?

They troop out with chairs, leaving Dickie to bring up the rear as usual.

INT. HALL/STAIRS. NIGHT.

They cross the hall with their chairs. George motions them to wait and he goes into the music room. Cut back to see Dickie in the drawing room still eating his pudding. He switches on his radio. The group is still waiting in the hall. George opens the door and beckons them in.

INT. MUSIC ROOM. NIGHT.

The entertainers are standing at the piano.

RUFUS I say. A piano. Does this spell music? How very civilised.

SUE (*coming in*) Oh, how lovely! What is it? Who are they?

PAULINE I think they must be going to perform.

The entertainers announce a song at the piano, which is listened to in absolute poker-faced seriousness by the group. Dickie as usual arrives late and doesn't bring his chair, so has to sit on one of the wide window ledges, and has his radio soon glued back to his ear. During the singing, Harold moves discreetly round the room with the silver jug of coffee, followed by Glyn with cream and sugar.

FEMALE ENTERTAINER Good evening, ladies and gentlemen. My accompanist, Mr Gervase Howard, and I would like to give you something from our repertoire. We would like to start with one of our favourites and hope it will soon become a favourite of yours.

Because you come to me
With notes of love,
And hold my hand
And lift mine eyes above,
A wider world of hope and joy I see
Because you come to me.

Because you speak to me
In accents sweet,

I find the roses waking round my feet,
And I am led through tears and joy to thee
Because you speak to me.

Because God made thee mine
I cherish thee
Through light and darkness,
Through all time to thee
And pray his love will make our love divine
Because God made thee mine.

*Towards the end of the song, Stella gets up abruptly and leaves
the room, still with one of her shoes off. Before she leaves, she gives
Glyn her cup. He stands with the cup for a moment after she has
left, then puts the cup down and follows.*

INT. HALL/STAIRS. NIGHT.
*Stella goes upstairs, pauses at the turn of the stairs to look back. Glyn
begins to mount the stairs after her. He takes out her shoe.*

INT. UPSTAIRS CORRIDOR. NIGHT.
*Stella goes along the corridor. Glyn follows her along the corridor.
He stops. Drops her shoe. Stella stops, comes back. Puts her foot into the
shoe. She opens the nearest door and goes into it, followed by Glyn.*

INT. OLD LADY'S ROOM. NIGHT.
*It is the room where the old lady is watching television. She takes no
notice. She is watching a travelogue. The fourth wall is again missing
and we see camera and crew. Stella draws Glyn to her. She takes off
her earrings. Glyn puts them in his pocket. Stella puts Glyn's fingers in
her mouth, one by one. The old lady frowns very slightly and turns the
volume up. Stella and Glyn sink down behind the television set.*

INT. HALL/STAIRS. NIGHT.
*Cut to the empty hall from the top of the stairs. The sound of applause
downstairs. Harold appears, leading the entertainers to the drawing
room. Cries of 'Bravo!'*

INT. MUSIC ROOM. NIGHT.
*George and Betty are now dancing together with Oscar and Sue.
Pauline is dancing with Peter. Rufus is settled in at the piano. Pauline
guides Peter out of the room and down the hall.*

INT. DRAWING ROOM. NIGHT.
Harold has given the two entertainers something to eat and they are
sitting at the dinner table, now cleared except for two plates.
MALE ENTERTAINER I thought that went very well. Didn't you?
FEMALE ENTERTAINER Very well. They liked you.
MALE ENTERTAINER They liked you too.
FEMALE ENTERTAINER I didn't think I was quite at my best
    tonight.
MALE ENTERTAINER I thought you were.

INT. CLOAKROOM. NIGHT.
Peter is sitting up on the mantelpiece and Pauline is standing by him
with her head against his knee.
PAULINE You see, you're so young. That's the thing about you.
    You're so bloody young.
PETER Oh, I don't know.
PAULINE Young neck. Young arms. Young legs. *Young.*
PETER Well, I suppose I am really.
PAULINE All you people. Young . . . *Young.* (*Lays her head against*
    Peter's knee.) We're not. We're not young. And never more shall
    be so. I love your young legs.
PETER Yes, Auntie Pauline.
PAULINE I'm not really your auntie, you know. That's just a
    name.
    They laugh.

INT. DRAWING ROOM. NIGHT.
A party at the card table.
SUE I think it's so sad.
BETTY What's sad?
SUE Your friend, Totty.
BETTY It is sad. It *is* sad.
OSCAR But one does die. That's what one does. Dies.
GEORGE And she's had a very rich life.
OSCAR Oh, yes.

INT. HALL/STAIRS. NIGHT.
Rufus comes out, looks around, moves towards kitchen. He passes
Dickie.

RUFUS Found it yet?

DICKIE What?

RUFUS What you're looking for.

DICKIE It's here somewhere.

RUFUS You'd better get a move on.

INT. KITCHEN. NIGHT.

Rufus enters the kitchen where Harold is eating.

RUFUS Thing that I admire about you actors, thing that puzzles me, is how you remember it all.

HAROLD Remember what?

RUFUS Shakespeare. Those great speeches. And not only Shakespeare. The newsreaders. Never stumble, do they? Never falter. And they *care*. You can see it in their eyes. Alone in this bloody little world of ours, they *care*.

HAROLD They're reading it. Every bloody word.

INT. DRAWING ROOM. NIGHT.

The entertainers are sitting at the table eating their supper while Betty, George, Oscar and Sue play cards.

BETTY She made those holidays. The children adored her.

OSCAR Two no trumps.

GEORGE They were the best holidays I ever had.

OSCAR Was that at Walberswick?

SUE Dear old Suffolk. Oh, pass.

BETTY I loved that house. The dogs, the children, and everybody on the veranda. Three hearts.

GEORGE It's another world. (*calling to the entertainers*) All right over there?

FEMALE ENTERTAINER Oh, yes. We're having a lovely time, aren't we?

MALE ENTERTAINER Oh, yes.

SUE It must have been wonderful.

Sound of distant howling.

INT. UPSTAIRS CORRIDOR. NIGHT.

Dickie is wandering down the corridor, looking at various pieces of newspaper.

DICKIE (*thoughtfully*) Zambia. Zambia. *Zambia.*

The noise of the howling is stronger.

INT. CLOAKROOM. NIGHT.
*Peter is still sitting on the mantelpiece, looking very blank. Pauline
walks round him howling like a dog.*

INT. KITCHEN. NIGHT.
*Harold is still eating, watched by Rufus. Glyn enters and goes to the
sink. Rufus turns as he hears Glyn pissing. Glyn comes over to Rufus,
buttoning his trousers, picks up the carving knife and cuts a large slice
of ham. The doorbell goes.*

INT. HALL/STAIRS. NIGHT.
The hall is empty. The doorbell goes, unheard.

INT. DRAWING ROOM. NIGHT.
Cut to silent shot of the bridge table. The doorbell goes.

INT. HALL/STAIRS. NIGHT.
Loud knocking on the front door. Betty comes out into the hall.
BETTY Why doesn't somebody answer the bloody door?
*Guests appear from their various locations as Betty opens the door.
An impressive woman is standing on the threshold.*
Totty! Totty!
GEORGE Hello! Totty!
*Totty comes in, stands monumentally in the hall. She is dressed in
flowing garments, rather like Dorelia John. A very 'Sladey' sort of
dress. She opens wide her arms.*
TOTTY I had to come . . . Hello, everyone!
*There is a moment's silence, then the party converges on the hall,
much as they did when Peter and Sue arrived.*
GEORGE Look everybody! It's Totty!
*And each person, with the exception of Dickie, comes downstairs or
appears, saying, 'It's Totty' or expressing surprise and pleasure. They
come up to her and kiss her, shake her hand and she says their
names, laughing and embracing.*
RUFUS Totty – darling!
TOTTY Hello, my love.
STELLA Is there one for me?
TOTTY Dear Stella.
OSCAR (*kissing her hand*) Que je suis enchanté.

TOTTY Oscar.

PAULINE I'm so glad you came.

GEORGE We're all glad you came.

RUFUS Hear, hear.

PETER Hello, Totty. Totty, you don't know my wife. Sue, Totty. Totty, Sue.

TOTTY Dear little Peter: yesterday you were playing with your bucket and spade.

She embraces Sue, who hadn't expected to be embraced.

GEORGE But ought you to be here?

TOTTY Oh, *yes.* I can do anything. Anything I want. It's wonderful.

PAULINE I'm glad you came.

GEORGE We're all glad you came.

RUFUS Hear, hear.

BETTY Take Totty's coat, somebody. (*She looks round for Glyn or Harold. They are not there.*) George. Take Totty's coat. Come through.

TOTTY So this is your new home?

They go through into the drawing room. George comes out of the cloakroom and follows them in. Door closed. Dickie now appears, and Harold in the passage leading to the kitchen.

DICKIE Did somebody come?

Harold doesn't answer. Dickie opens the door and we hear Totty say 'Dickie!' as the door closes again.

INT. DRAWING ROOM. NIGHT.

They are all gathered round Totty, who is sitting on a chair. Some are sitting at her feet, others stood behind her. Grouped.

GEORGE And not only is our stuff not here, it's apparently somewhere in Carlisle.

TOTTY Carlisle?

STELLA Oh don't go through all that. That's boring. What's been happening to you?

TOTTY Nothing's been happening to me. I'm so happy to be here.

She puts out her arms and takes them all in.

Us.

George has brought her a drink. And food. She toasts them.

TOTTY (*to George and Betty*) How's Giles? And Toby?

GEORGE Toby's fine.

BETTY And Giles is fine.

TOTTY And Duncan and the twins?

RUFUS They're just the same. Just the same. Alas! (*He laughs.*)

TOTTY And is Donald still in Mozambique?

STELLA Goa.

TOTTY Isn't life strange?

GEORGE Why?

TOTTY Having children. Bringing them up. Sending them out.
Wait a moment.

GEORGE What?

TOTTY There was something I wanted to say.

PAULINE What?

TOTTY No. It's gone. I was on my way here and I thought, when
I get there I'll tell them that. It'll come back.

BETTY What sort of thing? A message?

TOTTY Not a message, exactly.

GEORGE Nice or nasty?

TOTTY Oh, *nice*. Only it's gone.

GEORGE I was just about to have a little show.

TOTTY Oh, the old epidiascope – how splendid!

BETTY Are you sure? Because it's your party.

TOTTY I'd love it.

*The entertainers are watching the group round Totty. They are still
sitting at the table, and when George starts the slides, they turn and
watch those.*

GEORGE Lights.

Slide 1: a woman upside down.

Apologies.

Slide 2: a prison gateway.

Mmm. Can't think where that one is.

Slide 3: Lindsay's brother with cap.

Slide 4: a bandstand.

Slide 5: an anonymous airport.

Can't think why I took that.

Slide 6: a meal. Pauline reacts.

This won't mean much to you, I'm afraid.

FEMALE ENTERTAINER Oh, no, they're fascinating, aren't they?

MALE ENTERTAINER Yes.

Slide 7: a waiter.

ALL Mmmm.

Slide 8: a bear.

PAULINE That's Boris, dear old Boris.

Slide 9: a white dog.

STELLA That's Rex. Remember?

Slide 10: penguins. They all laugh.

Slide 11: policemen.

RUFUS Who are they?

Slide 12: a seashore.

SUE Is that Walberswick?

BETTY No, Tunis.

Slide 13: a woman raking.

TOTTY Who's that?

GEORGE That's you, Totty.

TOTTY Is that me? Poor me. If only I'd known.

GEORGE Known what?

TOTTY I don't know, just known.

Slide 14: two children by a pool.

RUFUS That child is now in the Foreign Office.

OSCAR She's dead.

Slide 15: Milos Forman.

STELLA That's Percival. Before he went to India.

Slide 16: a cadet walking past a brass rubbing.

DICKIE That boy trod on a land mine in Borneo.

Slide 17: a puppy in arms.

Side 18: a bike.

GEORGE My old Hercules.

RUFUS

And the sun went down, and the stars came out
Far over the summer sea
But never a moment ceased the fight
Of the one and the fifty-three.

Slide 19: an aeroplane.

DICKIE That's the Comet at Dar es Salaam.

STELLA

Up the airy mountain,
Down the rushy glen,

We daren't go a-hunting
For fear of little men.

PAULINE
  Wee folk, good folk,
  Trooping all together;
  Green jacket, red cap
  And white owl's feather!
  The slides continue.

OSCAR
  If you can talk with crowds and keep your virtue,
  Or walk with kings – nor lose the common touch,
  If neither foes nor loving friends can hurt you,
  If all men count with you, but none too much . . .

TOTTY
  No more Latin, no more Greek,
  No more extra work from Beak,
  No more beetles in my tea,
  Making googly eyes at me,
  No more science, no more French,
  No more sitting on a hard school bench.
  This time tomorrow where shall I be?
  The final slide is of a grinning mouth with bad teeth.

PAULINE Who's that?

GEORGE That's Angela.

STELLA No, it isn't. It's Hugo.

PETER It's Auntie Clare.

BETTY Rubbish, it's Percival. Surely it's Percival.

RUFUS Who do you think it is, Totty?

STELLA Totty?

PAULINE Totty?

GEORGE Totty. Totty. Is she asleep? (*Puts lights on.*) Totty?

OSCAR She's dead.

STELLA Oh, I don't think so.

OSCAR She is dead.

GEORGE She can't be. Totty? Totty. Totty.

BETTY Totty.

GEORGE Totty? Totty. Totty.

BETTY George.

GEORGE She's gone. She's just gone.

PAULINE Totty? Totty.

GEORGE No good.

OSCAR Have we got a mirror?

They lower the mantelpiece mirror and hold it with difficulty over her as Oscar checks. The entertainers help.

RUFUS Steady, steady. Totty? Totty.

STELLA Is she dead? What do you think, Oscar?

OSCAR It's death all right.

PAULINE She was having such a good time.

SUE She doesn't look dead. I've never seen anybody dead before. Have you?

PETER Only at school.

RUFUS We ought to lay her out flat. Can't just have her sitting there.

OSCAR Put her on the table.

GEORGE That's a good idea.

RUFUS Come on, everyone. All hands to the pumps. Prepare to lift – and lift.

They lift her up, like Hamlet in the final scene, and we have a top shot of Totty and her bearers, which takes in the set and the studio surroundings. The camera pans round to the gallery. From behind the director, assistants, etc., in the gallery, we see the scene in the monitors. The female entertainer starts to sing. The whole party joins in.

Goodnight, ladies.
Goodnight, ladies.
Goodnight, ladies.
We're going to leave you now.

Merrily we roll along, roll along, roll along,
Merrily we roll along,
O'er the deep blue sea.

Sweet dreams, ladies.
Sweet dreams, ladies.
Sweet dreams, ladies.
We're going to leave you now.

Merrily we roll along, roll along, roll along,
Merrily we roll along,
O'er the deep blue sea.

The entertainers move to leave.

GEORGE I'm so sorry.

FEMALE ENTERTAINER It's quite all right, we understand, don't
we?

MALE ENTERTAINER Yes.

George gives him an envelope.

Goodnight.

Stella indicates to Dickie that they should leave.

GEORGE You're not going?

STELLA Yes, we should.

BETTY Must you?

STELLA Yes, we really must. Dickie.

PAULINE We ought to.

RUFUS Yes. I have to be up in the morning.

BETTY You're not all going? She wouldn't have wanted you all
to go.

PAULINE She had such dignity.

RUFUS It wasn't your fault. It wasn't anybody's fault.

GEORGE Oh, no. It wasn't our fault. I'll have them get your coats.

SUE Yes. You have to be up in the morning.

BETTY Oscar, you can stay.

OSCAR One too must go. Alas.

INT. HALL/STAIRS. NIGHT.

*The guests are standing about waiting for their coats. George looks in
the cloakroom and comes out again. George and Betty go towards the
kitchen.*

INT. KITCHEN. NIGHT.

*George comes into the kitchen. It is empty. The large chest has gone. The
door is open, no sign of anyone ever having been there. George is
puzzled. Looks outside. Betty comes in.*

GEORGE They appear to have gone.

BETTY Gone? Did you pay them?

GEORGE No.

Betty picks up the carving knife.

I've seen that before. They'll be back. If they haven't been
paid. They'll be back.

INT. HALL/STAIRS. NIGHT.
George and Betty come back. Only Oscar is left in the hall, with Sue and Peter, getting their motorcycle helmets on.

BETTY Have people gone? Where is everyone?

PETER They went on.

OSCAR They all went off. They wanted to stay together. I go a different way.

PETER They said to say goodbye.

SUE We'd better say goodbye too. Goodbye – we did enjoy it.

PETER It was lovely seeing you all again.

GEORGE Goodbye.

PETER Goodbye.

BETTY Goodbye.

SUE Goodbye.

GEORGE (*seeing them through the door*) And take care.
George and Betty stand in the hall, the door still open.
George closes the door and bolts it.

INT. DRAWING ROOM. NIGHT.
George looks in the drawing room. Totty lying on the table. He goes up to her.

GEORGE Totty? Totty.
There is no response.
I think she enjoyed it.

BETTY Oh, yes.

OLD LADY (*out of vision*) George! Betty!
George turns the lights off.

INT. HALL/STAIRS. NIGHT.
The old lady is at the top of the stairs, walking with the aid of a Zimmer frame.

OLD LADY I can't get anything on my set. It's not working.

INT. UPSTAIRS CORRIDOR. NIGHT.
They go upstairs and along the corridor. George and Betty ahead of the old lady, who comes along behind.

INT. THE OLD LADY'S ROOM. NIGHT.
George stares at the set, which is showing only static. The old lady comes in.

GEORGE No good. Never mind. (*He switches it off.*)

OLD LADY Don't switch it off. (*Switches it on again.*) It may come on again.

George and Betty leave the room. The old lady continues to watch as the credits come up on the blank screen.

Afternoon Off

CAST AND CREDITS

Afternoon Off was first transmitted by London Weekend Television on 3 February 1979. The cast included:

FATHER	Benjamin Whitrow
MOTHER	Angela Morant
BERNARD	Philip Jackson
MARJORY	Harold Innocent
LEE	Henry Man
HARRY	Harry Markham
JACK	Jackie Shin
MAN IN GALLERY	Stan Richards
GALLERY ATTENDANT	Peter Postlethwaite
MISS BECKINSALE	Elizabeth Spriggs
CUSTOMER IN SHOE SHOP	Carol Macready
MISS BRUNSKILL	Joan Scott
SHIRLEY	Angela Curran
MR BYWATERS	Peter Butterworth
IRIS BUTTERFIELD	Patricia Baker
ERNEST FLETCHER	Douglas Quarterman
CHRISTINE	Janine Duvitski
STANLEY	Alan Bennett
MR TURNBULL	Richard Griffiths
ALF	Paul Shane
CYRIL	Neville Smith
VIC	Bernard Wrigley
DUGGIE	John Normington
JANE	Anna Massey
LIZ	Stephanie Cole
FIRST ORDERLY	Silvia Brayshay
SECOND ORDERLY	Vicky Ireland
MRS BEEVERS	Thora Hird
MR BEEVERS	Frank Crompton
OLD IRIS	Jeanne Doree
STAFF NURSE	Lucita Lijertwood
IRIS	Sherrie Hewson
Producer and Director	Stephen Frears
Designer	Frank Nerini
Music	George Fenton

PART ONE

INT. HOTEL DINING ROOM. DAY.

A northern spa or seaside town. Scarborough, perhaps. A large hotel dining room, empty except for a family (father, mother, two sons) having a late lunch: a half-holiday from school perhaps. There is a maître d'hôtel and two waiters: Bernard, who is local and Lee who is Cambodian or North Vietnamese. Bernard and Lee are at a loose end, watching the diners. Lee folds napkins into cones and puts them on the tables set for the next meal. Bernard waits to take away the dirty plates, and at the right moment Lee brings up the sweet trolley.

FATHER Well, family! Your father begins to revive. He feels fractionally better. Now, my friend, what have you in the way of puddings to tempt my starving brood?

The maître d'hôtel summons Lee with the sweet trolley.

So, brats, anything there that tickles your fancy? I should tell you – (*leaning in mock confidence towards the maître d'hôtel*) – my children are pigs.

SIMON Trifle.

JEREMY Cake.

FATHER This pig will have that and that pig will have this. Elspeth?

MOTHER I think, perhaps, one or two figs.

FATHER Figs for my lady wife.

Mother nudges him.

MOTHER (*mouthing*) No cream.

FATHER Senza crema per favore.

MAITRE D'HOTEL And for monsieur?

FATHER Yes. Monsieur. Monsieur will have . . . what will Monsieur have? Well, he'll have a heart attack if he has any of *that*. Ha ha. Still, it's my birthday this year, why don't I treat myself? Do I spy strawberries lurking there? Strawberries it is. Splendid. Know that you have the blessings of a starving man and his offspring.

INT. HOTEL KITCHEN. DAY.

*Lee, who has simply held the trolley impassively throughout this, now
wheels it into the kitchen through some swing doors. He watches the
cook putting the dishes from the sweet trolley into a fridge. Bernard, the
other waiter, comes in from the dining room.*

BERNARD 'Two cups of your excellent coffee and we shall have
the courage to face the world.' (*addressing the swing doors*) You
pillock. It's half past bloody two. I shall be on teas in five
minutes. And don't smile that inscrutable oriental smile,
Genghis. This is your afternoon off. And, moreover, today
is the day. Look at him, Marjory.

Marjory is the nickname of the cook, a fattish man of about fifty.
Portrait of a man about to have the best sexual experience
Scarborough (*or Harrogate*) has to offer. Does it show? Is it
written all over his face? Is it buggery.

Lee smiles.

That's my chicken.

MARJORY Who's the lucky recipient?

LEE Eilis.

BERNARD No, bollock-brain, Iris.

LEE Eilis.

BERNARD Skip it. I'll write it down. (*Takes the coffee tray.*) Here
we are. Two cups of the life-giving liquid. I'd like to pour it
very slowly up his nostrils. (*He goes through the swing doors into
the dining room.*)

MARJORY Do you like young ladies, then?

LEE Yes, yes. Very much.

MARJORY I thought you people didn't mind one way or the
other. Orientals. Same as you don't set much store by human
life. Or is that just the Chinese? I had a friend from Samoa
once. He was very catholic. Very catholic indeed. Ended up
in the air force.

LEE It is difficult.

MARJORY I know some nice people.

LEE Young ladies?

MARJORY Not exactly. But you never know. One thing leads to
another. That's always been my philosophy.

LEE I want to meet young ladies. English young ladies.

MARJORY You can't expect them on a plate. You can't expect
anybody on a plate. Ladies. Anybody.

LEE Eilis is Bernard's friend. She likes me. He showed her my
photograph.

*He shows Marjory the photograph. It is a passport photo of Lee,
grinning inanely.*

MARJORY There's a lot has to go into it in the way of preparations.
That is if you're thinking about bed. It has to be a roundabout
way of doing it. Are you thinking about bed?

LEE Yes. I have bought some chocolates.

MARJORY Chocolates? Chocolates? They won't do it for
chocolates. In Berlin, in 1945, then they might have done it
for chocolates. But this isn't Berlin, 1945. This is Scarborough,
1978. Things have changed. We're not a conquered nation.
There isn't a demoralised populace out there. They won't do it
for chocolates now. Berlin, you could have had anybody you
wanted for nothing. For Nescafé. They'd do anything for
Nescafé. Anything. And now I've got drums of the stuff.
It breaks your heart. A lot more has to go into it nowadays. I've
cooked soufflés and they've not done it. Scampi in a
hollandaise sauce. *Zabaglione.* And nothing. The cocky little
sods. I tell you, you'll want more than Dairy Box.

INT. HOTEL DINING ROOM. DAY.
Lee goes back into the dining room.

FATHER (*writing a cheque*) I think you'll find that if you present
this at any branch of Lloyd's Bank you will find yourself
adequately recompensed.

MAITRE D'HOTEL Sir.

FATHER Well, family! On your feet. Thus fortified let us sally
forth to see what the afternoon has in store.

*They go beneath the smile of Lee, the scowl of Bernard, and are
followed by the maître d'hôtel.*

INT. HOTEL STAIRS/CORRIDOR. DAY.
*Lee going upstairs through the empty hotel. Along corridors where a
maid is changing dirty sheets, with more sheets on a laundry trolley
outside the room, clean ones on another trolley.*

INT. ATTIC CORRIDORS. DAY.
More stairs. Through a door marked 'Private' and along, up and down attic corridors, round corners to his room.

INT. LEE'S BEDROOM. DAY.
Lee shaving at his little basin. Contents of his room: a map; smiling home photographs of a large family; a few battered paperbacks; a Playboy *nude behind the wardrobe door, which also has a mirror so that we see it incidentally while he is dressing. A box of chocolates waiting.*

INT. HOTEL KITCHEN. DAY.
Bernard is sitting in his white coat, with his feet up.
BERNARD Once again. Iris.
LEE Eilis.
BERNARD Iris.
LEE Eilis.
BERNARD You try, Marjory.
MARJORY Iris.
LEE Eilis.
MARJORY If she was called Kevin there wouldn't be any problem. Write him it down.
BERNARD (*shaking his head and writing*) What's her last name? I can't think of her last name. Anyway – (*writing down her name*) – she works in this shoe shop and she comes off at four.
LEE Eilis.
BERNARD (*to Marjory*) It's his skin that does it. She loves olive skin. Crazy for it. Olive skin makes her go mental. Me, I'm the great white whale.
MARJORY I like a texture to the skin, I must say.
Lee is going out.
Are you off then, Genghis?
BERNARD Ta-ra then, sugar. Give her one for Marjory and me.
Marjory looks unhappy.

EXT. HOTEL STAFF ENTRANCE. DAY.
Lee goes out through the staff entrance of the hotel. Dustbins. Great zinc containers. Cardboard boxes.

EXT. HOTEL FRONT ENTRANCE. DAY.
Then past the front entrance to the hotel.

EXT. TOWN. DAY.
The town is very quiet. Most of the shops are shut. It is early-closing day.

EXT. SHOE SHOP. DAY.
Lee tries to see in through the window, looking for Iris. He looks at a clock. Quarter past three. He is early.

EXT. STREET. DAY.
Lee stands in a deserted street. A man comes along and goes into an open doorway. Another man comes out. Lee watches as someone else goes in. He crosses the road.

INT. MEN'S CLUB: STAIRS. DAY
Lee going up a staircase.

INT. MEN'S CLUB: LIBRARY. DAY.
Two old men playing draughts. Lee watches them for a while but they take no notice.

INT. MEN'S CLUB: BILLIARD HALL. DAY.
We see two old men unlock a cue box, take their cues, put money in the meter to turn the lights on over one of the tables and start to play snooker. Lee watches them.

HARRY She was on at me again yesterday.

JACK Who?

HARRY My home help. She was proposing again. She keeps on proposing.

JACK While she's doing your housework?

HARRY Well, not while she's doing it. In the intervals between.

JACK *(to the ball)* Keep floating, keep floating. Oh, lovely stuff.

HARRY They're not supposed to do that, you know.

JACK Propose?

HARRY Take advantage. There was a meals-on-wheels woman had up. *(to the ball)* Kiss, you bugger, kiss. They reckon to have to maintain professional impartiality.

JACK One off the red. One in the bed.

HARRY 'Let's get married,' she keeps on saying. 'Let's go to Jersey.'

JACK Jersey?

HARRY I know. That's what I said. And she's only about forty.
Little woman. Blonde hair.

JACK Maybe you ought to be flattered. (*to the ball*) Very nice,
very nice.

HARRY If it goes on I reckon I'm going to have to contact my
social worker. She was invaluable over my rates.
Lee is going out.

JACK Getting quite cosmopolitan round here.

HARRY Ay. Who was he?

JACK He looked Chinese.
Harry goes and looks after him down the stairs.

HARRY It's happen one of these visiting delegations. (*coming back
to the game*) We had some people round last week from
Romania.

INT. ART GALLERY. DAY.
An attendant is sitting on a chair at the corner of an empty room.
*A man in a cap wanders through, obviously passing the time on. Stops
to talk to the attendant. The man is in his sixties, the attendant a bit
younger. The conversation is in progress when the camera catches them.*

MAN Now then, Neville. Not busy.

ATTENDANT Ay. Run off us feet.

MAN I could do with your job.

ATTENDANT It carries its own burdens. We get that much rubbish
traipsing through here now I feel like a social worker. This is
one of their regular ports of call, you know. Here and the
Social Security.
Lee appears, walking through the gallery.
They don't come in for the pictures.

MAN No?

ATTENDANT They come in for the central heating. Genuine art
lovers, you can tell them a mile off. They're looking at a picture
and what they're looking for are the effects of light. The brush
strokes. Economy of effect. (*watching Lee all the time*) But not
the lot we get. Riff-raff. Rubbish. Human flotsam. The detritus
of a sick society. Shove up half a dozen Rembrandts and they'd

never come near. Turn the Dimplex up three degrees and it's packed out.

Lee has sat down.

No sitting.

Lee doesn't understand.

No sitting. Ally-up.

Lee doesn't understand.

Keep moving.

He motions with his fingers, and Lee gets up.

MAN He looks like one of these overseas visitors.

ATTENDANT They think just because the Corporation provide seats that they're to be sat on. They're not. They're Chippendale.

MAN That's never Chippendale, is it?

ATTENDANT School of. Anyway, they've no business sitting down.

MAN Oh, no.

ATTENDANT We've got an added responsibility now. These explosive devices. I search bags. I have authority to search bags. I mean him. What's he *doing*? And they have a tradition going back to the kamikazies. No sitting. I've told you once.

MAN You've told him twice.

ATTENDANT I bet I know what he wants. You're not looking for the Turner?

LEE Sorry?

ATTENDANT No? That's what they all want to see. Anybody who has any idea. 'Where's the Turner?' Flaming Turner. I can't see anything in it. Looks as if it's been left out in the rain. And we've got all sorts in here. Penny-farthings. Instruments of torture. Plus the death mask of Charles Peace. Do they want to see any of that? Do they naff. We had Kenneth Clark in here once. Same old story: 'Where's the Turner?' I've never seen a suit like it. Tweed! It was like silk. Then some of them come in just because we have a better class of urinal. See the Turner, use the urinal and then off. And who pays? Right. The ratepayer.

MAN Wicked.

ATTENDANT Art students are another bugbear. They come in here and touch. Paw the pictures. Get their noses right up to them. Do you know what does most damage to pictures?

MAN No.

ATTENDANT Breath. Not chemical pollution. Human breath. And
which are students now? You don't know. A beard used to be a
good guide. Now they've all got them.

MAN Ay. Our Derek has.

ATTENDANT A beard? Your Derek? Has he given up the garage?

MAN Oh, yes. And the launderette. He's in these transverse
applicators, now, the other side of Darlington.
*And the conversation ends, trailing away as the camera follows
Lee out.*

EXT. SHOE SHOP. DAY.
*Lee walks along the street. Peers into the shop again. The manageress
sees him, and stares back. He looks at the clock. He still has twenty
minutes.*

INT. CHURCH. DAY.
*Lee wanders round. Monuments to dead worthies. The children's
corner. Pictures of Jesus. All somehow meaningless to this bland oriental
gaze. There is a woman arranging flowers in the chancel. He watches
her.*

MISS BECKINSALE I hate gladioli but at least they register.
Cornflowers are my favourite, but you'd need binoculars.
These are so vulgar. Almost as bad as blowsy old chrysanths.
Are you keen on churches?
Lee smiles.
This one's very dull.
*She goes away to do another vase somewhere else. Lee wanders after
her.*
Are you a stranger to these shores? Yes? I suppose you are,
going by the look of you. You aren't by any chance Buddhist,
are you?

LEE No.

MISS BECKINSALE Just a thought. Not that anybody cares a toss
these days, we're all so ecumenical. I had a great friend who
was a Buddhist. She lived in Stroud. Ploughing rather a lonely
furrow there, I always thought. The only Buddhist in Stroud.
Vegetarian too. Dear, dear, friend. Dead now.

LEE (*of the flowers*) They look nice.

MISS BECKINSALE Don't they? Not that the vicar will give them a second look. And they won't last five minutes. That much incense flying around. (*She gets up laboriously and carries her kneeling mat over to another spot and a fresh vase.*) Don't suppose it'll be long before all they have on the altar is a couple of rubber plants. Anything to cut costs. They come from round you, I imagine, rubber plants?
Lee smiles.
About the most boring plant in the world, I think. No offence.
LEE I am a waiter.
MISS BECKINSALE Jolly good. We also serve.
LEE I am meeting my girlfriend.
MISS BECKINSALE Good for you. I was going to offer you a cup of tea, but you're spoken for. Some other time. Done my duty by the mission field. Betty, this Buddhist I was telling you about, and me were going on a trip to the Far East. Just up sticks and off. Your part of the world. Palm trees, tropical shores. She'd been a WAAF there in the war. Just after the war, actually. I'm not that prehistoric. Going to be the journey of a lifetime. Deck tennis, flying fish, sarongs. Of course there were one or two things that had to be done first. Parents to look after. House too large. Sell the house. Mother in a home. Who's to visit. Yours truly. Never a clean slate somehow. We still used to talk about it over the cocoa, our trip. And then she died. Dear, dear friend. K. L. Singapore. Hong Kong. One of those big might-have-beens. And now it's Scarborough. Where is it they put garlands of flowers round your neck? Hawaii, is it? Fiji? Somewhere. Not Scarborough.
A clock strikes four. Lee hears it and begins to go.
If you go out, be careful and close the door. The vicar's got a big thing about saving fuel . . .

EXT. CHURCH. DAY.
Lee running out of the church and along the street as the clock strikes four.

EXT. SHOE SHOP. DAY.
Lee outside the shoe shop. It is ten-past four. No one has come out. Lee, after peering in through the window. eventually goes into the shop.

INT. SHOE SHOP. DAY.

The manageress, Miss Brunskill, is serving a middle-aged customer.

CUSTOMER I've always had eights ever since I can remember.

MISS BRUNSKILL Madam is a wide seven.

CUSTOMER I was told I was a narrow eight.

MISS BRUNSKILL Not by anybody with qualifications. This is a broad foot. (*She puts a shoe on it.*)

CUSTOMER It feels a bit short.

MISS BRUNSKILL It shouldn't. Here is madam's big toe. Acres of room.

The woman tries to walk on them, hobbles up and down. Shirley, the girl assistant, is up a ladder, putting shoes away. Lee is waiting for her at the foot of the ladder.

Miss Featherstone. You have a gentleman waiting.

SHIRLEY Can I help you?

LEE Iris?

SHIRLEY Sorry?

LEE Iris. Are you Iris?

SHIRLEY No. Shirley.

Lee looks doubtfully at Miss Brunskill.

LEE She's Iris?

SHIRLEY No, Iris left.

MISS BRUNSKILL The men's department is in the mezzanine, sir.

LEE I want to see Iris. Do you know Iris?

Miss Brunskill is about to answer when the customer hobbles up.

CUSTOMER Could I try an eight? I'm sure I'm not a seven. Sevens are torture.

MISS BRUNSKILL We don't stock that model in an eight. One moment. Whom did you say you wanted?

LEE Iris.

MISS BRUNSKILL Shirley. Alert Mr Bywaters.

Shirley goes unhappily downstairs.

If you'll take a seat, I will be with you in one moment.

Lee sits down.

I can show you something in suede.

CUSTOMER Suede makes my feet swell.

MISS BRUNSKILL (*whose attention is distracted by Lee*) There are preparations for that nowadays, madam.

The customer looks mystified.

Deodorants, madam.

CUSTOMER I said 'swell', not 'smell'.

MISS BRUNSKILL One moment, madam.

Miss Brunskill goes to meet Mr Bywaters, who has come halfway up the stairs. He waits there, surveying Lee. Behind Lee, Miss Brunskill indicates that Lee is the person in question. Shirley comes back up the stairs into the shop and looks sympathetically at him, before going on with her own work.

MR BYWATERS Is this the person, Miss Brunskill?

Miss Brunskill nods.

I understand you're looking for Miss Butterworth.

LEE Iris.

MR BYWATERS She is no longer in our employ.

LEE Not here?

MR BYWATERS I'm afraid not. We were forced to release her.

LEE Where is she?

MR BYWATERS Perhaps you could tell me? Miss Butterworth left taking with her some of our stock, namely one pair of thigh-length boots in crushed mimosa and fourteen packets of fully fashioned hosiery. The matter is now in the hands of the police. Do you know her? Is she a friend of yours?

LEE No.

MR BYWATERS You don't know her. Yet you are making enquiries as to her whereabouts?

LEE No.

MR BYWATERS No? Yes. She was a dishonest employee. I hope you're not on the same game. One of these foreign visitors who come over here for the express purpose of shoplifting, perhaps. Well, not here, young man. See that? That's a television camera. Every move you make is monitored. So don't come that game with me. If you have no intention of making a purchase I suggest you leave these premises forthwith.

Lee goes.

Where is Iris, indeed. I wish I knew. I say I wish I knew.

Miss Brunskill turns back to find that her customer has sneaked out after Lee.

EXT. SHOE SHOP. DAY.

Outside the shop. It is raining, so the customer and Lee shelter in the doorway.

CUSTOMER The blighters! They always want to rule you, shops. Wide seven! I'm a narrow eight. I have been ever since I got married. Well, I'm fifty-seven, and the beggars aren't going to rule me. I'm old enough to rule myself. Then saying they smelt. They never do. Only they would if I had to cram them into a seven. Preparations. I'd look well starting on that game my age.

Lee watches her go, but still waits, uncertain what to do. While he is waiting Shirley, the young assistant, comes out with a second customer who wants to point out a pair of shoes in the window.

SECOND CUSTOMER I think them's the ones I mean.

SHIRLEY Do you still want Iris?

LEE Iris? Yes.

SHIRLEY I think her dad works at Batty's. (*Gives him a piece of paper.*) Which?

SECOND CUSTOMER Them.

SHIRLEY Batty's.

SECOND CUSTOMER Who wants Batty's? You want Batty's? It's at the bottom of Dickinson Road.

The second customer takes Lee out and points out the way. No sound. Shirley watches as he goes and he smiles at her. We know that even though her name isn't Iris, she would have been quite prepared to fill the bill.

EXT. CHURCH HALL. DAY.

Lee is waiting at a bus stop outside the church hall. Behind him is a large notice-board, with a hand-painted poster advertising a pensioners' concert:

LADIES BRIGHT HOUR
SONGS AT THE PIANO
BY
IRIS BUTTERFIELD AND ERNEST FLETCHER
AT THE PIANO: MISS TATTERSALL
ALL WELCOME

The sound of distant music from the hall attracts Lee's attention. He looks at the poster. At the note in his hand. At the name 'Iris'.

INT. CHURCH HALL. DAY.
*An audience of OAPs. The two singers are giving their rendition of
'Pedro the Fisherman'. Periodically the old ladies join in and whistle
the refrain. The scene is intercut with shots of Lee coming up the stairs
backstage and eventually finding his way into the wings.*

> Pedro the fisherman was always whistling,
> Such a merry call;
> Girls who were passing by would hear him whistling,
> By the harbour wall.
> But our sweet Teresa who loved him true always knew
> That his song belonged to her alone.
> So they wandered hand in hand; you in love will
>   understand
> Why it was he whistled all the day.
> And in the evening when the lights were gleaming
> And they had to part,
> As he sailed his boat away,
> Echoing across the bay,
> Came the tune that lingered in her heart.
>
> But Pedro found the sea was drear and chose another
>   course
> He sold his boat and fishing gear and bought himself
>   a horse.
> He rode away to find the gold the sea could never bring,
> To buy a dress, a cuckoo clock, a saucepan and a ring.
> One day her father said to her, 'Oh dearest daughter mine,
> You'll never make a lot from fish, you make much more
>   from wine.
> Though Miguel is rather fat, his vineyard's doing well.
> So marry him and let your dreams of Pedro go to hell.'
>
> The organ peals
> The choirboys sing
> The priest is ready with the book and ring.
> So small and white
> Here comes the bride
> And stands by swarthy Miguel's side.
> 'Will you have this man to be your lawful wedded spouse
>   eternally?'

And suddenly the church is still.
They wait to hear her say, 'I will',
When through the open doorway a far-off sound disturbs
    the air . . .

The audience begin to whistle.
Iris has sent her partner, Mr Fletcher, offstage and now beckons him
on as the returning Pedro. Thinking she is welcoming him,
Lee ventures hesitantly on to the stage. Iris, who is plainly not the
Iris, is mystified. The old ladies, thinking it all part of the show, are
delighted and burst out clapping. Lee stands on stage very puzzled.

PART TWO

INT. GENERAL OFFICE. DAY.

Reception-cum-general office of a factory. A man and a woman in
the office, Lee sitting outside on the other side of an enquiries hatch,
but visible from the office. He has obviously been sitting there some
time.

CHRISTINE He's looking for someone called Iris. Have we got an
    Iris? I can't think of an Iris. Stanley.

STANLEY What?

CHRISTINE Nice face.

STANLEY Don't look at him, Christine. If you don't look at him
    he'll happen go away.
    Pause.

CHRISTINE Stanley.

STANLEY What?

CHRISTINE He's still there. (*She smiles at Lee.*)

STANLEY Course he's still there, with you doing all that silly
    smiling. Christine.

CHRISTINE What?

STANLEY Wasn't that Iris in Despatch?

CHRISTINE Which?

STANLEY She was in Despatch. She had a big mauve jumper.
    Her mother had a duodenal ulcer. They had a caravan at
    Skipsea. Did she have a caravan at Skipsea?

LEE Iris.

STANLEY Her mother didn't have a duodenal ulcer? Ran a little
    primrose mini. Crippled with indigestion.

CHRISTINE He may not have met her mother.

STANLEY She could have told him.

CHRISTINE She mightn't. If you're going out with somebody you
    don't kick off by saying, 'My mother's got a duodenal ulcer
    and we've got a caravan at Skipsea.' That's quite far on in the
    relationship.

STANLEY Anyway, I think that was Eirlys, not Iris.

229

CHRISTINE Men, they don't want to know about your mother. You tell them your mother's got a duodenal ulcer and that puts the tin hat on it straightaway.

STANLEY You'll find somebody one day, Christine. Raymond's not the only pebble on the beach.

CHRISTINE I just wish I'd not splashed out on all that motorcycle gear.

STANLEY Well, I thought you were being rather short-sighted at the time.

CHRISTINE Mind you, they make motorbikes, don't they?

STANLEY Who?

CHRISTINE The Japanese. Honda. Suzuki.

STANLEY He doesn't look particularly motorised to me. I just wish he'd go away. There'll be the Chairman of the CBI coming round in five minutes reconnoitring and we've got Aladdin stuck there. Have you no other data?

LEE Iris.

CHRISTINE Stanley. We could always ask Mr Turnbull.

STANLEY Yes. I could always put my head in the gas oven.

CHRISTINE Mr Turnbull knows everybody by name.

STANLEY So do I. There's a Maureen in Maintenance. An Eileen in Records. Two Karens in Costing.

CHRISTINE Debbie in the post room.

STANLEY Diane in the canteen. Wait a minute. Canteen. Canteen, Christine. *Canteen.* We did use to have an Iris. She worked in the canteen before Mr Turnbull had the big clampdown. That's right. *Iris.* They caught her going through the gate with some cooking fat under her coat. Her locker was piled high with Carnation Milk. Iris.

LEE Iris.

STANLEY Don't get excited.

CHRISTINE What happened to her?

STANLEY She got finished. She was one of the first casualties of the Turnbull era. But her dad works in the pressing shop. Butterworth. She's little Mr Butterworth's daughter. Iris Butterworth. Point him in the direction of the pressing shop. (*to Lee*) You want to be in the pressing shop. Off you go. Like the motto says: 'The difficult we can do straightaway; the impossible takes time.'

CHRISTINE Come on, love.
She goes out and almost immediately Mr Turnbull comes in.
MR TURNBULL Oh, yes, and who was that, the oriental gentleman?
STANLEY A potential customer. Enquiring about delivery dates
for South Korea.
MR TURNBULL South Korea. There you are. Exactly what I was
saying last week. It won't be long before the whole of the
Middle East is knocking at the door.
Christine comes back and doesn't at first see Mr Turnbull.
CHRISTINE I hope he finds her.
MR TURNBULL Finds who?

INT. PRESSING SHOP. DAY
*Some kind of machine shop. Not large. Noisy. Light engineering. About
half a dozen men working. Lee enters.*
ALF We've got a visitor.
CYRIL A trade delegation.
VIC It's Mao Tse-tung. How do you do?
ALF 'New lamps for old.'
All this above the noise of the machines.
Who is it you want? Who . . . do . . . you . . . want?
*Lee shows him his paper. Alf's face changes. Stops his machine.
Shows it to Vic, who stops his. Gradually the machines shut down.
There is silence.*
Iris Butterworth?
LEE Yes. Iris. Iris.
ALF Iris Butterworth doesn't work here. Her dad works here.
Iris's dad.
VIC He works here all right. Where is he?
CYRIL He's just paying a call.
VIC Lucky for you –
ALF I'd better tell him.
Alf goes to knock on the door of the toilet.
CYRIL Alf. Wait on. You'd not better. You know Duggie.
VIC Tell him, Alf. Go on.
CYRIL No. Nay, Victor, have a heart.
VIC Don't be soft.
CYRIL Listen, you'd better go quick, you.
LEE Iris. Iris's father.

CYRIL Yes, Iris's father.

VIC Go on, Alf.

Alf knocks on the door and Vic joins in the conversation.

ALF Duggie. You've got a visitor.

DUGGIE (*through the door*) What?

ALF You've got a visitor.

DUGGIE Who? I'm on the lav.

VIC (*winking*) He wants your Iris.

DUGGIE Who wants who?

VIC Your Iris. This feller. There's a feller here wants your Iris.
I want to see this.

DUGGIE What sort of a feller?

VIC A feller. You'd better stand back. He's a bloody tornado.
*Sound of a lavatory flushing. The door of the toilet opens very
slowly. A small timid man comes out, slowly fastening his braces.*

DUGGIE What about our Iris?

ALF This feller wants her.

DUGGIE Him?

VIC Him.

DUGGIE The Chink? Iris?

LEE Iris.

VIC (*mimicking him*) Ilis.

CYRIL Nay, Victor. He can't help the way he talks.

DUGGIE You, is it? You. Do you know who I am?

LEE No.

DUGGIE I'm Iris's father. Are you the one, then? Are you him?
You're him, aren't you?

LEE Him?

DUGGIE The one she's been knocking about with.

VIC He's one of these Disco Desmonds, Duggie.

DUGGIE That's right, Victor. I thought his sort were generally
Maltese.

VIC What, Duggie?

DUGGIE Pimps, Victor.

CYRIL Nay, Duggie.

DUGGIE Or else it's drugs. Is that it, drugs? Are you the last link
in the chain? Tibet to Scarborough. The outlet.

VIC Bite his ankles, Dug.

DUGGIE I expect you're getting her hooked, are you? The opium.

is it? I've seen them. The dull light in their eyes. All purpose gone. Scum. Scum.

LEE No. Iris.

VIC I think he's making fun of you, Douglas, pulling your leg, taking the Chinese piss.

DUGGIE She never let on he was Chinese. Else I'd have given her another hiding. You've got a nerve coming round here. What do you want?

VIC Her hand in marriage.

DUGGIE Marriage doesn't mean anything to these people, Victor. They just go behind a bush. Then they come over here and expect us to do likewise. She was a good girl.

CYRIL She was a grand girl.

DUGGIE Where is she now?

LEE (*nodding*) Where?

DUGGIE You little slant-eyed tup. If I thought you were worth it I'd give you the hiding of your life.

VIC I would. Me, I would, Duggie.

DUGGIE Victor, I would not soil my fingers.

VIC Put his head in the machine press, Duggie.

DUGGIE It's not his head I want to put in the machine press, Victor.

CYRIL Nay, Duggie. He looks as if he might be a nice lad, underneath.

DUGGIE Underneath what?

CYRIL Their different customs. He probably doesn't know any better.

DUGGIE You wouldn't be saying that if he came sniffing round your Christine.

Lee takes the paper with Iris's name on it from Duggie's trembling fingers.

You see, look at him. He's shameless. No shame.

LEE I am looking for Iris.

VIC The nerve, Douglas. Of all the Chinese nerve. Clock him one.

LEE Where is she?

DUGGIE Don't ask me where she is. I know where her mother is. In her grave. With a broken heart. Iris. She's a scrubber. She's a bloody scrubber. (*Starts crying.*) My daughter's a bloody scrubber.

CYRIL Nay, she's not.

DUGGIE What do you know about it, you soft article?

ALF (*to Lee*) You've upset him now. It's you that's done that. He was as right as rain till you came in. Coming in, upsetting him. You've no business. He's highly strung. He's on tablets.

CYRIL I should take your teeth out, you'll feel better.

DUGGIE I don't want to take my teeth out. I thought I'd seen everything when she fetched home a bloody Zambian. Now it's Wishee-Washee. Where did we go wrong, Betty? Where did we go wrong?

CYRIL I think the nuns do the damage. It's all right when they're right little, but come puberty they allus break out. Look at Carmen Lockwood.

DUGGIE Nuns? Nuns? She's never been near no nuns, Iris.

CYRIL She went to Crossgates. Crossgates is nuns.

DUGGIE It never is. Crossgates is comprehensive.

CYRIL But nuns' comprehensive.

DUGGIE It isn't nuns. How many more times? There were no flaming nuns.

CYRIL Sorry. My mistake.

DUGGIE Nuns. Chinks. What a day.

VIC And he's just standing there, the cause of the chaos.

DUGGIE Doesn't he understand? I've disowned her. She is not my daughter. There is no person called Iris in my life.

CYRIL It's tragic because she was a wonderful girl. Loved the open air.

ALF I blame television.

DUGGIE She never watched television. She was never in for long enough. She'd come in after her work, plaster herself up with make-up, then get off out to a disco or something similar, then pole in at half past two in the morning. Well, I tell you, I don't care. It serves her right. Scrubbing floors in the hospital. Running errands for Paki doctors. That's all she's fit for. A hospital skivvy, Chiang Kai-shek, that's what Iris is. One of these ancillary workers.

LEE Hospital?

DUGGIE Yes, *hospital*. You want Iris, go up the Royal and look round the gerry wards. That's what she's doing, emptying slops, cleaning out bedpans. And it's all she's fit for. My daughter.

The boss has come in. It is the Mr Turnbull who came into
Reception.

MR TURNBULL Hello. I thought I was coming into the pressing
shop. I find myself in a church. Silent. All activity at a standstill.
One machine, idle. Another machine, idle. Idle, idle, idle. Are
we getting the country back on its feet? Is this the year of the
beaver? It seems not. It seems not. And you. What are you
doing still on the premises? What do you want? To ruin our
schedules? Bugger up our norms? You're not another one from
ASLEF, are you? Because I can't understand what you are
doing here. Get out. Get out get out, get out, get out, get out.
Do I make myself plain? I am saying to you, 'Get out.' And
don't smile at me. Not funny. Not funny, not funny, not funny,
not funny.
He ushers Lee through the factory and out.
A thought strikes me. You haven't been sent round to check on
the fire precautions? No. Such subtlety is beyond the
municipality. Carry on, Miss Dunbar. I'm just seeing this
person off the premises. Do not come back. Come back do
not. No. Not back here. Come, no. Out. Off.

LEE Where is the hospital?

MR TURNBULL What hospital? No hospital. All hospital. This
place is a hospital. The sick, the lame, the halt. Bedridden.
Work? Nowhere. Work, the disease. We cure them of it. That's
what this place is, a hospital. Sick, sick, sick. We're all sick.
Mr Turnbull goes off muttering to himself. Lee goes, very sadly.
England is mad.

INT. COFFEE SHOP. DAY.
Cut to a smart culinary shop. Elizabeth David pots, teacloths, wooden
utensils, etc. One part of it is a coffee place. Lee sits there. Most of this
scene is shot on him, his increasingly doleful face. Perhaps a tear even
as the scene goes on. Jane, who runs the shop, is talking to Liz.

JANE The genesis of this place, the germ of the whole thing,
I mean, the real seed, as it were, was when I was trying to find
a decent double-boiler. You know, just an ordinary *bain-marie*.
I scoured the whole of the town, and nobody's even *heard* of
them. Which is ridiculous because they've been making
double-boilers since the dawn of civilisation, practically. So

one night I said to Geoffrey, 'Look, Geoffrey, I can't find a double-boiler for love nor money. You've got your pension and I've got those few pennies Auntie Lucy left me, adventure is the spice of life, why don't we blue it all on a shop that sells them? I mean, not exclusively. Other things as well. And that was how the whole thing started. Of course we've branched out a lot. Lots of pots, mostly French, you know, sort of thing you used to be able to pick up for a few francs any town in France any market day. Cost a bit more now, alas. But still heaps better than anything you get here. And, you know, I don't think I'm being fanciful, I think they make the food taste different. Then Geoffrey came up with the idea of making this little back place we had in the shop into a tea/coffee place, served in the crocks we have on sale in the shop, open sandwiches, little snacks, cakes, etc., all strictly of the home-made variety . . . which we did . . . and, you know . . . it's become quite a little meeting place. It's called the Pop In because . . . well . . . you know that's what people do . . . just pop in . . . except old Geoff says it's called Pop In because Pop's always in, which he is, he has to be, look after the place . . . he's actually out just this minute, popped along to the bank, popped in there, ha ha, drawing out not depositing, because there's no money in it, we manage of course but what I think is that we perform a service. Then Vanessa helps out.

A very miserable girl is washing up.

I mean, I pay her a wage, but she does it very much on a friendly basis. Nice girl. Nervous. Bit anorexic. At least she doesn't eat the cakes. But, you know, the really satisfying thing is that one feels one is fulfilling a social need, and old Geoff says the same, because that's always been a big strong point with him. I mean, that's what the army was, really, you know, performing a service. I mean, I don't think there are enough little places like this, you know, *nice* places, places where the pots are nice and the cakes are nice and the people are nice. Where, really, you know, it's nice. So one does feel one is making a contribution and even taking into account VAT (which does make one's life sheer misery) even including VAT I think it's been worthwhile. (*to Lee, who is going*) Coffee and one cake. Seventy-five p.

LEE Where is the hospital?

JANE Are you ill?

LEE Tell me the way to the hospital.

JANE There are lots of hospitals. The Royal's at the top of the
hill. Do you mean the Royal?

LEE The hospital.

LIZ He means the Royal.

JANE Try the Royal.

Lee goes out.

Was he crying? I thought he was crying. I didn't think they did
cry. I thought that was the point about them.

INT. HOSPITAL SLUICE ROOM. DAY.

*The sluice room off a hospital ward. A woman orderly is washing up
bedpans and bottles. Another orderly comes in.*

FIRST ORDERLY You work in a hospital and they think you're
anybody's. I'm always finding that. Soon as I told him what
I did he just went mad. No please or thank you.

SECOND ORDERLY It's the body. They think you're not shocked
by the body. They think you've seen it all.

FIRST ORDERLY Well, I'm not shocked by the body, but I still
like to be treated like a human being. It can get so clinical.

SECOND ORDERLY I wish mine had been more clinical. He kept
wanting a running commentary. Who was he?

FIRST ORDERLY Smallish feller. Bit on the ginger side. Said he
ran a string of dry cleaners.

SECOND ORDERLY I've heard that before.

First Orderly goes out and comes back straightaway.

FIRST ORDERLY You seen Iris?

SECOND ORDERLY Not on this afternoon. It's Tuesday.

FIRST ORDERLY There's a little Chink wants her.

SECOND ORDERLY A little Chink?

She goes and has a peep at Lee, dejectedly waiting.

No. That won't be for that Iris. He looks too nice for her. It'll
be the other Iris. Our Iris. They're students. They send them
round visiting. Lonely students they send round seeing lonely
old folks. Like Bob-a-Job. Not Bob-a-Job. What do I mean?
Samaritans. Something voluntary. I'll see to him. Come on,
love. Follow me.

LEE Iris?

SECOND ORDERLY Yes, Iris is here.

INT. HOSPITAL WOMEN'S WARD. DAY.
*Mrs Beevers, a woman in her sixties, is wearing a little bedjacket and
being visited by her husband.*

MRS BEEVERS I've watched her picking her nose all afternoon.
It's just been pick pick pick. She's in with one of these
unwanted pregnancies. Have you brought me anything?

MR BEEVERS Yes. I brought you the parish magazine.

MRS BEEVERS Parish magazine! *Food.* Have you brought me any
food?

MR BEEVERS Nay, Daisy, you're on a strict diet.

MRS BEEVERS You love this, don't you? Watching me tortured.
I could murder a Kunzle cake.
*The second orderly brings Lee down the ward to the bed opposite
Mrs Beevers in which there is an old lady asleep.*

SECOND ORDERLY Iris. Iris. Wake up, love. Come on, sleeping
beauty, here's the prince.

LEE No. No.

MRS BEEVERS Go on, love. Wake her up. Iris. Iris. Don't let her
sleep. It's months since she had anybody to see her. Iris! She's
got two daughters and they never come near and one of them's
in a real tip-top job with Hotpoint. Come on, Iris. Shake her.

OLD IRIS What?

MRS BEEVERS Got a visitor.

OLD IRIS Where?

MRS BEEVERS Here. Him. This young man.

OLD IRIS Him? He's a Jap.

MRS BEEVERS She forgets. Sit down a minute, love. She'll come
round in a bit. She'll surface eventually. Mind you, she's not
been all that clever. In fact she died last week. They got the
priest to come and give her the last rites and do you know five
minutes later they're along with the trolley to resuscitate her.
It's what I was saying to you. (*her husband*) Hospitals, there's
no liaison.

OLD IRIS Are you one of these Japs? I didn't know I knew any
Japs. It just shows you who you come across. You're not from

our Gerald, are you? He was in a Jappy camp during the war.
He came out a skeleton.

MRS BEEVERS That's all done with now. They've turned over a
new leaf. They make television sets. Our Bertram's got a Jappy
car. (*to her husband*) Fancy coming to see Iris. This is Iris. And
I'm Daisy. All we want now is a Buttercup and we'd be a right
bunch.

OLD IRIS Nay, Buttercup's a cow's name.

MRS BEEVERS Ay, well. (*peals of laughter*) You've got some nice
hair. Hasn't he, Bert? Got nice hair? My sister-in-law's hair
was a bit like yours.

MR BEEVERS Only she wasn't Japanese.

MRS BEEVERS I wasn't saying she was. I'm just saying her hair
was on a par with his.

MR BEEVERS He looks a bit lost to me.

MRS BEEVERS Well, he'll be a student. He'll be one of these
foreign students.

OLD IRIS He's not to do with the blackie vicar, is he?

MRS BEEVERS No. We've got this black vicar comes round. He's
black and yet he's Church of England. But beautifully spoken.
And lovely hands. Course it's all in the melting pot now, isn't
it? Foreign doctors. Black vicars. The physio's Hungarian and
Muriel over there, she has a home help that comes from
Poland.

MR BEEVERS Not every week?

Mrs Beevers looks at him.

Comes from Poland. Not every week.

MRS BEEVERS Is that a joke? It's all right, isn't it? I'm lying here
with suspected gallstones and you're on top of the world.
(*Pause.*) I bet the house is upside down.

MR BEEVERS It never is. I did the kitchen floor this morning.

MRS BEEVERS Which bucket did you use?

MR BEEVERS The red one.

MRS BEEVERS That's the outside bucket. I shall have it all to do
again. Men, they make work.

*Lee is sitting there unhappily. He looks at his chocolates, looks at
Old Iris, who has dropped off again, and gives her the chocolates.*
Isn't that nice? See, Iris. He's fetched you some chocolates.

He's fetched some chocolates. (*Gets smartly out of bed.*) Are they Jappy chocolates?

MR BEEVERS Nay, they're Dairy Box.

MRS BEEVERS They're probably Jappy Dairy Box. That's what they do, pinch our labels and make their own. Let's have a look.

OLD IRIS No. They're mine. He fetched them for me. Reparations.

MRS BEEVERS Well, let me undo them for you. She'll be all day wrestling with the cellophane.

OLD IRIS I can't do with hard ones.

MRS BEEVERS What's the index say?

OLD IRIS Coffee creams are the ones I like. I'd have them all coffee creams.

MRS BEEVERS That's coffee cream.

OLD IRIS It never is. Bloody nugget.

She chucks it away and Mrs Beevers gives her another.

MRS BEEVERS You want to squat these, Iris. Get them in your locker quick. Do you want one, Bert? They won't last five minutes in here. Somebody's on the pinch. I think it's the nurses. I know one thing: every time I go to spend a penny the level of my Lucozade drops.

OLD IRIS Hand round the hard ones. Save us the soft ones.

Mrs Beevers makes to give one to Lee.

Don't give him one. I don't know him. Who is this Jappy feller?

MRS BEEVERS He brought you the chocolates.

OLD IRIS I thought they had a funny taste.

MRS BEEVERS Hand them round, love, go on.

Lee hands round the chocolates, going round the beds.

Nice-looking young feller. Still, it'll take more than Dairy Box to erase the memory of Pearl Harbour.

The West Indian staff nurse enters.

STAFF NURSE Do you bin mind informin me what you is doin distributin de chocolates round de beds, man? En diabetics, man. En no sugar. Dis lady to whom you give de chocolates she bin in a coma last week cos some lady take pity on her and done give her some jelly, man. I jus don resuscitatin her, man. I don wan to re-resuscitate her. We're in a shortstaffin situation, man.

LEE I want Iris.

STAFF NURSE Don't rubbish me, man. Iris. (*Goes over to her.*) Iris, gel. You en no friend of Iris, man. You in doin her no good turn. Wi de Dairy Box.

MRS BEEVERS He gave us all some, didn't he, Bert? He fair insisted. I told him I was on a strict diet, but he wouldn't take no for an answer.

MR BEEVERS They can't, you see. It's to do with losing face.

STAFF NURSE (*while trying to fetch Old Iris round.*) Resuscitatin and re-resuscitatin, I don wan de doctors crawlin round my neck all de time. Am I on de bum or de bonce? What you doin on de ward anyway? En no visitin hours. En no relation of Iris. Iris en no foreign relations. Out of here, Chinese man, or I gwan call de biggest black man you ever seen in yo life, and he beat de shit out of you, man, Third World or no Third World.

Lee leaves hurriedly.

EXT. HOTEL STAFF ENTRANCE. DAY.
Lee going dejectedly in at the staff entrance.

INT. HOTEL CORRIDOR. DAY.
Along the narrow up-and-down corridor towards his room. He stops at his own door, then goes to one opposite and knocks. He knocks again.

BERNARD (*out of vision*) Yes.

LEE It's me. Lee.

BERNARD (*out of vision*) Hold on.

INT. BERNARD'S BEDROOM. DAY.
After a bit Bernard opens the door. He has a towel round his waist. He nips smartly back into bed once Lee comes in. There is a blowsy girl in bed, and there are a pair of bright yellow boots in the corner.

LEE Hello.

GIRL Hello.

LEE I did not find her. Iris. I could not find her.

BERNARD I know you didn't find her. Course you didn't find her. This is her. This is him. Iris, Lee. Lee, Iris.

IRIS Pleased to meet you. (*whispering*) Who?

BERNARD The one I was telling you about. You know. Olive skin.

IRIS Oh. Him.

BERNARD She came round here after work. Came round for tea, didn't you? Tea, bread and butter, scones and jam. Plus something from the trolley.

LEE I went to many places. Nobody knows her.

BERNARD Nobody knows Iris? Everybody knows Iris. Don't they, Iris?

IRIS Oh, yes. They all know me.

BERNARD You can't have gone to the right place. He can't have gone to the right place.

She turns over on her stomach and mutters.

What?

IRIS I wouldn't have fancied him anyway.

BERNARD No? He's a nice lad, aren't you, Genghis? Shy, but nice.

IRIS I think they're a bit creepy.

She turns over and looks at him boldly. Bernard also. Lee goes.

INT. LEE'S BEDROOM. DAY.
Lee lies on his bed, having taken everything off except his underpants. His hand moves slowly down his body to rest on his thigh.

INT. HOTEL DINING ROOM. EVENING.
Both waiters on duty. Lee with the sweet trolley. The dining room is very busy and full of diners. Credits over.